Experiences of Women Students with

Disabilities in Kenyan Universities

Disability in Society, Gender and & Higher Education

Challenges

Bathseba Opini

Nsemia

First Edition: February 2012
Published by Nsemia Inc. Publishers (www.nsemia.com)

Edited By: Bathseba Opini
Cover Concept Illustration: Robert Kambo Maina
Cover Design: Danielle Pitt
Production Consultant: Matunda Nyanchama

Note for Librarians:
A cataloguing record for this book is available from
Library and Archives Canada.

ISBN: 978-1-926906-17-1

DEDICATION

To all my study participants
and
my dear family

This work was submitted in partial fulfillment of the requirements for the Degree of DOCTOR OF PHILOSOPHY in the Graduate Studies Program at Ontario Institute of Studies in Education, University of Toronto supervised by Professor Sandra Acker, (Sociology and Equity Studies in Education) and examined by Professors Njoki Wane (Sociology and Equity Studies in Education) and Roy Moodley (Counselling Psychology) in June 2009.

Reader comments

Bathseba's book focuses on key scholarship on female students with disability within the Kenyan university system. This significant work challenges everyone to think about what it means to make education and learning environments truly inclusive and all encompassing. The research narratives dispel stereotypical ideas and misrepresentations of women living with a disability. The fundamental question addressed by this book is the notion of what it means to have a disability. This book is critical, powerful, and insightful. Bathseba reminds individuals and institutions alike that it is indeed time to listen and act if education is to be made accessible to everyone not just in postsecondary institutions in Kenya but also in global contexts
- ***Dr. Erica Neeganagwedgin, Toronto.***

This book is an outstanding sociological exploration of gender, disability and higher education in the African context. The women's stories come alive in this brilliant and sensitive interpretation of challenges and accomplishments of women students with disabilities in Kenyan universities. By giving voice to those who are rarely heard, Bathseba contributes to a comprehensive understanding of the student experience
– ***Dr. Sandra Acker, Professor Emeritus, Ontario Institute for Studies in Education, University of Toronto***

TABLE OF CONTENTS

ACKNOWLEDGEMENTS

This book grew out of my doctoral research in the Department of Sociology and Equity Studies in Education at the Ontario Institute for Studies in Education, University of Toronto. My sincere gratitude goes to the many people who contributed toward the success of this project in different ways. First and foremost, I want to thank the participants of my research without whom this book could not have been produced. Thank you for sharing your experiences with me. I dedicate this book to you.

I am very thankful for the intellectual mentorship of Sandra Acker and Njoki Wane in my academic path. I would also like to thank Immaculate Tumwine, Roy Moodley, Tanya Titchkosky and Sheryl Bond for their feedback on early versions of this book. My sincere thanks go to Nsemia Publishers for their decision to publish this work. I owe special thanks to Taylor and Francis for their permission to reprint several parts of the article "Examining the motivations of disabled women's participation in higher education in Kenya" *Scandinavian Journal of Disability Research* 45, 1-18 by Bathseba Opini (2011) and the Association of Higher Education and Disability for their permission to reprint parts of the article "Barriers to Participation of Women Students with Disabilities in University Education in Kenya" in *Journal of Postsecondary Education and Disability* 25(1), 2012 by Bathseba Opini. I am also grateful to Esther Nyang'ate, AnneMarie Grant, Erica Neegan, Nimo Gulleid, Lincoln Chivaraidze and Mikel Missakabo for their friendship, informative dialogues and encouragement while doing this work.

I wish to thank my beloved dad, mom and siblings for inspiring me to pursue an education and for their love, support, patience and believing in me. Special thanks to my husband Arnold Getaro whose unwavering love and support saw this publication come into fruition. Finally, I am grateful for the many friends I have met and made in my academic, social and spiritual journey. You have all been precious and a great source of inspiration.

About the Author

Bathseba Opini teaches at the Ontario Institute for Studies in Education and the African Studies Program, University of Toronto. She is the author of the Children's Book "Africans Thought of It: Amazing Innovations" (with Richard Lee). Her other published works can be found in the *International Journal of Inclusive Education*, the *Scandinavian Journal of Disability Research* and the *Journal of Postsecondary Education and Disability*.

PREFACE

This book examines the experiences of women students with disabilities in university education in Kenya. It investigates the situation of women students with disabilities enrolled in two selected universities in Kenya; identifies the challenges these women face in their educational lives and the coping strategies they have developed to deal with those challenges.

The book is based on an ethnographic study done in Kenya in 2006 which employed qualitative interviews with 20 women students with disabilities and four officials from two public universities. The research also benefited from an in-depth analysis of university policies and statements incorporated in the universities' websites, strategic plans and student handbooks to unearth the experiences of women students with disabilities at the selected institutions.

Drawing on the African feminist perspectives, Erving Goffman's notion of stigma and Michel Foucault's ideas of power and knowledge, the book demonstrates how individual and institutional ableism limits women students with disabilities' efforts to pursue a university education. The narrative findings reveal some of the measures taken by the women interviewed to counter this ableism. It is also shown that although women students with disabilities in Kenya perceive higher education as a crucial stepping stone to a better life, few have the opportunity of accessing, experiencing and participating in that education. The book stresses the need for higher education institutions to encompass more inclusive and comprehensive policies/disability statements, support services and actions in their efforts to eliminate practices that reinforce societal prejudices against people with disabilities.

CHAPTER 1

INTRODUCTION

The World Health Organization (WHO) (2008) estimates reveal that about 650 million people globally experience some form of disability; approximately 80 to 90 percent of these people live in low-income countries, are themselves poor, and have limited access to basic services (McConkey & O'Toole, 1995; WHO, 2007). Considering these numbers, people with disability are, and will continue to be, key members of our society. Disability is the "most human of experiences, touching every family *vicariously* (my addition) and – if we live long enough – touching us all" (Garland-Thomson, 2002). As Brueggemann, Garland-Thomson and Snyder (2002) put it, "the fact that many of us will become disabled if we live long enough" is one of "the fundamental aspects of human embodiment" (p. 2). Disability and the disabled body are no longer alien conditions but realities of our lives (Brueggemann, et al, 2002; Davis, 2002).

The WHO (2008) also documents that majority of disabilities are chronic conditions, the result of such diverse causes as cardiovascular and respiratory diseases, cancer and diabetes; injuries due to road accidents, falls, landmines, war and other violent events; mental illness; HIV/AIDS; poverty and malnutrition, and other infectious diseases (Coleridge 1993; Elwan, 1999; Oliver, 1996; Turmusani, 2003). Furthermore, the WHO predicts that the population of persons with disability around the world will continue to increase because of: (i) increased aging populations due to medical advances that preserve and prolong life (Anderson, 2004; Asch & Fine, 1988; Beresford, 1999; Wendell, 1996); (ii) violent conflict (see also Whitehead, 2004) and (iii) illness including HIV/AIDS and other diseases. Thus, an individual could become disabled any time, even when born non-disabled (Davis, 2002; Brueggemann, et al, 2002; Kozma, 2005). This is why Garland-Thomson (2002) emphasizes the need to acknowledge and to understand issues of disability. She argues that "disability studies and disability advocacy should never be a concern of only persons with disabilities but a concern for all of us" (p. 5), whether we are disabled or not.

Nonetheless, and in spite of the reality that disability occurs in every society throughout the world (Kisanji, 1998; McConkey & O'Toole, 1995) and touches all of us (Garland-Thomson, 2002), many non-disabled people have not yet accepted this truth (Linton, 2006). Society continues to assume that disability is solely the concern of persons with disabilities (Garland-Thomson, 2002). Many non-disabled people prefer not to face the issues

1

raised by people with disabilities and avoid the topic of disability. Rarely do non-disabled persons acknowledge that the world favours them (Linton, 2006) at the expense of those with disabilities. Davis (2002) explains the lack of acknowledgement of disability by non-disabled people as follows:

> What people fear is that disability is the identity one may become part of but didn't want. This is the silent threat that makes folks avoid the subject, act awkwardly around people with disabilities, and consequently avoid paying attention to the current backlash against disability rights. (p. 4)

Consequently, the lives of people with disabilities the world over continue to be made more difficult by the way society interprets and reacts to disability (WHO, 2008). Common responses to disability by the non-disabled population remain largely those of shame, prejudice and exclusion of the disabled from community life (McConkey & O'Toole, 1995). In both Western and non-Western societies, prejudiced attitudes and reactions toward disability and people with disabilities are evident (Amosun, Volmik & Rosin, 2005; Chimedza, 2000; de Klerk & Ampousah, 2003; Kabzems & Chidmeza, 2002; Ghai, 2003). Disability is often represented as a "deficiency" (Michalko, 2002). This representation becomes the defining characteristic of people with disabilities, symbolically representing lack, tragic loss, dependency and abnormality (Amosun et al., 2005; Chimedza, 2000; Ghai, 2003; Rioux, 1991; Saito & Ishayama, 2005). These negative representations inform the *ableist* biases and practices that people with disabilities face. As Peat (1997) remarks, "society is driven by norms that are based on the experiences, views and biased interpretations of non-disabled people" (p. 657). Biased interpretations of disability make it difficult to create a society in which people with disabilities live full and active lives, similar to that lived by non-disabled persons (Saito & Ishayama, 2005). As a result, people with disabilities continue to experience disenfranchisement and have limited access to essential services, such as health care, education, employment and recreation etc. (Driedger, 1996; Peat, 1997; Turmusani, 2003).

Especially valuable to this book is the body of existing literature which offers a discussion of the manner in which disability intersects with other forms of representation, such as gender, race/ethnicity, class, language, age, religion and sexuality (Durst & Bluechardt, 2001; Garland-Thomson, 2002; Stienstra, 2003), and literature that highlights further challenges to full integration of people with disabilities into mainstream society. For example, alluding to intersections between race and disability, and referencing First Nations urban persons with disabilities in Canada, Durst and Bluechardt (2001), noted that Aboriginal people with disabilities are severely marginalized by virtue of being both Aboriginal and disabled. Durst and Bluechardt (2001) similarly demonstrated that Aboriginal women with disabilities are further marginalized because of their gender. This is also true of other aspects of difference such as gender, age, religion, class etc. For instance, scholars researching gender and disability have pointed to the fact that, although discrimination of people with disabilities is a global phenomenon, girls and women with disabilities suffer added discrimination because of their sex (Froschl, Rubin & Sprung, 1999; Gerschick, 2000; Ghai 2003; Thomas, 1999; Ziesler, 2002). This added oppression of women with disabilities manifests itself in different forms. For example, women with disabilities are significantly poorer than both men with disabilities and women without disabilities (Froschl, Rubin & Sprung, 1999; Gerschick, 2000; Meekosha, 2004); more women with disabilities are unemployed, compared to disabled men and non-disabled women (Asch & Fine, 1988; Gerschick, 2000); women with disabilities earn less monthly income than other groups (Froschl, Rubin & Sprung, 1999; Gerschick, 2000; Meekosha, 2004); and jobs for women with disabilities cluster around service occupations and unskilled labor, rather than managerial or professional work (Gerschick, 2000; Lonsdale, 1990). Women with disabilities are less likely to hold high school or college degrees, and their vocational training and counseling is often gender-stereotyped (Fulton & Sabornie, 1994; Mason, 2004). Women with disabilities are also less likely to marry than non-disabled women, and when they do marry, are more likely to do so later in life and more likely to become divorced (Asch & Fine, 1997; Gerschick, 2000).

The discrimination towards women with disabilities is so insidious and extends even to mainstream women and women's movements, which have been subject to criticism (Disability Awareness Action, 1996). As some feminist disability activists have noted (Asch & Fine, 1988; Ghai, 2003; Meekosha, 2004; Morris, 1996; Thomas, 1999; Wendell, 1996), women with disabilities have, for a long time, been rendered invisible in the feminist discourse. Women with disabilities are further subject to marginalization within the disability movement, this time on the basis of their gender, as these groups are often driven by male-centric agendas (Asch & Fine, 1988). This is why a majority of women and girls with disabilities remain a silenced group, whose concerns are rarely voiced, and whose rights are often overlooked (Meekosha, 2004). Zeisler (2002) writes that the situation is even bleaker for women with disabilities and girls in low-income countries. This is because women and girls with disabilities in low-income countries are more affected by poverty than their non-disabled counterparts; they are more vulnerable to domestic violence; they are less likely to access education and jobs etc. (Disability World, 2007; Meekosha, 2004; Zeisler, 2002). Additionally, women and girls with disabilities in developing countries are also sometimes affected by the complexities created by the cultural beliefs and practices toward disability, since, in many incidences; persons with disabilities are perceived as lacking the potential to learn and to further develop through learning (Zeisler, 2002). It is for this reason that many children with disabilities, especially girls with disabilities, are under-represented in school, regardless of whether or not their specific form of impairment affects their ability to learn (Ziesler, 2002). This discrimination has resulted in limited access for women and girls with disabilities, which has, in turn, contributed to high levels of unemployment for most women with disabilities in low-income countries (Dawn Ontario, n.d.).

In Africa, natural disasters, accidents, conflicts/wars, landmines, poverty, inadequate nutrition, limited access to health care, unsafe working conditions, inadequate safety regulations and HIV/AIDS are identified as some of the primary causes of disability (O'Toole, 2000; Tomlinson & Abdi, 2003; UNAIDS/UNICEF/USAID, 2004). Nonetheless, there are no clear accounts on the numbers of people with disabilities in the African continent. The African Decade 1 (2005) estimates that there are about 80 million people with disabilities in Africa (cited by Malakpa, 2006). Other estimates put the numbers at about 300 million people (Malakpa, 2006). Regardless of the numbers, it has generally been noted that people with disabilities in Africa continue to be discriminated against and are largely excluded from social, economic and political activities (Malakpa, 2006). The limited literature available shows that up to 70 per cent of people with disabilities in Africa are poor and live in the rural areas (Chimedza, 2001; O'Toole, 2000; Statistics South Africa, 2005). The literature also reveals that a great percentage of people with disabilities in Africa also have limited formal education and, therefore, limited chances of accessing employment (Abang, 1986; ILO, 2004; Tembe, 2001; Statistics South Africa, 2005). As in many other parts of the world, women with disabilities in Africa experience further discrimination and greater exclusion than men with disabilities (Kiyaga & Moores, 2003; Statistics South Africa, 2005; Zimbabwe Women's Resource Center and Network (ZWRCN) and Southern African Research and Documentation Center (SARDC), 2005). Some literature has also shown that women and girls with disabilities in Africa also experience sexual abuse, giving them heightened vulnerability to sexually transmitted diseases and HIV/AIDS (ZWRCN/SARDC, 2005). In terms of education, while commendable efforts are being made to reduce illiteracy among girls and women in Africa, not much has been done to address the needs of girls and women with disabilities. More disabled girls are out of school compared to non-disabled girls (see ZWRCN/SARDC, 2005) and consequently, fewer and fewer female students with disabilities move up the education ladder.

In Kenya, the low enrollment rate of girls and women in the universities remains a challenge (Ministry of Education, 2006), let alone the enrollment of the small percentage of women with disabilities who make it to university. Even though there are a few studies that examine under-representation of women with disabilities in universities (Barile, 1996; Nosek, 1996; Traustadottir, 1990), they are not focused on Kenya. It is in this context that this study was designed to investigate the experiences of women students with disabilities in university education in Kenya. The goals of this study were to: (i) understand ways in which women with disabilities perceive their participation in university education in Kenya; (ii) understand how disability impacts the lives and education of women students with disabilities (iii) examine policy issues and generate recommendations for enhancement of inclusive practices in education, aimed at promoting access to higher education for women with disabilities in Kenya.

OVERVIEW OF DISABILITY IN KENYA

There is no definite information about the numbers of people with disabilities in the country (International Labour Organization, 2004; Republic of Kenya, 2004). Very few studies have been undertaken to determine the conditions of persons with disabilities in that nation (Oriedo, 2003; Ndurumo, 2001). These few studies fail to provide a precise picture of the current situation in the country.

For example, the 1999 census done in Kenya, with official figures released in January 2001, put the Kenyan population at 28.7 million people, with a population growth of 2.9% (Government of Kenya Central Bureau of Statistics Office, 2001). However, this census release did not provide any account of people with disabilities in the country. The 2010 census results showed that there are 38,610,097 people in the country (Basse, 2010). Of the 38.6 million, 1,330, 312 have disabilities (647,689 males; 682, 623 females). This is way below the UN estimates that 10% of population is likely to be living with a disability (which would translate into over 3 million people). It should thus be noted that the numbers from the census may not be very accurate because families tend to define and identify their disabled members differently. Some communities in Kenya, for instance, may not use disability as criterion for classifying people and, therefore, see a child as a child (Talle, 1995; Ogechi & Ruto, 2002) and will count them as so.

This is the first time the government officially accounted for the number of people with disabilities in the census exercise. The lack of accurate information on disability which persisted in Kenya for a long time supports Melissa Whitehead's (2004) assertion that people with disabilities in Africa remain "an invisible community and that not enough attention is paid to address their needs and rights" (p. 12). It also echos Tom Oriedo's (2003) observation that, in Kenya, "disability is not considered a significant priority in the country's economic development planning" (www.cec.sped. org/intl/state). There is a need for more contemporary research studies to provide up to date information for better planning, resource distribution, service delivery and integration of people with disabilities into mainstream society.

With regard education, the little information available reveals that, in Kenya, most persons with disabilities are poor and live in the rural areas, with limited access to schooling (Republic of Kenya, 1993). Oriedo (2003) reiterated that the majority of people with disabilities in Kenya have limited or no access to education, healthcare, employment and other basic services. Pointing to the education of students with disabilities in primary and secondary education in Kenya, a survey conducted by a task force on special needs education[1], appointed by the permanent secretary, Ministry of Education, Science and Technology in July 2003, indicated that the majority of students with disabilities do not receive any special education services and are either at home or in regular schools without any support (National Development Plan 2002-2008 cited in Republic of Kenya, 2003; Republic of Kenya, 2003). A draft report issued by the Ministry of Education on special education affirms that special education has not received adequate attention and that education for learners with special education needs continues to be insufficient (Republic of Kenya, 2006). Therefore, in spite of the acknowledgement that education and life-long learning opportunities can fill the gaps in economic and social development that effectively marginalize individuals with disabilities (Republic of Kenya, 2006), people with disabilities in Kenya continue to receive limited attention and also remain underrepresented in educational institutions. According to documentation from the African Decade for Persons with Disabilities (2001) cited by Whitehead (2004),

> It would be incorrect to assume that this lack of attention is merely due to the lack of human and infrastructure resources, weak organizations of persons with disabilities, little or no policy

and legislation, and negative attitudes towards disabled Africans. Poverty and its implications is the major problem in the developing world; both as a cause and consequence of disability. (p. 12)

As demonstrated in chapters five and six of this book, poverty is a real impediment to women students with disabilities' participation in higher education. In Kenya, as in other African countries, there is a tendency for the government to issue policy directives and then defer responsibility for implementation to institutions and non-governmental organizations (NGOs) (Whitehead, 2004). This has mostly been the government's approach to dealing with disability issues. There persists a troubling, colonially-rooted assumption, on the part of government, and even in the wider society, that disability is an issue that is largely to be addressed through charitable organizations (Stone, 1999). This assumption pushes people with disabilities to the periphery when it comes to government planning/budgeting and service provision.

Following this marginalization, few people with disabilities successfully complete elementary education in Kenya, let alone secondary and university education. Commenting on the limited access to education for people with disabilities in Kenya, Nkinyangi and Mbindyo (1982) reported that "persons with disabilities in Kenya at one time in their life had very high aspirations for educational achievement; desiring to complete high school and to proceed to college or university" (p. 23). Unfortunately, due to barriers including finances, societal prejudices against disabled people, the majority of people with disabilities in Kenya remain either illiterate or have progressively become so after their basic primary schooling (Nkinyangi & Mbindyo, 1982). Many children with disabilities do not have access to education, and many of those who enroll drop out due to negative societal attitudes; rigid curriculum content; inadequate infrastructure, poor facilities (Republic of Kenya, 2006) and scarcity of resources, all of which force poor parents to make difficult choices in deciding how to invest their limited resources (Gathenya, 2003). In times of adverse economic conditions when both public and private investment in education are threatened, the first people to suffer are the already marginalized groups, such as girls, the poor, the disabled and other minorities (Gathenya, 2003; Republic of Kenya/Ministry of Education 1998). These prioritizations may explain, in part, why gender differentials, with respect to access to education, remain pervasive in many African countries. Males enjoy better access to education and training because they are considered to be the heirs and future bread-earners of the family, whether disabled or non-disabled (Njeuma, 1998; Rathgeber, 2003; Republic of Kenya, 1993;

Sifuna, 2006). Thus, although disability limits opportunity for schooling among all persons, its effects are felt more acutely by women than by men (Republic of Kenya, 1993).

In fact, a 1993 survey on the situation of people with disabilities in Kenya by gender showed that the greatest majority of people with disabilities are found in the category of "no-education." The survey also revealed that girls with disabilities were underrepresented in the entire educational system (Republic of Kenya 1993). These findings are consistent with prevailing national trends in gender differences in educational opportunity, whereby males dominate, with respect to the number of educated persons at all levels of education in Kenya (Bunyi, 2004; Kamau, 1996; Kiluva-ndunda, 2000; Sifuna, 2006). A major gap in these studies, though, is that they either take a totalizing approach and speak of women as a homogenous group or fail to address, in depth, the situation of women with disabilities in university settings (Republic of Kenya, 1993). Given the clear connection between educational opportunities and social, economic and political empowerment there is a need for studies that examine the experiences of women with disabilities in Kenyan higher education.

Moreover, although disability awareness continues to receive increasing publicity and attention in higher education institutions, particularly in Western countries, students with disabilities remain a small minority group within the student population at most higher education institutions (Connor et al. 1996 cited in O'Connor & Robinson, 1999, p. 88; Hurst, 1993). This is true of universities in Africa, Kenya included. There is also a dearth of information on gender differentials when it comes to participation of female students with disabilities in higher education. Only a few studies examine the issue of women with disabilities and university education and the majority of the existing studies have focused on the situation of women with disabilities in developed countries (Ferri & Gregg, 1998; Fichten, Barile & Reid, 1999; Nova Scotia Advisory Council on the Status of Women, 2006). Furthermore, there has been inadequate research examining the intersection of disability with other markers of social difference including class, ethnicity, sexuality, age, and religion etc. This book, therefore, fill the gaps in the literature concerning women students with disabilities in a developing world context. It focuses on the voices of a range of women with impairments, as they seek to overcome the combined effects of their disability and other socially marginalizing factors.

DEFINITION OF CONCEPTS

Access

Most governments around the world have expressed commitment to promoting access to education, and have made access a national policy. But what do they exactly mean by access? The meaning of the word "access" varies with the context in which it is employed. According to the Oxford Dictionary of Current English, access refers to the means or opportunity to approach or enter a place. Access also means the right or opportunity to use something or to see someone. Lelei (2005) defined access as "... the opportunity for individuals to enroll in and complete successive levels of education and training" (p. 155). Lelei noted that this is dependent on the availability of spaces in educational institutions for persons of the corresponding age and grade level as well as on their capacity or that of their families to pay any costs associated with enrollment (e.g. fees, uniforms, books and materials etc.). Lelei further suggested that:

> Access is reflected in the enrolment rates of students at each level of school and the rates of transition from one level of an educational system to another. Access also refers to transition into the labor market based on received education, and training that prepares students for suitable employment. It includes consideration of social protection for students, who may be disadvantaged in ways (e.g. income, gender, disability, ethnicity, place of residence) that would prevent them from being enrolled in educational institutions. (p. 155)

Joy Kwesiga (2002), likewise, emphasized that, in educational terms, access can be measured in degrees by observing the proportion of a particular group who enroll at a particular educational level. Kwesiga identifies literacy rates and enrollment rates as the two main indicators of access. Writing about people with disabilities and access opportunities to higher education in a British context, James Palfreman-Kay (1998) argues that: "the purpose of *access* is ... to attract ... *specific groups of adults in the community which have been identified as under represented in higher education... those groups who have been least well-served by the school system and who face particular barriers to entry to higher education...*" (emphasis in the original). Palfreman-Kay concluded that the goal of *access* is to provide an entry route into higher education for non-traditional groups such as people with disabilities and ethnic minority groups. This book adopts a combination of Kwesiga's (2002), Lelei's (2005)

9

and Palfreman-Kay's (1998) definitions of access and takes into account enrollment, completion, transition, individual differences and provision of entry route into higher education for non-traditional groups, in this case women with disabilities.

Disability

The question of "what is disability?" and "who is disabled?" is a complex one (Ghai, 2003; Thomas, 2004; Wendell, 1996). This is mainly because of the differences in the ways that societies and individuals gather information about disability as well as differences in understanding of what in fact constitutes a disability (Wendell, 1996). Since disability is more than a description of a specific health issue, definitions of disability are affected by people's cultures, social institutions, and political environments etc. (World Bank, n.d.). Different models have been proposed to explain the concept of disability. These contrasting models allow for an examination of disability in different ways and under different conditions (Finkelstein, 2004). In this book I discuss two models of disability. These are (i) the medical model and (ii) the social model.[2]

The medical model of disability

The medical model seeks to compartmentalize disability into the medical trilogy of sickness, disease and rehabilitation (Bichenback, 1993; Barnes, Mercer & Shakespeare, 1999; Llewellyn & Hogan, 2000). That is, persons with disabilities are perceived as sick and weak in their present state and the focus of therapeutic intervention is on improving the disability as a precursor to improving themselves (Bichenback, 1993). Oliver (1996) argues that the medical model focuses on bodily "abnormality," disorder or deficiency, and on the way in which these conditions relate to disability or to functional limitation (see also Titchkosky, 2003). Disability is seen as something arising from biological limitations or malfunctions. In this light, to be disabled is to be unable to do what "normal" people do (Thomas, 1999). Disability is, thus, cast as a personal tragedy where the individual concerned must depend on others for support (Barnes, et al., 1999). Titchkosky (2003) remarks that the medical model fails to recognize that, "while people with disabilities may not do some things in ways that non-disabled people do, or may not do some things at all, it is equally true that disability highlights the background expectancies that order this doing in a culture" (p. 16). This is because "disability is much more significant than simply the doing or the non-doing of things, as it bears social, political, cultural, and economic constructions" (Titchkosky, 2003).

Scholars critical of the medical model argue that the model is "a form of biological determinism, which looks at disability as a physical, behavioral, psychological, cognitive and sensory tragedy" (Gilson & Depoy, 2000, pp. 207-208). In the medical model, the problem to be addressed by disability services is situated within the disabled individual, a practice that gives rise to discourses of personal pathology, individual difficulties and dependency (Goodley, 2001; Oliver, 1996; Shakespeare & Watson, 1997). Barnes et al. (1999) add that the medical model proposes curative and rehabilitative medical intervention by "experts", such as physicians, psychologists and educationalists, as the solution to disability. These experts diagnose an individual's condition and identify the needs of that individual and how they should be met so as to minimize, the negative consequences of the individual's disability (p. 21). The individual who cannot be 'fixed" by professional intervention remains forever "deficient" (Gilson & Depoy, 2000). People are, therefore, defined, not only by their diagnosed conditions, but also by the degree to which those conditions are barriers to their ability to function in "normal" life roles (Gilson & Depoy, 2000). With such emphasis on the individual, the medical model fails to consider the social environment as part of the "problem" of disablement (Barnes, et al. 1999; Bickenbach, 1999; Oliver, 1996).

The social model of disability

The social model of disability focuses on examining the social processes and forces that cause people with perceived impairment to become constructed as disabled and/or as a minority group in society (Priestly, 2003). The social model of disability has roots in the UPIAS (Union of the Physically Impaired Against Segregation) – the organization of people with disabilities, founded by Vic Finkelstein and Paul Hunt, among others, in the U.K. in the mid-1970s. According to the UPIAS (1976), disability is a concept which is imposed on top of individuals' impairments which justifies unnecessarily isolating individuals and excluding them from full participation in society. People with disabilities, thus, become an oppressed group within society (UPIAS, 1976, cited in Finkelstein, 2001b, p. 1). Mike Oliver took up the ideas of UPIAS and encapsulated them in the notion of the social model of disability (Thomas, 2004).

The social model focuses on the degree to which an individual's incapacity to function may be related to a disability hostile environment in which barriers clash against personal choice (Gleeson, 1997 cited by Gilson & Depoy, 2000, p. 208). In this model disability is conceived as the outcome of social arrangements which work to restrict the activities of people with impairments by placing social barriers in their way (Abberley, 1987; Thomas; 1999). The social model challenges the fundamentals of

11

the medical model, whereby medicalization is key (see Oliver, 1996). This is not to deny the significance of germs, genes and trauma, but rather to point out that the effects are only apparent in real social, political, economic and historical contexts (Abberley, 1987). The focus is no longer on individual limitations of whatever kind but, rather, on society's failure to provide appropriate services and to adequately ensure that the needs of people with disabilities are fully taken into account in its social organization (Oliver, 1990). Thus, the social model "navigates notions of social problems, of societal/environmental difficulties and of independence in the face of self-advocacy" (Goodley, 1997, p. 373). The social model calls for alternative understanding, societal adjustment, and individual and collective responsibility among all societal members to redress disabling environments (see Oliver, 1995 cited by Goodley, 1997, p. 373).

The social model, like the medical model, is not without criticism. Some disability theorists arguing from a feminist viewpoint (Morris, 1991; French, 1993; Fawcett, 1999; Thomas, 1999), as well as from a postmodernist perspective (Marks, 1999; Shakespeare, 1994) raise questions about its negation of discussions of impairments and personal experience when analyzing disability. Additionally, and as Turmusani (2003) argues, "while the social model is about social issues, this does not imply that disabled people do not have medical needs. The medical model does play a vital role in explaining and in dealing with impairment" (p. 10). So what is disability then?

How different models define and explain disability has implications for policy making (Turmusani, 2003). The various models of disability are often in conflict with each other. One of the early definitions put forward in the 1980s by the World Health Organization (WHO) is broadly consistent with the medical model of disability and revolves around the official classification of impairment, disability and handicap or what is known as the International Classification of Impairment, Disability and Handicap (ICIDH). The ICIDH definition of impairment, disability and handicap presented by the WHO is as follows:

> *Impairment*: any loss or abnormality of psychological or anatomical structure or function.
>
> *Disability*: not being able to perform an activity considered normal for human beings. Any restriction or lack (resulting from impairment) of ability to perform an activity in the manner or within the range considered normal for a human being.
>
> *Handicap*: the inability to perform a normal social role and is defined as: a disadvantage for a given individual resulting from an impairment or disability that limits or prevents fulfillment of a role

that is normal (depending on age, sex, social or cultural factors) for that individual. (cited in Turmusani, 2003, p. 11)

The above definition has been criticized by disability activists who argue that its medical orientation results in development of programs and policies that are biased toward creating institutions to contain impairments, rather than facilitating the social inclusion of disabled people (Marks, 1999; Turmusani, 2003). Following these criticisms, the WHO revised the definition as follows:

Impairment: any loss or abnormality of a psychological or anatomical structure or function. Impairments are disturbances at the level of the organ.

Disability: any restrictions or inability (resulting from an impairment) to perform an activity in the manner or within the range considered normal for a human being. This describes a functional limitation or activity restriction caused by impairment. Disabilities are descriptions of disturbances in function at the level of the person.

Handicap: any disadvantage for a given individual, resulting from an impairment or a disability, that limits or prevents the fulfillment of a role that is normal...for that individual. The classification of handicap is a classification of circumstances that place individuals at a disadvantage relative to their peers when viewed from the norms of society. The classification of handicap deals with the relationship that evolves between society, culture and people who have impairments or disabilities, as reflected in people's life roles. (cited in Titchkosky, 2003, p.14; and also Turmusani, 2003, p. 15-16)

In the new definition, impairment and disability are defined in terms of capability rather than limitation and thus takes into account the notion of human capabilities and functioning. The revised definition also takes on board the issue of environment, and recognizes the role of social factors in the production of disablement (see Turmusani, 2003).

This book draws on the social model of disability and adopts the revised definition of disability because the revised definition recognizes that people with disabilities possess the same rights and privileges as all other citizens and their differences should not be ignored, nor should they be elevated to the status of a defining feature. My adopting of a social model is in line with Moore, Beazeley and Maelzer's (1998) emphasis that:

... only a critical approach to disability research, rooted firmly in social model discourse and practice, enables a human rights perspective to be given to issues which affect disabled people's lives. It is only with this approach that research can explore the extent to which fundamental rights, such as equal access to equal opportunities and [access] to full inclusion in society are recognized and promoted in the face of prejudice and excluding practices. Research which is structured in relation to the social model of disability is not 'disabled people blaming' but calls a disabling society to account. (p. 13)

Taking this social model stance allows for an interrogation of the influence of such factors as physical, communicative barriers and social barriers governing the definition and treatment of people with disabilities, and social stereotypes and attitudes of disability on the experiences narrated by the disabled women students (Charlton, 1998; Oliver, 1990).

MAPPING THE BOOK

Chapter one, the introduction, provides an overview of disability and people with disability, a brief overview of the discussion topic under study and sets the stage for the subsequent chapters.

Chapter two provides the historical, social and political contexts of Kenya. The chapter outlines the various changes that have occurred in the country through history and the implications for education. This history is important in understanding how women's education has been shaped over the years and the implications for women with disabilities' education. The chapter also offers a summary of the participation of women in general and that of women with disabilities in particular in Kenyan higher education.

Chapter three focuses on the frameworks that guided the analysis of the research findings and the methodology employed in the study. The first part discusses the three theoretical frameworks that informed the study i.e. Goffman's notion of stigma, Foucauldian notions of power and knowledge and African feminist perspectives). The second part outlines the ethnographic approach taken and also describes the sampling procedures, the objectives of the data collection, the participants and institutions selected.

The narrative analyses of the research data starts in chapter four. The chapter begins with a discussion of research findings relating to the the the women's choices to pursue a university education. It looks at the factors that influence women with disabilities in Kenya to pursue a university education and how they select the universities they attend together with the programs of study. The narratives show that while some of the motivations of women with disabilities to go to university are similar to

14

those of non-disabled individuals, women with disabilities have to struggle much harder to accomplish their goal because of societal barriers and prejudices towards people with disabilities.

Chapter five examines the lived experiences of the women students with disabilities in university. It looks at the factors, condition and structures that enable these women to participate in university education and their experiences in the areas of curriculum, interpersonal relations and physical access.

The sixth chapter looks at the facilitators and barriers to succeed in university. The chapter points out ways women students with disabilities manage the challenges they face. The seventh chapter examines the policies put in place to address the needs of women students with disabilities in the universities under investigation. A summary of the university officers' views on the existing disability statements/policies, together with the services and support systems offered to students with disabilities in their institutions, is also provided. These findings are compared with information gathered from the university documents reviewed and from the narratives of the women students with disabilities interviewed.

The eighth chapter analyzes the women students with disabilities' and university officer's recommendations for improving access to and participation of students with disabilities in university education. This chapter also offers suggestions and directions for future research.

CHAPTER TWO

Education and Social Institutions in Kenya

"... genealogy (historical investigation) does not pretend to go back in time to restore an unbroken continuity that operates beyond the dispersion of forgotten things; its duty is not to demonstrate that the past actively exists in the present that it continues secretly to animate the present, having imposed a predetermined form of its vicissitudes" (Michel Foucault, 1977, p. 147).

In order to better understand the marginal position of women with disabilities in Kenyan universities, it is useful to enter into some historical space and provide an account of the social and political history that has kept these women out of higher education. African feminist Ogundipe-Leslie (1994) emphasized the centrality of history when conducting studies on women in Africa in the following excerpt:

> Whatever studies we make of women in Africa, we should be aware of the need to "periodize" African history adequately. It is also necessary to recognize various social and historical categories which would affect our analysis of women's positions in Africa. We need to see problems in their class perspectives in both present day and past economic formations. In present day Africa, we should bear in mind that problems differ from society to society, depending on their ethnic history and specific relation to capital and neo-colonialism... Another variable in our ... studies should be religion – the various cultural effects of Islam, Christianity and the traditional religions on women's positions in Africa. (p. 32)

This chapter attempts to provide just such an historical context by examining how various societal actions and institutions resulted in the discriminatory state of social affairs evident in Kenyan universities today. The historical contextualization of this study aims at showing that there is an inextricable link between the past and the present (Foucault, 1977). The focus on history also seeks to address Oliver's (1990) concerns that history has largely been absent in most discussions of disability and, if at all discussed, it is done from a medical model perspective (p. xi). Little is known about the role of history in shaping the lives and experiences of disabled people in contemporary Kenya. In this study, I made attempts to make connections between what happened historically in educational contexts in Kenya to explicate the experiences of marginalization of disabled people, particularly the disabled women. The historical analysis also tries to show that, as Verstraete (2007) indicated, "disability is a complex and intertwined framework of relations. That is, disability is not simply located in the bodies of individuals but is a socially and culturally constructed identity" (Longmore & Umansky, 2001, p. 19 cited by Verstraete, 2007, p. 57). My historical analysis, thus, points to the fact that attitudes and practices regarding the marginality of people with disability have been historically and socially produced and reproduced.

KENYA'S DEMOGRAPHIC CHARACTERISTICS

Kenya lies in east-central Africa on the coast of the Indian Ocean, straddling the equator. It borders Somalia to the east, Ethiopia to the north, Tanzania to the south, Uganda to the west, and Sudan to the northwest. The 2009 census indicated that Kenya has a population of 38,610,09 people (www.mwakilishi.com). There are close to 50 ethnic groups in the country. Although each of these groups uses their own unique indigenous language, English and Kiswahili are used as the official languages.[3] On the whole, Kenyans are a religious people. About 80 percent of Kenyans are Christians, 10 percent Muslim, while about 10 percent follow traditional African religions or other faiths (U.S. Department of State, Department of African Affairs, 2008). The majority of the population lives in rural areas. However, recently there has been an upsurge in the urban population, due to rural-urban migration by high school and college/university graduates seeking jobs in the cities. These movements from rural to urban areas have had serious implications for access to services, such as education and healthcare (Ministry of Education, 1996).

THE POLITICAL SYSTEM

Kenya attained independence from the British in 1963 with the Kenya African National Union (KANU) as the ruling party, while the Kenya African Democratic Union was the main opposition party. At independence, KANU pledged to promote democracy and to fight against poverty, disease and ignorance (Amutabi, 2003). However, the federal system adopted at independence was soon abandoned by the KANU regime in 1964 with the support of the nascent KADU opposition, which voluntarily dissolved itself thereby ending any semblance of opposition to KANU (Amutabi, 2003, p. 128). According to Amutabi (2003), the dissolution of KADU marked the beginning of "the seeds of autocracy, tyranny and single-party dictatorship, which continued to prevail in the succeeding years of Kenyatta's rule" (p. 128), extending to Moi's reign which began in 1978, and now Kibaki's era (2002 to date). During the first few years of independent Kenya there was virtually no opposition to Kenyatta's regime (KANU) until 1966 when there was a fall-out between Kenyatta and his vice-president Jaramogi Oginga Odinga. Odinga formed the Kenya Peoples Union (KPU) party and he, together with his friends, was detained for attempting to rival KANU for power (Amutabi, 2003, p. 128). By 1969, Kenya was firmly established as a de facto one party state, and the KANU regime abandoned any pretensions to democratic ideals (Amutabi, 2003, pp. 128-129). This status quo prevailed till December 1991, when multi-party democracy was re-introduced. Since then, there has been an emergence of several political parties, each with a different agenda (Mucai-Kattambo, Kabeberi-Macharia & Kameri-Mbote, 1995). The first multi-party election was held on December 29, 1992, and incumbent president Daniel Arap Moi won amid domestic criticism that the election was unfair. In 2002, Kenya held the second multi-party election, which was hailed by international and local observers as democratic and fair. This marked the end of Daniel Arap Moi's 24–year rule. The presidency and the parliamentary majority passed from the KANU party that had ruled Kenya since independence to a coalition of new political parties (National Rainbow Coalition – NARC). This move towards democracy was disrupted in the December 27, 2007 election in which the incumbent Mwai Kibaki won amid allegations of massive rigging/irregularities. Life was never the same again for many Kenyans whose lives were marred by ethnic violence sending the message that multi-party democracy in Kenya faces significant challenges. Emerging democratic institutions in Kenya continue to struggle against the country's corrupt political system and intimidation, largely based on patronage and ethnic alliances (Human Rights Watch, 2002). Corrupt leaders and officials continue to plunder state resources, plunging the country into deeper poverty. The majority of Kenyan people have poor access to opportunities such as health care, education, housing and employment.

The post-election violence in Kenya in 2007 rattled the peace and tranquility that the country had long enjoyed and had been known for (Masakhwe, 2008). The crisis not only played out as a corollary of political flaws, but it also invigorated the long-standing ethnic differences, historical injustices and imbalances dating back to colonial times, particularly the problem of access to and distribution of national resources and opportunities (Masakhwe, 2008). Many Kenyans died; others were severely wounded, left disabled for the rest of their lives. There was widespread destruction of property, crops, grain stores, and other forms of human livelihood, particularly in Western, Rift Valley and Nyanza provinces, posing high risk of serious food shortages in the country. Hundreds of thousands of people were displaced and had to live in camps for the internally displaced with limited access to food and medical care, a situation that contributes to disability. To date, a number of those who were displaced have not returned to their homes.

Worth mentioning is the fact that people with disabilities were rendered invisible by the government, and by the media and relief organizations in the 2007/2008 crises in Kenya. In describing the difficult situation that disabled people were facing in the various camps for the internally displaced persons in the country, Masakhwe (2008) observed:

Over the past few weeks I have visited various camps and witnessed first hand the difficult conditions that disabled people are facing. They are often unable to access food and water as they are not physically strong enough to queue or even at times [strong enough to] push through the crowds to get supplies. Many disabled people had to abandon their wheelchairs and crutches, etc. in the flight from their homes and were carried to camps by friends and relatives. They are now confined to sitting in the same spot all day, dependent on friends and family to feed and clothe them. For many, not only have they lost their homes, but also their independence and livelihoods. (www.independentliving.org/#masakhwe20080124)

Masakhwe, who is himself disabled, lamented that many camps failed to recognize that people with hidden disabilities such as diabetes or epilepsy, had urgent health care needs. Some children with disabilities died because of lack of health care which their lives depended on. Masakhwe (2008) further noted that a number of parents, relatives and friends reported about leaving their relatives and friends with disabilities at home or on the road when they were fleeing for their lives, simply because they were unable to carry them. Masakhwe called on the media to report on the situation of people with disabilities and to publish their stories in an effort to raise awareness and to lay emphasis on what was happening with this vulnerable segment of the population. He also called on the Disabled People's Organizations (DPO) to work with relief agencies and government to explain the importance of recognizing and prioritizing the needs of people with disabilities in emergency situations.

In spite of Masakhwe's observations, it still remains unclear to date how many people with disabilities were affected by the post-election violence in Kenya. Twelve days after Masakhwe's analysis, on February 5, 2008, one of the country's daily newspapers, the Daily Nation Newspaper, carried a story that mentioned the plight of people with disabilities in the crises in Kenya. The story talked about the mediation process led by former United Nations Secretary General Kofi Annan and also outlined the measures that the Government and opposition (ODM) mediators[4] had agreed to take in an effort to resolve the political crisis in the country. These measures included:

- Setting up a Truth and Reconciliation Commission to aid in the healing process and also to encourage and help displaced people to settle back in their homes or other areas.
- Providing adequate security and protection, particularly for vulnerable groups, including women and children in the camps.
- Providing basic services for people in displaced camps – ensuring that there was adequate food, water, sanitation and shelter within the affected communities (both those in displaced camps and those remaining in their communities).
- Providing medical assistance with specific focus on women, children, people living with HIV and Aids, and on the disabled, currently in camps for the displaced.
- Ensuring all children had access to education. This would involve reconstruction of schools and encouraging return of teaching staff, provision of learning materials, and helping children to return to the institutions.
- Providing information centers where the affected could get information regarding the assistance that was available to them and how to access it, for example, support for reconstruction of their livelihood, or tracing of family members.
- Operationalizing the Humanitarian Fund for Mitigation of Effects and Resettlement of Victims of Post 2007 Election Violence expeditiously by establishing a non-partisan, multi-sectoral board to streamline procedures to disburse funds rapidly.
- Ensuring that victims of violence in urban areas were not neglected.
- Ensuring that inclusive Reconciliation and Peace Building Committees were established at grass roots levels, involving the provincial administration, councils of elders, women, youth and conflict resolution or civil society organizations.

(www.nationmedia.com/dailynation/nmgcontententry. asp?category_id=1&newsid=116165).

In the above recommendations, there was a mention of people with disabilities but only with respect to provision of medical assistance. Other basic needs, such as food, security, education etc. were not covered.

The recommendations were great but very general and, thereby, failed to appropriately cater for specific needs of vulnerable groups, such as people with disabilities.

Following the post-election violence, in 2009, The National Council for Persons with Disabilities (NCPWD) represented the interests of persons with disabilities in the "One Kenya, One Dream: The Kenya We Want" Conference held at the Kenyatta International Conference Centre on 4–6 February 2009. This conference evaluated the progress made regarding Kenya's national reconciliation efforts and the reforms needed to resolve diversity issues and improve the country's legal, economic, social, and political systems (NCPWD, 2009). The conference provided an important opportunity for persons with disabilities to contribute to defining the country that Kenyans want. NCPWD Acting Director Phoebe Nyagudi highlighted the effects of post-election violence on persons with disabilities and the consequences of conflicts on disabled people (NCPWD, 2009). She urged the government and civil society to consider the plight of persons with disabilities more seriously and ensure their protection and safety in situations of armed conflict and other crises. Nyagudi presented a number of recommendations to enhance participation of persons with disabilities in peace-building and national development which included: ensuring government preparedness in situations of emergency; gazettement of the remaining sections of the Act and the Rules and Regulations; full implementation of the Disability Act with appropriate budgetary allocation; finalization of the Disability Policy; domestication and implementation of the UN Convention of the Rights of Persons with Disabilities; mainstreaming of disability issues in policies dealing with education, health, and HIV/AIDS among others; appointment and involvement of persons with disabilities in decision-making bodies; inclusive and free primary education for children with disabilities; and accessible tourism for persons with disabilities (NCPWD, 2009).

As for gender, disability and political representation in Kenya, although women account for slightly half (about 52%) of the country's population they are grossly under-represented in the social, political and economic arenas in the country (Oanda, 2005, p. 89; International Knowledge Network of Women in Politics (iKNOW Politics), 2007). Since gaining independence from Britain in 1963, women have played a marginal role in Kenya's political life (Achieng' 1998). Women have not had equal opportunities as men to contribute to society, especially in decision making as leaders (iKNOW Politics, 2007). For example, with regard to parliamentary representation, in the 2002 general elections, only nine women were elected as members of parliament (MPs) in Kenya. In addition to the nine, there were also eight nominated female MPs, meaning that, in the last parliament there were only 18 women out of 222 MPs. Of these 18, there was none with a disability. In the general elections held on December 27, 2007, fifteen women were elected to parliament and none of them had a disability. It was hoped that the numbers of women MPs would rise if the different political parties nominated more women (Kinoti, 2008) but this did not happen. It should be noted that, even with this relative progress in terms of women's representation in Kenyan parliament in 2008, compared to the year 2002, Kenya still lags behind its neighbours in eastern and central Africa (Kinoti, 2008). Rwanda ranks first globally in women's representation in parliament with 56.3 percent women legislators; Burundi is 22nd with 31.4% of female legislators. Tanzania and Uganda were 16th and 17th with 30 percent women in parliament. Kenya's ranked 115th globally, and was in the 4th worst in Africa" (pajamasmedia.com).

There is a concern that the marginalization and under representation of women in Kenya persists in spite of the country being a signatory to some of the most important international instruments that affirm equality of sexes and fundamental human rights, such as the Universal Declaration of Human Rights; the International Covenant of Civil and Political Rights; the Convention for the Elimination of all forms of Discrimination against Women, and the Beijing Platform for Action (iKNOW Politics, 2007). Perhaps the question to ask is, why should countries then be allowed to be party to ratifying some of these conventions if they do not live up to their obligations? There is laxity on the part of government to promote rights and freedoms of women in Kenya. This laxity has led to women's limited participation in governance and decision-making in all spheres of life, whether in educational management, industry and commerce, in the professions, or in national politics. Consequently law-makers have largely not been women, and have rarely had the perspective of women in the process (Mondoh & Mujidi, 2006, p. 60). According to iKNOW Politics (2007), the patriarchal society in which Kenyan women operate ensures male domination of political and public life (www.wedo.org/files/kneya. doc). In some communities, it is a taboo for a woman to compete with a man and, in such circumstances; male politicians do not face any competition from a woman for electoral positions (Toroitich & African Women and Child Information Network, 2004). This is because of the prevailing patriarchal attitudes in the Kenyan society, whereby a lot of times male leadership is validated at all levels as the only legitimate leadership (Kariuki, 2006; Wane & Opini, 2006). In most Kenyan communities, males are socialized to see themselves as the breadwinners and leaders in society (Wane & Opini, 2006). Although Kenyan women are beginning to upset some of these patriarchal practices by ascending to leadership positions previously dominated by men (Kariuki, 2006), the culture of patriarchy in Kenya remains deeply entrenched, thus ensuring male domination in much of the political and public life. Consequently, women in Kenya have not had equal opportunities to contribute to society especially in decision-making or leadership arenas (Toroitich & African Women and Child Information Network, 2004). I agree with Kariuki's (2006) argument that the more we understand the effects of the patriarchal culture in Kenya, the more we are likely to understand the roots of the marginalization that women in Kenya experience and, in this context, disabled women students (pp. 65-67).

On 4 August 2010, the people of Kenya voted to adopt a new Constitution which addresses among many other issues gender equality and disability. Article 27 (3) states that "Women and men have the right to equal treatment including the right to equal opportunities in political, economic, cultural and social spheres." Section (4) says that: "The State shall not discriminate directly or indirectly against any person on any ground, including race, sex, pregnancy, marital status, health status, ethnic or social origin, colour, age, disability, religion, conscience, belief, culture, dress, language or birth." While this is an important step forward, implementation is key.

There have been limited efforts by the government to promote gender equality and participation of both men and women equally and moreso those with disabilities in all spheres of life. Considering the state of affairs in Kenya today, I argue that, until the government takes more interest in women and in disabled people and, until it specifically focuses on the promotion of efforts to better represent women and disabled people in the government and in other key leadership positions in the country, they (women and disabled persons) will continue to exist as marginal persons with minimal say and influence on the affairs of the nation. This goal could be achieved through, among other means, lobbying for better representation and for the enforcing of the international human rights rules and regulations spelt out in the Charter of Human Rights. Otherwise, only limited efforts will be made on the part of government to push agendas, policies and legislation to address the plight of marginal groups in the country.

EDUCATION IN PRE-COLONIAL KENYA

Indigenous educational systems existed in African societies prior to the coming of the Europeans (Esu & Junaid, 2008; Nathani, 1996; Omolewa, 2007; Wane, 2005). Such education was aimed at preparing Africans for responsibilities as adults in their communities (Boateng, 1983). Children and members of society learned by living and doing (Nyerere, 1967; Dei, 1996b; Kenyatta, 1961/65; Marah, 2006; Mbiti, 1990). Unlike the educational systems of the colonialists, African traditional education was inseparable from other segments of life, as it was not only there to be acquired, but also to be lived (Wane, 2008). Indigenous education in Africa had clearly identifiable principles and goals. Adeyemi and Adeyinka (2002) identified these goals as follows: (1) To develop the child's latent physical skills; (2) To develop character; (3) To inculcate respect for elders and those in position of authority; (4) To develop intellectual skills; (5) To acquire specific vocational training and to develop a healthy attitude towards honest labour; (6) To develop a sense of belonging and to participate actively in family and community affairs; (7) To understand, appreciate and promote the cultural heritage of the community at large. In other words, indigenous African education sought to prepare children and young people for the places they were to occupy in that society (Nyerere, 1967, p. 2; see also Boateng, 1983; Kenyatta, 1961).

Education in African indigenous societies was done by elders/adult members of society and according to age groups (Esu & Junaid, 2008; Nathani, 1996; Omolewa, 2007). The elders employed traditional oral literature, secret societies, and other religious practices in the education of youth, a practice that ensured intergenerational communication (Boateng, 1983, p. 323). Felix Boateng (1983) defines intergenerational communication as:

> ... the smooth transmission and continuous preservation of the values and traditions of a society from one generation to the other. Intergenerational communication ensures a peaceful transition from youth to adulthood, and creates an understanding between the generations of the proper roles of each in the society. ... this was achieved through a network of traditional institutions and a set of norms, mores, and folkways that produced understandings-an essential element in cultural growth and stability. (pp. 322-323)

However, folktales, legends, myths, and proverbs could not achieve their maximum efficiency as educational and communicative tools without the proper orientation of boys and girls toward their traditional roles in society (Boateng, 1983, p. 332). Girls were socialized to learn the roles of motherhood, wife, and other gender-specific skills. Boys were socialized to be hunters, herders, agriculturalists, blacksmiths, etc., depending on how the particular ethnic group, clan or family derived its livelihood (Marah, 2006, p. 15; also Kenyatta, 1965). These roles were acquired in stages and according to age. In the early years of childhood, the child's education was largely in the hands of the biological mother, and the community assumed a larger role as adolescence approached (Marah, 2006, p. 20).

With the advent of European missionaries and colonialists in Africa, indigenous education in Africa started to fade out. This is because, as Puja (2001) reveals, missionary and colonial educators tried to eradicate the existing indigenous forms of education when designing education for African people (p. 47). Puja adds that the missionaries and colonialists made Africans feel that their way of life was inferior to that of their colonial masters, and that this belief was responsible for the destruction of much of indigenous African knowledge and education in Tanzania and other African countries (p. 48). Boateng (1983), commenting on this hierarchization of races and its implications for education, observes that colonial interruption in social relations left a vacuum in the lives of African people that was filled with confusion, loss of identity, and a total break in intergenerational communication (p. 334).

As for individuals with disabilities, the literature about the education of children and youth with disability in African traditional societies is limited. Some authors argue that "a child with a disability was provided with an extended care system within the African traditional system because education was a family matter involving grandfathers, grandmothers, father, mother, uncles, aunts, brothers, sisters, cousins, nephews and nieces" (Kenosi, 2000). Others argue that children with disability were special spiritual beings and that there were rituals accompanying their education and living in society. Some writers indicate that disability was believed to be a result of witchcraft or parents violating traditional standards and/or values (Hops, 1996). Thus there were feelings of fear, pity and isolation, often resulting in the neglecting of children with disabilities. Disability deteriorated into inability under those conditions. The differing perceptions are examined further in chapter four in the review of literature on indigenous attitudes and reactions to disability in Africa.

COLONIAL EDUCATION IN KENYA

The establishment of "formal western" schooling in Kenya is often traced back to the 19th century, when the Church Missionary Society established a school at Rabai in Mombasa in 1846. The early "western-oriented" schools in Kenya were established to promote Christian evangelism. Later, these schools developed into instruments for producing labour for white settler farms and clerks for the colonial administration (Mungai, 2002, p. 3). As in many African countries, colonial education in Kenya was characterized by racial stratification and sexual segregation (see Mianda, 2002; Musisi, 1992). There were schools for Europeans, Asians and Africans (Mungai, 2002).

Chege and Sifuna (2006) argue that, even though the existence of a dominant patriarchal arrangement was typical in many traditional (pre-colonial) African communities, the claim that the underlying ideology translated exclusively into the exploitation of women is inaccurate. This is because there were matriarchal societies in Africa in which women held positions of power that were linked to age and experience that gave them reverence in the community's economic, political and religious life (Chege & Sifuna, 2006; Obioma, 1998; Oyewumi, 2003; Sudarkasa, 1996). Women were queen-mothers, queen-sisters, princesses, chiefs and holders of other offices in towns and villages, and they were even occasional warriors. Women were also noticeable in the economic life of their societies, being involved in farming, trade or craft production (Oyewumi, 2003). Chege (2001) argued that the colonial administration imported models of Western education which propagated notions of female inferiority, exploitation and oppression, resulting in the marginalization of African women in most societies, relative to their male counterparts, in ways that were unprecedented in the recorded and oral history of the colonies (see Amadiume, 1987; Sofola, 1998). Western education employed an exploitative capitalist ideology that was not only racist but also sexist, and ignored the diversity of African cultures and disrupted the functional traditional pedagogy that had regulated gender relations among African societies for generations (Chege, 2001). The colonialists gave priority to males and especially sons of chiefs and local administrators in education provision (James, 1953, cited in Kabira & Nzioki, 1993, p. 30). Men received instruction (and in the language of the colonizer) so they could work for the colonial government (Mungai, 2002; Bogonko, 1992). Women's education was offered in indigenous languages and focused on the acquisition of home-making skills and the reinforcement of supposedly feminine characteristics, as defined by Christian morality (see Musisi, 1992). Thus, the first modern African social and political elites were exclusively men (Musisi, 1992).

The missionaries, too, gave preference to male education because, as Kabira and Nzioki (1993) note: "... education was a means to provide Christian personnel to carry out evangelization in remote areas, a task which was not favorable to women" (p. 30). Kabira and Nzioki add that, later, "the missionaries realized that education of women was crucial for survival of the church. The majority of men left home in search of wage employment and those who received missionary education left missionary service to take up 'white collar' jobs in towns". Neither could the educated African men find the right (Christian) wives (p. 30). Thus, missionary actors in education were not interested in educating women for employment; they believed that the main aim of education was to prepare women for marriage (Ogundipe-Leslie, 1994).

The colonial administration was determined to clearly define the gender divide in a way that was more advantageous to men than women (Chege & Sifuna, 2006). Although some scholars have described the arguments that colonialism privileged men as inaccurate (Zeleza, 1997, 2003), from the above examples, it is evident that African men did benefit more than women in terms of higher education (Kanogo, 2005). On the few occasions that higher level educational opportunities were offered to women they were geared towards employment mainly as nurses, lady physicians, schoolmistresses and secretaries. Even in these selected areas, women were denied access to any position requiring them to exercise authority over men, a policy which was ironically justified on the basis that the idea would be "too foreign" to Africans (Chege & Sifuna, 2006). Feminization of these occupations was consistent with gender roles in Victorian England, where women's employment positions were thought of as being inferior to those of men. This institutionalized gendering of occupations continues to negatively affect the education and employment of women in present times (Chege & Sifuna, 2006, p. 24). It is, thus, clear that, and as Musisi (1992) infers, colonization improved and perfected the gendered positions of men by according them more privileges than women in political, judicial, economic and social domains. Mianda (2002) concludes that "this discrimination against women shows why girls' education continues to lag behind that of boys, because girls have been trained primarily for domesticity" (p. 144). The social marginalization effected by colonial education is only magnified in the case of disabled women. There is a definite need for future research documenting the place and status of women with disabilities in colonial Kenya.

EDUCATION AFTER INDEPENDENCE

Until 1960, education in Kenya was offered to three distinct demographic populations: African, Asian and Arab, and European (Anderson, 1970; Bogonko, 1992). The colonial government's greatest interest was in educating the European and Asian populations and, therefore, by the time of independence educational infrastructure was more highly developed in these areas (Anderson, 1970). When Kenya attained independence in

1963, the government sought to reform the education system to meet local needs (Bogonko, 1992). In order to achieve this goal, a number of Commissions were established to chart the way for reforms that would make the education multi-racial and enhance access to education for Kenyans. These commissions include: the Ominde Commission of 1964; the Ndegwa Commission of 1971; the Gachathi Commission of 1976; the Mackay Commission of 1981; and the Kariithi Commission of 1983 (Bogonko, 1992; Rotich, 2004). There was also the Presidential Working Party on Education and Manpower Training for the Next Decade and Beyond in 1988 (Kamunge Report) and the Koech Report of 2000. All of these commissions have shaped Kenyan education policies and practices in various ways.[5] Here, I focus on the Ominde Commission, the Kamunge Report and Koech Reports which had significant implications for the education of students with disabilities.

The Ominde commission of 1964 sought to reform the education system inherited from the colonial government to make it more responsive to the needs of the country (Ngigi & Macharia, 2006). The Commission proposed an education system that would foster national unity and the creation of sufficient human capital for national development. The commission recommended bringing to an end the segregation of schools by race, and the unification of the curriculum in all schools (Rotich, 2004, p. 177). It also recommended universal primary education in the country to enhance access to many learners.[6] As for disability, the Ominde Commission recognized the disability sector as needing attention in terms of education and training (Republic of Kenya/ Ministry of Education, 2006, p. 10). The Commission recommended measures to address the Government's role in coordination and improvement of service, quality and delivery strategies. According to the Republic of Kenya/ Ministry of Education (2006), the recommendations of the Ominde report set the pace for Government leadership in the provision and in the coordination of services to persons with disabilities. The report also marked the beginning of the provision of technical, industrial and vocational education for young adults with disabilities in Kenya (p. 10-11).

The Kamunge Report of 1988 (Report of the Presidential Working Party on Education and Manpower Training for the Next Decade and Beyond) focused on improving education financing, quality and relevance of education as a whole to local and international needs (Republic of Kenya, 2005). Recommendations from this Working Party (Kamunge Report) led to the production of "Sessional Paper No. 6 on Education and Training for the Next Decade and Beyond." This led to the policy of cost-sharing between government, parents and communities (Ngigi & Macharia,

2006), otherwise described as the downloading of costs from the national government to community organizations. The government was to meet salaries of teachers and education administration as well as fund some limited school facilities while parents were to provide for tuition, textbooks, activity and examination fees. The communities, on the other hand, were to be responsible for putting up physical structures and ensuring their maintenance (Owino & Abagi, 2000). This shift had implications for disabled students, especially those from poor backgrounds, because parents lacked the finances to support them. Consequently, they had to make choices of which children to invest in when it came to paying school fees. In most cases non-disabled children were prioritized while those with disabilities often ended up being sent to vocational schools to train in courses such as tailoring and craft work.

The Koech Report of 2000 (Commission of Inquiry into the Education System of Kenya) was mandated to recommend ways and means of enabling the education system to facilitate national unity, mutual social responsibility, accelerated industrial and technological development, life-long learning, and adaptation in response to changing circumstances. The Report also attempted to address issues relating to the structure of education, arguing that the 8-4-4 structure, although appropriate and well-intentioned, was implemented in a hasty manner (Republic of Kenya, 2003). The Koech Report, perhaps overly ambitious, proposed 558 recommendations, most of which have not yet been accomplished. The Report reiterated that the education system in Kenya faced major challenges and that it had been difficult to achieve the objectives of Education for All (EFA) initiative for the last ten years. The report revealed that many school-age children did not attend school; half of those who entered primary education dropped out by grade 6; the quality and relevance of education had not met the hopes and expectations of the people. Additionally, the cost of education had been rising and had become unaffordable to half of Kenya's population.[7] The Koech Report recommended a policy proposal it termed: Totally Integrated Quality Education and Training (TIQET) to reflect the need for Government and other players (including households, communities, NGOs, religious organizations and international agencies) to adopt a holistic and inclusive approach to the problems facing education (Abagi, 1997; Abagi, et al, 2000). In the Koech Report (Koech, 1999) efforts were also made to highlight disability, with a focus on special educational needs of each category of disabled people and to increase participation in day-to-day human activities while reducing the degree of dependence on others (Ochoggia, 2003, p. 309). While the Government did not undertake all the recommendations advanced by the Koech Report, citing of lack of money, some recommendations, such as curriculum rationalization, have been adopted and implemented (Ngigi & Macharia, 2006).

The above reports, in spite of their shortfalls, made commendable contributions that helped to advance the discussion over education policy, particularly policies affecting students with disabilities in one way or the other. The recommendations of the Ominde Report (Republic of Kenya, 1964); the Kamunge Report (Republic of Kenya, 1988) and the Koech Report (Koech, 1999), made attempts to address the issue of disability, thus, prompting the Kenyan Government to recognize the existence of persons with disabilities among its citizenry (Ochoggia, 2003). As a result, some considerable efforts have been made to increase government involvement and interest in special education in the country (Ndurumo, 1993) with greater focus centered on primary education and some beginning initiatives in secondary education.

However, policies which explicitly address the educational needs of the disabled at secondary schools and higher levels of education are yet to be formulated. When the Commissions addressed issues of disability, emphasis was laid on disabled children being provided with support services at primary school levels. Little was mentioned about secondary and post-secondary education. There is, thus, reason to conclude that, in Kisanji's (1993) words, disability and special education continue to occupy a low profile in Kenya's national planning and post-secondary level educational development initiatives. Indeed, there is no clear distinction between disability studies and special education, as many of the recommendations made in the Reports are immersed in the medical model of disability, thus minimizing the role of society and environment in producing disablement. This distinction is important in moving forward the project of disability as an issue of equity and social justice. Moreover, in order to accord people with disabilities their full respect and dignity, government policy must focus, not only on the early years, but also must contemplate a path through secondary and post secondary education and eventually to the labor market. This is not to deny the commendable steps that have been made toward addressing the needs of disabled people in Kenya, as seen, for example, in the passing of legislation such as the Persons with Disabilities Act (PDA) - ACT NO. 14 of 2003 and the preparation of a draft policy on special needs education for children with disabilities in Kenya (Republic of Kenya/Ministry of Education, 2006), described below. The argument, however, is that more needs to be done, particularly in terms of enforcing these laws and policies.

PERSONS WITH DISABILITIES ACT (PDA) - ACT NO. 14 OF 2003

The Persons with Disabilities Act was enacted by the Kenyan parliament on December 2003. The Act seeks to provide for the rights and rehabilitation of persons with disabilities, with the ultimate goal of achieving equalization of opportunities for persons with disabilities. The PDA also provides for the establishment of the National Council for Persons with Disabilities (NCPD) to be the focal point for all issues relating to persons with disabilities; to implement and ensure the implementation of the rights of persons with disabilities covered in the Act, and to formulate and develop measures and policies designed to ensure that persons with disabilities are educated, employed and participate fully in sporting recreational and cultural activities. The Act states that the Council will implement projects that will promote sheltered employment, regular or self-employment opportunities for persons with disabilities (ILO, 2004; Kenya Law Reports, n.d.). In 2004, the National Council for Persons with Disabilities (NCPD) was established. According to the Act, the NCDP is required to have up to 27 members, composed as follows: representatives of disabled persons' organizations (8), Government (9), organizations providing services to persons with disabilities (3), employers' and workers' organizations (2). The Council sought to conduct research on diverse disability-related issues in the country and to work towards a barrier free and disability friendly environment. It was, and still is, also responsible for the registration of persons with disabilities and disabled people's organization (DPOs) in the country (http://www.ke.undp.org/disabilities.htm).

The Persons with Disability Act prohibits all manner of discrimination against persons with disabilities (AFUB, KUB & CREAD, 2007, p. 20). The PDA prohibits discrimination on the basis of disability in areas such as education, employment and health etc., and in service provision in both the public and private sector (AFUB, KUB & CREAD, 2007, p. 20). Discrimination is defined as "according different treatment to different persons solely or mainly as a result of their disabilities and includes using words, gestures or caricatures that demean scandalize or embarrass a person with a disability" (http://www.kenyalawreports.or.ke/kenyalaw/klr_app/frames.php). Discrimination in education is specifically prohibited by the Act. Section 18 of the PDA stipulates that: (1) No person or learning institution shall deny admission to a person with a disability to any course of study by reason only of such disability, if the person has the ability to acquire substantial learning in that course; (2) Learning institutions shall take into account the special needs of persons with disabilities with respect to the entry requirements, pass marks, curriculum, examinations, auxilliary services, use of school facilities, class schedules, physical education requirements and other similar considerations (Kenya Law Reports, n.d).

With respect to employment, Section 12 prohibits discrimination against people with disabilities as follows: (1) No person shall deny a person with a disability access to opportunities for suitable employment; (2) A qualified employee with a disability shall be subject to the same terms and conditions of employment and the same compensation, privileges, benefits, fringe benefits, incentives or allowances as qualified able-bodied employees; (3) An employee with a disability shall be entitled to exemption from tax on all income accruing from his employment (Kenya Law Reports, n.d.; see also AFUB, KUB & CREAD, 2007; ILO, 2004). The Act provides for wide-ranging benefits and incentives for persons with disabilities, including exclusion from paying tax on income from jobs. For examples, materials, articles and equipment that are modified or designed for use by disabled people, are exempted from import duty and from value added tax (ILO, 2004). In addition, both public and private sectors are required to reserve five per cent of jobs for disabled persons. The Act stipulates that a private employer who employs a person with disability who has the required skills or qualifications will be entitled to apply for a deduction from his/her taxable income equivalent to 25 per cent of the total amount paid as salary and wages to such an employee (ILO, 2004).

Pointing to accessibility, Section 21 states that "... persons with disabilities are entitled to a barrier-free and disability-friendly environment in order to enable them to have access to buildings, roads and other social amenities, and [are entitled to] assistive devices and other equipment to promote their mobility" (Kenya Law Reports, n.d). To make the work place environment more accessible, the Act allows for an employer who improves or modifies physical facilities for the benefit of employees with disabilities additional deduction from his net taxable income. This deduction is equivalent to 50 per cent of the direct costs of improvements, modifications or special services (ILO, 2004).

The PDA also has provisions which prohibit discrimination against persons with disabilities in areas such as television programs, telephone services and postal charges (AFUB, KUB & CREAD, 2007, p. 20). Following the enactment of the PDA, some efforts have been made towards enhancing access to education for disabled people in Kenya, but more needs to be done especially in higher education. Although the PDA represents the government's efforts to address the needs of people with disabilities in the country, there are still some gaps that need to be addressed. In the area of education, the Act provides a very general explanation of the discriminatory practices that are not allowed and also calls for establishment of special schools and institutions to cater for the needs of the disabled. In as much as all these provisions are important, they can be improved further by identifying some key aspects that educational institutions, especially universities and colleges, ought to address to improve access to education for disabled people. For example, disabled people share some common discriminatory experiences but it is also important to remember that disability intersects with other aspects of difference like class, gender, ethnicity/race, religion etc. meaning that different individuals will end up having different experiences. The Act is silent when it comes to provisions that acknowledge and address these differences. This is an important area that needs to be looked into.

DRAFT POLICY ON SPECIAL NEEDS EDUCATION FOR CHILDREN WITH DISABILITIES IN KENYA

The provision of education for children with special needs has not been easy in sub-Saharan Africa, including Kenya (East African Standard, 2007). In Kenya, the Government has expressed commitment to the attainment of Education For All (EFA) by 2015, in line with the right to education for all Kenyans, as spelt out in the Sessional Paper No. 1 of 2005[8] (Republic of Kenya/Ministry of Education, 2006). In working towards this EFA goal, the Government has made efforts to promote inclusive education by, for example, calling for the restructuring of the education system in terms of physical facilities, curriculum and instruction and teacher preparation to allow all children access to education (Republic of Kenya/Ministry of Education, 2006). Nevertheless, a report on the status of access to education in Kenya, issued by Elimu Yet Coalition (2007), indicated that many disabled children were still at home and did not receive the required assistance to pursue their basic education. There was also lack of a clear policy and lack of coordination of the activities and services for disabled people. Subsequently, there was duplication, substandard and unregulated service provisions to learners with special needs. Consequently, in 2006, the government embarked on the development of a special needs education policy with the vision of moving toward attaining a society in which all persons with disabilities would have access to and equally exercise the right to quality education and training (Republic of Kenya/Ministry of Education, 2006, p. 13). The draft policy, which in my view, draws largely from a medical model of disability, identifies the goals of special needs education as follows: (i) to improve skills, values and attitudes aimed at habilitation, rehabilitation and adjustment to environments; (ii) to identify, assess and provide early intervention for correction and rehabilitation; (iii) to promote awareness of the needs of persons with disabilities and the methods of alleviating the effects of the various disabilities; (iv) to promote integration and inclusion of children with disability in formal and non-formal education and training; (v) to promote provision of specialized facilities and equipment; (vi) to promote measures to prevent impairment in order to limit the incidence of disabilities; (vii) to put in place measures that would reduce effects of impairment; (viii) to promote provision and use of specialized facilities, assistive devices, equipment and teaching/learning materials (Republic of Kenya/ Ministry of Education, 2006, p. 14). The policy also identifies the objectives of the special needs education policy as follows:

- To develop a range of special needs education services capable of responding to the needs of all learners with disabilities
- To systematize all learning approaches and techniques required by each category of learners with disabilities across all levels of education
- To harmonize and standardize use and application of terms, measurements and assistive technology
- To develop suitable curricula, examination procedures, certification and management processes to facilitate the efficient provision of quality special needs education services
- To remove environmental and other barriers affecting access to education by learners with disabilities
- To provide suitably trained personnel for each category of special needs education learners at all levels of education including pre-primary, secondary, tertiary, universities, technical, non-technical education
- To develop institutions of excellence for the training of personnel, development, adaptation and maintenance of assistive technology and conducting research into various aspects of special needs education
- To provide relevant and appropriate equipment, teaching/learning materials and assistive devices to all categories of children and learners with special needs
- To enhance parents', families' and community participation in education of children with special needs
- To respond to the greatest extent possible to changing circumstances of children and learners with special needs
- To provide specific legislation to govern the provision of special

needs education services and related materials

- To promote linkages and collaboration with individuals, institutions and other special needs service providers for efficient and effective utilization of resources
- To enhance access to technical, vocational, entrepreneurial and professional training in formal and non-formal settings in order to promote functional skills for persons with disabilities (Republic of Kenya/Ministry of Education, 2006, pp. 14-15).

The objectives of this draft policy are great but also very generalized and say little about the needs of disabled students in higher education. For example, the policy identifies "systematizing all learning approaches and techniques required by each category of learners with disabilities across all levels of education" as one of its objectives, but what does this really mean and how is the goal to be achieved? Moreover, the draft policy does not address issues of intersectionalities and thus leaves a lot to be desired. There is a need to simplify the above objectives and to provide more tangible goals that are achievable and that can be easily evaluated. The section that follows discusses contemporary higher education in Kenya and explains how women fare in higher education in the country.

CONTEMPORARY HIGHER EDUCATION IN KENYA

After four years of secondary school education, students in Kenya sit for the Kenya Certificate of Secondary Education (KCSE), which is administered by the Kenya National Examinations Council. Students who obtain a minimum aggregate grade of C+ and above are eligible to go to university. However, this minimum entrance grade keeps changing from year to year depending on students' performance for that particular year. There are also secondary schools that still offer the 7-4-2-3 education system and most of their graduates go to overseas countries for post-secondary education. Those who do not qualify typically join two or three year colleges for certificate, Diploma and Higher National Diploma programs, and can later apply to join universities as mature students. The two or three-year colleges include teacher training colleges (TTCs), Kenya Medical Training colleges (KMTC), Polytechnics, and many others. Postsecondary institutions in Kenya are set up by various Acts of Parliament (Association of African Universities, 2004, p. 215). The focus of this book is on university education.

University education in Kenya is predominantly offered through public universities that have been established by Acts of Parliament (some of them with constituent colleges). University education in Kenya is also offered through private institutions with a charter (fully accredited), through private universities with a letter of Interim Authority, and through private institutions without a charter. Currently, there are seven public universities (the University of Nairobi, Kenyatta University, Jomo Kenyatta University of Agriculture and Technology, Egerton University, Moi University, Maseno University and Masinde Muliro University of Science and Technology – formerly Western University College) and 17 private universities operating in the country (Nyaigotti-Chacha, 2004).

Admission decisions concerning entrance into an undergraduate degree program are undertaken by the Joint Admissions Board (JAB) (Teng'o, 2003). The JAB is a centralized body which coordinates the admission process for all public universities in Kenya. The admission requirements for undergraduate programs are determined by the performance of students from year to year. However, the minimum requirement is an aggregate of C+ in the Kenya Certificate of Secondary Education (KCSE) examination or its equivalent. Applicants must also meet specific degree program subject cluster points. The entry requirements are regarded as the minimum, which do not entitle an applicant to a place in public universities. The Joint Admissions Board (JAB) sends application forms to all high school students in their final year. Application forms are also available from the websites of some of the universities and from the office of the Joint Admissions Board in Nairobi (Teng'o, 2003; www.ku.ac.ke/admissions/jab.htm). Those who meet the aggregate grade set for that particular year get admission into university as "regular students" and are entitled to a student loan from the Higher Education Loans Board (HELB) of Kenya. Students who do not meet the aggregate grade set for admission for that particular year, or those who want to join university as mature entrants, have to do so as "self-sponsored students". These students either collect application forms directly from their university of choice or apply online through the universities' website. A student wishing to join university as mature entrants qualifies for the HELB loans if they are below 25 years of age. If they are over 25 years and are mature entry students, the university has to make a case for them for HELB loans to be granted. Some of the reasons offered during that advocacy include disability, low social economic status, etc. Most of my study participants (80% - 16 out of 20) fell under this category (self-sponsored).

It is important to also note that student enrollment in Kenyan universities has increased tremendously over the years since independence. This is because, as Aisemon (1992) indicated, at independence, the government of Kenya emphasized investments in higher education as a means of forming "high level" human capital (p. 157). Consequently, the country experienced rapid expansion of the public university system (see Eisemon, 1992;

Oketch, 2004). In the 1980s, the number of undergraduate students grew so rapidly that the Kenyan government was unable to provide the same level of financial support that higher education institutions had received in the 1960s and 70s (Eisemon, 1992, p. 157). Oketch (2004) remarked:

> ... The official enrollment at the state universities increased from 571 students in 1963/64 academic year to an all time high of 42,360 in 1995/96. State universities witnessed the largest increment in enrollments in 1987/88 when student population went up by over 100% for undergraduate enrollment as a result of a presidential declaration for double intake (*i.e. state universities admitted twice the number of students that would have been admitted under the stipulated yearly capacity*). The year 1990/91 also registered a sharp increase in undergraduate enrollment to 36,691 from the previous year of 24,164 when the first group of the 8-4-4 education system joined the university with the last group of the former advanced level system. The universities continued with their growth in student population in the subsequent years until the 1996/97 academic year when it declined to 37,212. By the 2000/01 academic year, the student population at the state universities had dropped from an all time high of 42,360 in 1995/96 to 34,955. But this figure does not include the students who have been enrolled in the public universities under the parallel degree programs which were initiated in 1997/98. (p. 121)

The high enrollment rates in Kenya's public university system meant that the government was unable to admit and finance all qualifying students. In response to this problem, the Kenyan government allowed the development of a private higher education sector to help take pressure off of the public system (Eisemon, 1992). Furthermore, in an effort to accommodate expanding enrollments in public universities, during the 1997/98 academic year, the self-sponsored programs (also called parallel programs or Module II programs) were initiated as a means of financial diversification (Oketch, 2004, pp. 121-122). In Kenya, therefore, there are two ways a student can enter the public university: (i) through the Joint Admissions Board (JAB) and (ii) through the parallel program. As already noted, the JAB (regular entry) admissions are done by the joint admissions board while the self-sponsored (parallel) admissions are done by individual universities. The latter allow admission of high school graduates (and mature entrants who want to come back for higher education) who meet the minimum university entry requirements but whose examination results are not competitive enough to warrant them government tuition loans and bursaries (Oketch, 2004). Parallel students are, thus, self-sponsored and directly pay the full cost of their university education. They can take their lectures separately in the evening and weekends or together with the regular students (Nyaigotti-Chacha, 2004). Critics of this program call it the "private wing" of Kenya's public universities that is serving the rich group in the country who, after all, still pay far less than what they would pay for private universities or universities abroad. To the universities, it is an alternative revenue stream (see Oketch, 2004).

WOMEN AND HIGHER EDUCATION IN KENYA

Without a doubt, the Government of Kenya recognizes the importance of education in reducing poverty and in encouraging economic growth. Education is seen as an important exit route from poverty (Republic of Kenya, 2005). This importance has heightened the attention paid to education as a policy issue and contributed to the series of educational reforms implemented since independence. Such reforms have dealt with problems afflicting the education sector such as the need to find ways to improve student enrollments, regardless of gender, economic status or location of residence (rural, urban, arid or semi-arid). Many schools have been built to promote access. The number of both private and public universities has also grown (Lelei, 2005, p. 154). Enrollment and growth in universities has been increasing since the establishment of the first Kenyan university, the University of Nairobi, in 1970. The total enrollment in public universities has increased from 3,443 students in 1970 to 58,017 students (18,317 females and 39,700 males) in 2003/04. However, despite these increased enrollments, the sector is still faced with issues of access, equity and quality (Republic of Kenya, 2005 cited in Lelei, 2005, p. 155). As Lelei (2005) writes, "in many urban slums and rural areas of Kenya, children have limited access to education" (p. 155). Girls face major challenges resulting in low participation in education at the secondary education level (Republic of Kenya, 2004, cited in Lelei, 2005, p. 155). At university levels, female students constitute 32 per cent of the total enrollment in public universities and 54 percent in private universities (Republic of Kenya, 2005 cited in Lelei, 2005, p. 155).[9]

The table below shows the representation of women in different levels of education for the years 2004 to 2006:

Table 1

Student enrolment by type of educational and training institutions and sex (1000s)

	2004		**2005**		**2006**	
	M	**F**	**M**	**F**	**M**	**F**
Enrolment in primary school	3,815.5	3,579.3	3,902.7	3,688.8	3,896.6	3,735.5
Enrolment in secondary school	490.5	435.6	494.2	440.0	546.1	484.0
Enrolment in universities (1)	**58.0**	**33.6**	**58.8**	**33.5**	**68.3**	**43.9**
Enrolment in other institutions (2)	45.7	44.6	47.1	45.7	47.8	46.0

(1) Kenyan students in national Universities and accredited Universities

(2) Includes teacher training colleges, Polytechnics, technical schools and institutions of science and technology

Source: Kenya National Bureau of Statistics (2007, p. 26)

The above statistics show that a greater population of men than women was enrolled in universities in Kenya between 2004 and 2006. Some studies have shown that female student enrolment is much higher in private universities, where they register well above 50 per cent (Chege & Sifuna, 2006; Lelei, 2005). For example, Lelei (2005) observes that, in Kenyan private universities the total enrollment for 2003/04 was 9,541 students (5,128 females and 4,413 males) (p. 155). Chege and Sifuna (2006) wrote that the higher enrollment of women in private universities is a result of the fact these universities offer more arts-based programs (Bachelor of Arts programs) and more women are likely to go into such programs (p. 85), compared to programs that offer math and science-based subjects (see also Wesonga et al., 2003). According to the European Mollecular Biology Organization [EMBO] (2007), there is no one clear single cause for the low enrollment of women in sciences, rather, there are many different causes tied to one another. In Kenya, gender stereotypes and differences in socialization have been identified as some of the factors that limit women from excelling in math and sciences (Eshiwani, 1993; Kiluva-Ndunda, 2000). Lack of social and professional support for women throughout their careers are other reasons (Sifuna, 2006).

In relation to students' background, Chege and Sifuna (2006) wrote that most of the women who attend universities come from economically advantaged backgrounds and that this has been a characteristic of Kenya's higher education over the years (p. 85). There are also variations in participation rates of female students across the various faculties. Most female students tend to prefer law, teaching and arts subjects over science, engineering, technology, agriculture and medicine (Kamau, 1996). In his paper *Reforming higher education in Kenya: Challenges, lessons and opportunities*, Chacha Nyaigotti-Chacha (2004) acknowledges that the participation of women in higher education in Kenya remains low. Nyaigotti-Chacha goes on to state that women are not only poorly represented in higher education as students but also as workers. Gender disparities are evident in teaching and in the administration of higher education institutions in Kenya proving Bond's (1997) assertion that "the principle and practice of full and equal partnership of women and men (*in higher education*) although a significant reform in gender roles, is yet to be achieved" (p. 2). The few women academics in Kenyan universities are there are concentrated in the lower ranks of the hierarchy and in the traditional "female" social science and education disciplines (see also Kamau, 1996; 2004; Onsongo, 2006). For example, a survey conducted by Onsongo (2002) on women's participation in university management revealed that women were a minority in university management both in public and private universities in Kenya, as seen in the tables below:

Position	M	F	Total	% of females
Vice Chancellor (VC)	6	0	6	0
Deputy (VC)	13	2	15	13.3
Principal	7	2	9	22.2
Director	42	18	60	30
Dean of Students	3	2	5	40
Dean of Faculty	38	5	43	11.6
Finance Officer	6	0	6	0
Librarian	6	0	6	0
Head of Dept (HOD)	208	35	243	14.4
Council Members	119	18	137	13.1
	462	82	544	14.6

Source: University calendar and staff lists cited by Onsongo, 2006 (p. 36)

Table 3: Status of women in management in four Kenyan private universities

Position	M	F	T	% of females
VC	3	1	4	10
DVC	8	1	9	11.1
Registrar	2	3	5	5
Human resource manager				
	2	1	3	33.3
Director	2	1	3	33.3
Dean of students	2	1	3	33.3
Dean of Faculty	11	1	12	8.3
Finance Officer	4	0	4	0
Librarian	2	2	4	50
HOD	35	17	52	32.7
Total	**71**	**28**	**99**	**100**

Source: University calendars and staff lists compiled by Onsongo (2006, p. 36)

Similar findings were reported by Kamau (1996) in her study on the experiences of female academics in five public universities in Kenya. Thus, women in Kenya do not enjoy educational and leadership opportunities equal to those enjoyed by their male counterparts. The few women who become academics and administrators face numerous challenges arising from policies and practices of the institutions. These challenges include discriminatory appointment and promotion criteria, lack of opportunities for further training, resistance from men, hostile work environment, sexual harassment and sex role stereotyping (Onsongo, 2006, p. 36). These findings are in agreement with findings from studies on gender and higher education from other parts of the world. For example, in her analysis of the situation of women in higher education in western contexts (British and North American), Acker (1992) remarked that the problem of marginalization of women in higher education lies in sex-typed socialization; family-career conflicts; under-investment in women's education; sex discrimination and career structures, and the workings of capitalism and patriarchy (p. 57). Acker further noted:

> ... although the representation of women as *students* has increased considerably, and many institutions have made gestures in the direction of equal opportunities, women academics are relatively disadvantaged, and the universities remain dominated by men. Feminist scholarship has been superb, but some disciplines and some individuals have barely heard of it. (p. 71)

The situation is true of Kenya. Although gender and feminist studies courses have been introduced in virtually all public universities; gender equality is far from being realized. In her study on the educational experiences of women in Kilome, Kenya, Kiluva-Ndunda (2001) reported that "gender continues to play an important role in determining who is given time and resources to gain educational skills and thus participate in economic roles in the public sphere" (p. 91; see also Kamau, 1996; 2004). Kiluva-Ndunda further noted that girls have limited access to existing educational opportunities. The choice of who is to be educated is based on gendered cultural assumptions about femininity and masculinity and is also influenced by the availability of funds. Girls continue to be seen primarily as potential mothers with the major responsibility of childbearing and childrearing, while sons are seen as future heads of households, breadwinners and bearers of the family name (Kiluva-Ndunda, 2001, p. 97-98). Indeed, the increasing economic difficulties accompanied by structural adjustment programs have had negative impacts on education and have undermined efforts to equalize educational opportunities in Kenya (Chege & Sifuna, 2006; Nyaigotti-Chacha, 2004). With the implementation of structural adjustment policies (SAPs) in the early 90s, the government reduced public expenditure in education and in other social services. Women and girls were the first victims of these structural adjustment policies (Kiluva-Ndunda, 2001). The SAPs disproportionately affected female participation in education, and therefore affected survival strategies of poor households (Buchmann, 1996). These reforms have translated into familial decision making processes whereby, because of cultural factors, education of male children ends up being prioritized in times of scarcity of resources (see Lelei, 2005). The cost of education in Kenya increases as one moves up the education ladder, and parents have to make difficult choices based on scarce resources. Under these circumstances, males are often given priority over females (Chege & Sifuna, 2006). This may explain why gender disparities in education access are more pronounced at university levels. For example, in 2001, only 60,612 of the 188,175 citizens who had attained university education were women (Daily Nation, 2001). Only 0.7 per cent of girls who enroll in Standard One (grade one) complete university, compared to 1.6 per cent of boys (Daily Nation, 2001).

Lacking in much of the literature on women in higher education in Kenya is information on women and girls with disabilities, who also face negative societal attitudes and stigmatization. Making this problem difficult to analyze is the fact that, in spite of the information available about the rate of participation by women in Kenyan higher education, none of these analyses attempts to provide even a rough account of the participation of disabled women at any level, primary through post-secondary. During the course of conducting research for this study university officers were asked for information about the number of disabled students enrolled in their university and they had no clear statistics. Percentage estimates such 1 to 2 percent was the response from one of the staff that were interviewed. Overall, the literature indicates that enrollment of disabled students in schools is generally low (Republic of Kenya, 2005). A report issued by Elimu Yetu Coalition (2007) revealed that approximately 25 percent of the 3.5 million disabled people in Kenya are school-aged children and youths (about 825,000). About 80 to 90 percent of this population does not receive any services to help them engage in education more successfully (see also Republic of Kenya, 2005). In addition, on average, disabled children go to school when they are older than their counter parts, for example, eight years and above (Elimu Yetu Coalition, 2007). They, thus, become adults before they complete their educational programs. Low enrollments of disabled children at lower levels of education in Kenya have implications for their access to higher education. Indeed, at postsecondary educational levels in Kenya, the enrollment level of people with disabilities is very low, a situation which must be addressed by enforcing policies that enhance disabled persons' access to postsecondary education.

Moreover, for a long time, in Kenya, schools for children with disabilities have been segregated, with special institutions for those with visual, hearing and intellectual impairments (Oriedo, 2003). Most of these institutions are concentrated in towns and cities, and not many parents can afford to pay for residential services. If they do, in most cases, preference goes to boys; girls with extensive physical disabilities have less opportunity for schooling. This practice of institutionalizing individuals with disabilities has been critiqued. Writing from a Western perspective, Oliver and Barnes (1998) argue that, historically, disability has been considered a charity issue, such that few government provisions were targeted to people with disabilities. Available provisions did not give them the right to access education, employment, etc. Instead, it was left to the good will of civil society to provide disability services voluntarily. So long as education for people with disabilities is largely confined to a segregated system, only a few girls and women with disability will benefit. Above all, this practice of creating a parallel system helps to reinforce the perception that they are the "other".[10]

On the whole, there is no precise information as to whether participation in higher education by women with disabilities matches their presence in the Kenyan population as a whole. In Western contexts, it has been observed that data collection for higher education is dependent on a participant's willingness to identify themselves as having a disability

(Frieden, 2003; Parker, 1999). However, there is barely any literature that suggests that the same applies to students with disabilities in higher education in Kenya. Furthermore, there is a lack of data and/or records to show what support systems have been put in place to enhance disabled students' access to and participation in university education in Kenya. This lack of knowledge makes a study on disability and higher education in Kenya all the more essential.

CONCLUSION

Following the above contextualization of education and social institutions in Kenya, it is clear that patriarchy impacts on the lives and experiences of women in Kenya. It is also clear that women with disabilities are more affected and remain highly invisible in research studies examining issues of gender inequities and higher education in Kenya, calling for more focused studies in the area.

Additionally, although the numbers of women joining universities are increasing, especially in private universities, which are now boasting of increased enrolments of women (Oanda, 2005); these institutions should also be wary of how they are perpetuating ableism and classism. This is because the percentage of women students with disabilities in these universities is infinitesimal. The increasing numbers of women they are talking about are non-disabled women and from middle and upper class families. Students from poor backgrounds (which comprise, among others, students with disabilities, as existing literature has revealed and as evident in findings in this study) cannot afford the cost of academic programs and are rarely admitted. What are these universities doing to address these inequities? Like Kamau (1996) and Oanda (2005), I argue that increasing the number of women accessing higher education, though important, needs to be critically examined. Which women are accessing university education and which ones are not? Very few women with disabilities have managed to make it to private universities, and this gap needs to be addressed. Moreover, institutionalized patriarchal attitudes and practices prevalent in Kenyan leadership should be examined. Simply increasing the numbers of women in leadership will not necessarily guarantee change. Government and societal institutions need a total reorganization.

Most of all, there are considerable gaps in the literature on disability and disabled persons in Kenya. Without appropriate knowledge, people with disabilities in Kenya will continue being marginal subjects, fighting for their rights. The stipulations of the Disability Act 2003 and the new constitution ought to be enforced in order to improve the quality of life of disabled people in the country.

CHAPTER THREE

Framing the Research and Methodology

PART I: FRAMING THE RESEARCH

This section of the book discusses the theoretical approaches that guided the analyses of the research data from the study. Acker (1994) defines theory as "perspectives that guide the search for answers to a central series of questions and dilemmas" (p. 43). Three theoretical perspectives informed the research: (i) Goffman's theory of stigma; (ii) Foucault's ideas of "power/knowledge"; and (iii) African feminist theory. Using a combination of theoretical approaches provided a broader base for examining the different forms of marginalization faced by female students with disabilities. The use, in this study, of a combination of theories allowed for an inquiry about the experiences of disabled women students in Kenyan universities and a reflection on the meanings these women attributed to their participation in higher education (see Titchkosky, 2007). The combination of frameworks was useful in capturing the variety and complexity of issues that emerged from the research, such as the way in which social, cultural, political, economic, pedagogical factors intersect to influence disabled women's access to education. It also provided for additional opportunities and perspectives from which to examine those issues. Given the range and scope of themes that arose, a single framework would have been too limited in the task of interpreting the data. Multiple frameworks thus allowed for a more nuanced reading of the emerging data and provide more opportunities for a fine-grained analysis (Zine, 2005). Garland-Thomson (1997) also urges researchers to invoke several theorists when analyzing disability noting that: "theories best suited to examine disability were those that fuse questions of identity politics and knowledge and which take into account history and the complex relationship between society and the body" (p. 30). Drawing on multiple frameworks is, hence, in sync with Garland-Thomson's recommendation.

Goffman's Theory of Stigma

Central to Goffman's (1963) work on stigma is his assertion that, in every society, some persons have greater power than others and that those with power generally impose their norms, values and beliefs on those that are without power (see also Tompkins, 1996). Those with power, in this instance the non-disabled, set the standards that are to be expected of all individuals within a given culture. They also determine how each member of that culture is to be categorized (Becker & Arnold, 1986). Goffman identified three forms of stigma which act to mark the less powerful as "different": (i) abominations of the body or various physical deformities, (ii) blemishes of character or weak will, domineering or unnatural beliefs, values and attitudes, and (iii) tribal stigma or race, nation and religion (see also Titchkosky, 2003). Each of these instances of stigma marks the individual who bears them as having "undesired differentness". That individual, thus, becomes perceived as being "deviant" or not quite human (Goffman, 1963). These different forms of stigma show how stigmatization creates a shared, socially maintained and determined conception of a normal individual (the normate), sculpted by a social group attempting to define its own character and boundaries (Garland-Thomson, 1997). For example, the rich stigmatize the poor as lazy and superfluous people living off the taxpayer's money. Coupled individuals perceive and stigmatize the widowed as a threat to their relationships, while racial and ethnic minorities are stigmatized and discriminated against as lesser people, hence less is expected of them academically, economically, politically, etc. These examples illustrate some of the ways in which dominant groups construct stereotypes which stigmatize groups that they deem inferior and thus facilitate the exercising of authority over them (Goffman, 1963; Ainlay, Becker & Coleman, 1986). This process also governs the treatment of people with disabilities in society. The dominant groups (who often happen to be the non-disabled) create standards, and those who do not fit those standards are seen as "different". This "differentness" is abstracted or reinforced by stigmatization, and this stigma facilitates social influence and control. One will find stigmatizing terms such as " 'cripple', 'crip' and 'gimp' and descriptors such as 'victim', 'unfortunate' and 'helpless' being used, wittingly or unwittingly, to reinforce the status of people with disabilities in society" (Tompkins, 1996, p. 38). These terms reflect the dominant group's tastes, opinions and idealized descriptions of what is normal (Garland-Thomson, 1997). Stigma, therefore, is a comparative or scaling tool that is used to construct "in" and "out" groups in society.

Although Goffman's theory does not provide further explanations as to why society responds to people with disabilities in negative ways (Abberley, 1987; Barnes, 1996; Oliver, 1990; Titchkosky, 2003), his work still "underpins the nascent field of disability studies in the social sciences" (Garland-Thomson, 1997, p. 32). Goffman's theory places disability in its social context in order to show that disability is a result of complex intersecting social and cultural relations. The theory, thus, provides an understanding of the ways in which power relationships between the disabled and non-disabled are structured. It underpins the ways in which the non-disabled construct the disabled as "deviant" by making rules and standard labels that render the latter as "outsiders". Such domination limits disabled people's access to wealth, power and other opportunities in society. Goffman's theory, therefore, promotes a critical engagement with the relations of power embedded in societal institutions/structures that serve to reproduce and maintain social discrimination and inequities. Such a perspective is important in understanding the marginality of women with disabilities in university education in Kenya.

Foucault: Discourse, Power and Knowledge

This book also employs Michel Foucault's notions of discourse, power and knowledge. Foucault (1974) writes that ... discourses are "... practices that systematically form the objects of which they speak.... Discourses are not about objects; they do not identify objects, they constitute them and, in the practice of doing so, conceal their own invention" (p. 49). Similarly, drawing on Foucauldian ideas, Stephen Ball (1990) remarks that.... "Discourses are about what can be said and thought, and also about who can speak, when, and with what authority. Discourses embody meaning and social relationships; they constitute both subjectivity and power relations" (p. 2). They are a form of social practice that produces meaning, which includes activity and systems of behaviour as well as dialogue (Yates, 2005, p. 67). According to Preece (1999), discourse is a mechanism of power and domination, which, if studied carefully, may yield an explanation of how power relations operate through rules, norms and authorized practices as well as conveying certain meanings behind words and actions (p. 38). Discourses are, therefore, shared practices by a community of people and cannot be defined in the absence of a particular community (Foucault, 1980).

Foucault's approach to explaining power relations and domination intersects with Goffman's theory of stigma, as both authors point to societal power structures, practices and social relations as vantage points by which to examine the oppression of the powerless in society.

A Foucauldian analysis of "discourse" is especially relevant in considering educational institutions. Ball (1990) noted that educational institutions are generators of a historically specific (modern) discourse. That is, higher education institutions are sites which generate validations of, and exclusions from, the "right to speak" (p. 3) because often times they are privileged and validated as spaces of "truth" (knowledge) seeking.

These validations and exclusions may be obvious in terms of the rules and regulations formulated to govern an institution, but they influence the kind of knowledge produced via, for example, research. Research work and findings from higher education institutions are often validated as legitimate knowledge. This legitimization has implications for the kind of curriculum offered, the kind of students who have the opportunity to access the knowledge produced etc. For instance, only certain kinds of students join university, that is, those who "pass" a particular kind of exam or who attain a particular level of education and hence have been 'differentiated' from other student populations. Students who join university are assumed to, in the long run, be able to participate in the process of knowledge production and validation. Those that do not qualify to join university are expected to conform to particular norms, for example by finding ways of getting there through upgrading to meet the set requirements. Hence, McHoul and Grace's (1993) observation that "a Foucauldian discourse analysis is intimately connected with how human subjects are formed, how institutions attempt to "normalize" persons on the margins of social life, how historical conditions of knowledge change and vary..." (p. 41). McHoul and Grace's (1993) quotation above can be applied to persons with disabilities. The quotation is important in understanding the historical construction of modern thinking about the disabled body. It provokes the following important questions: How have historical and contemporary representations of disability shaped the treatment and forms of marginality that women students with disabilities experience in Kenyan universities today? How does this marginality impact on the participation of these women in higher education? What strategies could be employed to end this practice? In order to answer these questions and enrich our understanding of the situation of women students with disabilities in Kenyan universities, some analysis of the Foucauldian notions of power and knowledge is imperative.

Foucault on power and knowledge

Foucault (1980) conceptualizes power as a practice that is internal to all relationships. He argues that power is not held or exercised by individuals; rather, it is developed through interaction in various relationships. Foucault further notes that we all act within some scheme of power relations which varies according to our locations within different periods of history or social context. In his discussion of the relationship between power and knowledge, Foucault (1980) focuses on the "how" of power. He describes the ways in which power is used to define what is acceptable knowledge and what is not, what belongs and what does not. For this reason, Preece

(1999) notes that Foucault's neologism of power/knowledge means that power and knowledge relate to each other in a reciprocal manner. Yates (2005) adds that Foucault sees power and knowledge as validating each other, reproducing each other and sustaining each other's authority (p. 66). Foucault explores the system of relations within which power/knowledge functions, and through which power/knowledge is formulated and promoted. He draws examples from localized and institutional forms of power to suggest lessons about how macro-systems and behaviors work. Foucault's study of power and knowledge, therefore, is an analysis of the conditions through which "knowledge" emerges and how that knowledge becomes a medium for creating and sustaining control and domination over others (Foucault, 1980). His power/knowledge neologism has certain elements in common with Goffman's (1963) theory of stigma. Both Foucault and Goffman's theory of stigma contend that power is a social fact established by individuals or groups who hold positions within society or within particular social structures. However, Goffman's and Foucault's conceptualizations of power can also be contrasted. According to Goffman, power can be classically understood as the ability of group A (the powerful) to make group B (the less powerful) do some thing C (e. g. obey or live up to the rules and standards set by A). Goffman seems to be saying that power is the person A (or group A) making group B think that it wants to do thing C. For Foucault the notion of power is abstracted even further. In Foucault's theory, power is not something that gets "done" to someone, as it can constitute and create A's understanding of himself/herself, same to B and C. Nonetheless, both frameworks seek to unmask the ways in which power operates in different societal settings to maintain different forms of inequality.

Foucault also discusses the social relational conceptualization of power, asserting that power is seen as operating from the bottom up, in a low-profile manner, typified by everyday social relations or "micro practices", rather than in a top down way which might require a high-profile presence to enforce it. In this, Foucault establishes a postmodernist stance. Foucault's idea is that the operation of power can be best understood by examining the power relations exercised within everyday social practices (Foucault, 1980). Barbara Fawcett (2000) argues that by "social practices", Foucault means the planned, unplanned and taken-for-granted interactions of everyday interactions. Fawcett notes that, "to understand how power is operating, all "micro-practices" or everyday interactions and social relations have to be viewed or analyzed in their discursive contexts" (p. 97). Such an analysis will entail a detailed examination of historically specific social contexts, in an attempt to dissect what social rules were followed, what is taken for granted, and how these distinctions came to be considered important (Fawcett, 2000).

In the context of disability, an examination of power relations within everyday social practices requires that one take into consideration the social construction and reading/interpretation of the disabled body. As Foucault (1975) noted, the human body lives in the episteme – it lives in a culturally constituted world. That is to say, the human body is constructed by society and, like society, these constructions change over time. For example, and as will be shown in the subsequent chapter, in Africa, readings and interpretations of the disabled body before colonization, during colonization and after colonization (and now in the neo-colonial era) may have similarities, but they are also different. Attending to these historical changes is important in order to understand the manner in which certain social practices have been sustained and others changed (see Foucault 1980).

Criticisms and applications of Foucault's ideas to the study

It has been asserted that Foucault focused on "how" power is manifested in social practices, at the cost of properly addressing "why" social practices operate in particular ways (see Fawcett, 2000). Critics argue that Foucault's view of how power operates tends to be somewhat indifferent to the value that can be attached to particular claims and historical accounts of the operation of power, accounts which have a tendency to equate power with domination (McNay, 1992). Foucault has similarly been criticized for failure to recognize, for example, women's specific experiences of power. He is noted to be "gender-neutral and fails to recognize the significance of gender in the play of power" (King, 2004). What Foucault seems to be more interested in is how power works than what happens to people as a result of power relations (see Deveaux, 1994).

For this book, adopting the African feminist perspective will help address some of the limitation in Foucault's theory. For example, the African feminist theory can help address "why power operates to invest, train and produce bodies that are gendered, raced, classed, disabled etc." (King, 2004). This can be achieved through a contextualization of the practices of marginalization against women with disabilities and also by examining the history behind this marginality. It will address the disabled women's realities of marginalization which are a consequence of forces such as slavery and colonialism, neo-colonialism etc.

In spite of its limitations, a Foucauldian analysis is useful as it challenges us to interpret disability and similar categories in terms of the power relations which created it as a category (Hughes, 2005). Such an analysis may help disabled women students to challenge the dominant belief structure that currently inhibits them when they attempt to use their voices, their embodied experiences and their collective efforts to establish and exercise their rights and to overcome discrimination (see Hughes, 2005, p. 80). The history of people with disabilities has largely been one of pathologization, institutionalization and supervision. In the 19th century, people with disabilities were constructed as a passive and docile population (Garland-Thomson, 1997; Hughes, 2005). Foucault's work is important in illustrating the medical, administrative, legal and now educational practices that reified this status.

Drawing on Foucault's notion of discourse as a form of social practice, and on his relational model of power (Foucault, 1980), one can gain insights into the forms of knowledge by which people with disabilities are objectified, the interventions societies uses to regulate them, and the forms of authority to which they are subject. A Foucauldian analysis, therefore, unmasks power relations that directly affect the extent to which certain voices (e.g. those of people with disabilities) are silenced, and it exposes the dangers of defining and speaking for an entire class of individuals. Foucault's analysis teaches us that there is a danger in speaking for others about their situation and in formulating programs of resistance for them (see Yates, 2005). As such, the role of the researcher lies in working with people with disabilities in order to bring to light the actions of power and subjectivity that they experience and in turn to problematize those actions. In the field of higher education, such problematization involves ensuring that the people who plan higher education no longer regard as "natural" or unproblematic the ways in which they operate and that the forms of power that circulate within institutions do not remain hidden or go unquestioned (Yates, 2005). Ultimately, Foucault's work calls upon us to consider how "the very existence of disability as a classification affects the process of self-definition and conceptions of moral agency for individuals who are so-labeled" (Carlson, 2005, pp. 138-139).

African Feminist Perspectives

The feminist movement focuses on issues of justice for women and has challenged the subordination of women over the past century. For much of its existence, feminist activism and the feminist movement concentrated on issues affecting women in Euro-Western contexts. Consequently, the feminist movement became laden with Euro-Western ideologies, driven largely by White middle-class women (Oyewumi, 2003). Non-white feminists have, thus, argued that the feminist movement had excluded the experiences and plight of non-White women, leading to marginalization of the difficulties facing non-Western women (Collins, 1998; hooks, 1988; Oyewumi, 2003). Non-White feminists emphasize that feminism speaks to women in different contexts and locations differently. This means that feminism in Africa would differ from feminism in Asia, the Middle East, North America, Europe etc. (Akatsa-Bukachi, 2005; Mbire-Barungi, 1999; Oyewumi, 2003). In this study, the use of an African feminist analysis of disability offered an alternative emphasis by, for example, providing insights on how disability has been shaped by historical forces (e.g. colonization) which are quite different from those that have influenced feminism in Euro-Western societies.

According to Maerten (2004), in Africa, African feminism grew from a long tradition of female integration in collective structures. This differs significantly from the West, where feminism grew from middle class individualism and as a response to patriarchal structures, mainly in a (post) industrial society (see Nnaemeka, 1998). As Patricia MacFadden (2002) argues, African feminism has been strongly influenced by its tradition of resistance to colonial rule and racist ideologies. African feminism thus reflects a different experience than that addressed by western feminists (see Amadiume, 2000; Beoku-Betts & Njambi, 2005; Kamau, 1996; Oyewumi, 2003). This explains Oyewumi's (2002) caution about drawing on western feminist ideas to explain the situation of women in Africa because when the realities of African women are interpreted via western feminist discourse there are bound to be distortions (in language, beliefs etc) which lead to misrepresentations of African women. This is not to imply that western feminism is not beneficial; it is extremely valuable and we can gain a great deal from transnational co-operations between women's groups (see Mbire-Barungi, 1999). The argument here is that, it is also important to account for the huge diversities of women globally. Utilization of African feminism in this study, therefore, seeks to interrogate the unified notion of "woman" which generalizes the experience of all categories of women, irrespective of race, class, religion, language, disability and cultural differences etc (Beoku-Betts & Njambi, 2005).

Utilizing an African feminist perspective in examining disability and higher education also provides an opportunity to focus on the understanding of disability at the individual and community level and what it means to be disabled in the African cultural context (see also Groce, 1999). Interpretations of disability in Africa differ across cultures, but African cultures are also not static (Mikell, 1997). So, while beliefs about disability in African contexts may be long-standing and intricately woven into many other aspects of the African indigenous cultures, it is also possible that these belief systems have nonetheless changed over time. This may explain why there are differences in the ways some parents perceive and support their disabled children when it comes to education provision as discussed in chapters five, six and seven.

It is also important to note that women's experiences across the African continent are not monolithic. However, "despite the existence of differences among African women, there are common features and shared beliefs that under gird them" (Nnaemeka, 1998, p. 5). In this study, the conception of African feminism drew on these fundamental commonalties that unite African women (Mbire-Barungi, 1999). These commonalities are primarily the continent's historical realities of marginalization and oppression brought about by slavery; colonialism and globalization (Adeleye-Fayemi, 2004, p. 107). The interconnectedness of gender, women's oppression, race/ethnicity, poverty, class, disability is important in my analysis. Adopting an African feminist perspective is also central to understanding the effects of Kenya's patriarchal political structures (highlighted on in chapter two) and the existing socio-cultural practices on women's educational experiences. Patriarchy is used to reference the organization of social life and institutional structures in which men have ultimate control over most aspects of women's lives. It is important to understand how local and global patriarchal actors have contributed to the marginalization of disabled women students from the colonial era through the neo-colonial era. Such an understanding requires a critical reflection of the ways in which local and international social, political and economic activities and interactions impact on the lives of female students with disabilities.

African scholars (e.g. Amadiume, 1987; Kamau, 1996; Mama, 1995; Nnaemeka, 1998; Ogundipe-Leslie, 1994; Oyewumi 1997) have attempted to unravel the complex constructions of African women's gender identities. These authors maintain that in pre-colonial times, the gender roles between females and males in African societies were indistinct and that a flexible gender system placed women in a more favorable position with respect to the acquisition of wealth and formal political power and authority (Amadiume, 1987; Oyewumi, 1997). This structure of the African woman's world changed during colonization, as Euro-western ideals about gender roles were pushed upon African societies, rendering African women powerless and stripping them of their place in society (Amadiume, 1987; Oyewumi, 2003; Tamale, 2004; 2006). To date, African women remain alienated from traditional sources of power in society, socially, economically and politically. Although they may benefit from some opportunities, such as access to education; still their participation rates are lower than those of men. The use of African feminism in this study, thus, acknowledges this complex history and experiences of colonialism and neo-colonialism which have played an important role in reinforcing the multiple oppressions that African women are continually subjected to. Application of this analysis to women students with disabilities shows how the marginality and oppression of African women is historically located and rooted in differential power relations (Oyewumi, 2003). This overlaps with Foucault's (1980) ideas that power relations of domination and oppression reside in the complex network of interpersonal relations and societal structures.

In Kenya, feminist organizing dates back to the pre-colonial period during which women formed self-help groups and work parties to assist one another during periods of economic and social stress (Oduol & Kabira, 2002). Membership in these groups was based on friendship, kinship networks and common need (Oduol & Kabira, 2002). These organizations provided a means by which women resisted and coped with the burdens of oppression, particularly the unequal gender division of labor in society (Oduol & Kabira, 2002, p. 397). Women realized that their marginalized position in society resulted in shared problems not experienced by men and these issues could be better dealt with by forming cooperative networks. The women also expressed their dissatisfaction through songs, poetry and dance (Oduol & Kabira, 2002, pp. 381-382).

During the colonial period, women's organizations in Kenya evolved into a more militant role, resisting colonial domination, which denied them control of their lives and disrupted the mechanisms that organized society. The women also resisted patriarchal structures which marginalized them while providing almost all social and political opportunities to men (Oduol & Kabira, 2002, p. 385). At independence, women continued to experience a hostile political climate which was not conducive to organized protest or challenges to state policy (Oduol & Kabira, 2002, p. 380). Women's movements in Kenya, as is in other parts of Africa, have aimed to improve conditions for women in all spheres of life. Their activities have manifested in individual efforts, self-help groups, occupational associations, non-governmental organizations, business enterprises and social welfare activities etc. (Oduol & Kabira, 2002, p. 376). Women's organizing poses a significant threat to male superiority and dominance in Kenyan society. This threat has been taken so seriously as to provoke direct response from some Kenyan political authorities. For example, the Maendeleo Ya Wanawake (MYWO)[11] was co-opted when politicians appointed their own wives, relatives and partisan women leaders to ensure they could control votes during election periods (Oduol & Kabira, 2002, p. 389). This practice limited women's participation in the decision-making process.

It is, thus, clear that patriarchal power poses many challenges for African women. Male authority and power is located in, and is exercised through the capitalist economy, government systems, religion, marriage practices and gender relations, as well as the family. Each of these is rooted in colonial history and was often exploited to the benefit of the colonizers (Amadiume, 2000; Gordon, 1996). Women were literally excluded from the public political realm of formal-decision making. This history is important in understanding the exclusions of disabled women's voices from the corridors of power, where important decisions are made (see Tamale, 1999). As shown in chapters five, six and seven, the devaluation and assumptions of incapacity that female students with disabilities experience intersects in a powerful way with long held notions of "normality" and "ability", which have implications on education and the processes of knowledge production.

Furthermore, political leadership in Kenya has largely been for men and by men. The lingering effects of colonialism have adversely influenced political leadership structures in the country. The British divide-and-rule legacy, largely responsible for ethnic fissures, polarization and uneven regional development, left deep-seated and destabilizing effects in Kenya, which are evident in today's fractured politics. Part of the colonial legacy has been the marginalization of the voices of Kenyan women, particularly those who hail from north-eastern Kenya. Unfortunately, the post-independent leaders have continued to sustain this legacy. Some parts of the country have better access to educational services while others are left out. In chapter seven, Afya, a visually impaired woman, explains the implications of this unequal distribution of resources on disabled people especially in North Eastern Kenya. We cannot, therefore, negate the effects of patriarchal leadership on disabled women's access to education in the country.

Another challenge evident in Africa/Kenya has to do with the effects of economic globalization. African feminism provides an explanation of unjust international economic systems and leadership problems that have affected the Kenyan economy via the forces of globalization. Although the women in this study did not mention globalization directly, factors such as economic downturns, democratic representation, resource distribution and everyday financial flows in the country were indirectly problematized. Disabled women continue to be disadvantaged the most, in spite of increased emphasis on the full integration of disabled people into mainstream society and especially into the market economy.

PART II: RESEARCH METHODOLOGY

THE STUDY

This was a qualitative research situated within a critical ethnographic methodology. Qualitative research seeks to understand social phenomena through the study of people's stories, behaviors, and beliefs (Strauss & Corbin, 1990). According to Gall, Gall and Borg (2005), qualitative research takes as its starting point the ontological assumption that reality is socially constructed, complex, and ever-changing (p. 305; also Glesne, 1999). Qualitative research seeks to understand individuals' perceptions and interpretations of reality (Gall, Gall & Borg, 2005).

Critical ethnography emerged as a result of dissatisfaction within social accounts of structure such as class, patriarchy and racism in which real human actors never appear (Anderson, 1989, p. 249). Critical ethnographers endeavour to analyze power centers and the mechanisms that help produce various forms of resistance (McLaren, 1995). These aspects tie into my study which examined how power, class and gender play out in the lives of women students with disabilities. According to Thomas (1993), the term critical in critical ethnography describes both an activity and an ideology, implying that it can be a means to unsettle the status quo by analyzing systems of oppression and unmasking dominant traditions and interests (Zine, 2008).

Critical ethnography critiques scientific rationality and seeks to use knowledge for social and educational change. Critical ethnographers recognize that research ought to be used for social and political transformation. They thus place human actors and their experiences at the center of analysis (Anderson, 1989). This shows that critical ethnographers view subjects as social actors who are aware of and resist dominant structures and practices. They give power to the voice of social actors and the way they construct meaning (Madibbo, 2006, p. 49) together with their participation in challenging the status quo. Central to this study, therefore, was an effort to find out how the disabled female students interpret their participation in university education and their involvement in transforming things in their educational lives.

RESEARCH STRATEGIES

This section explains the various techniques used to collect, analyze and interpret the data. As already noted, the study utilized an ethnographic approach. The strategies of inquiry used included personal interviews

58

and observations and document analysis. The interviews involved both semi-structured and open ended interviews which were intended to gather descriptive data in the subjects' own words (Bogdan & Biklen, 2006, p. 103). With regard to document analysis, official university documents; including statements of philosophy; students and strategic plans; as well as websites of the universities in question were reviewed (Bogdan & Biklen, 2006, p. 133). The goal was to investigate the stated policies and support systems put in place to address the needs of disabled students and also issues of disability in the selected universities. One of the main issues that emerged from the interviews with the disabled women students was the gap between university mission statements and the realities of campus life. The document review enabled corroboration and triangulation of the words of the students and those of university officers interviewed leading to recommendations of how the existing gaps could be bridged.

PARTICIPANT SAMPLING

Mason (2002) suggested that a key question when considering a research sample community is whether that sample will provide access to sufficient data and with the correct focus to enable the researcher to draw conclusions. Mason further noted that decisions about sample group involve questions of the variable reliability and relevance of particular sources, be they people, texts, organizations or events (p. 132). Creswell (2005) added that, in qualitative inquiry, the intent is not to draw generalizable conclusions about a population but to develop an in-depth exploration of a central phenomenon. According to Creswell, in order to draw out the best understanding of a particular phenomenon the qualitative researcher has to select individuals and sites according to some organizing principle (p. 203). In this study, research participants were first recruited by contacting faculty known to me in the selected sites and requesting them to assist in identifying potential interviewees, both students and university officers. These faculty were provided with copies of the recruitment notices for distribution to potential study participants. I chose this method because I am an alumna of one of the public universities in Kenya and had contacts with some faculty in one of the selected sites. Following this initial recruitment initiative, three disabled women students offered to participate. The study goals and outcomes were explained to them and they all agreed to participate. After interviews with these three participants, I adopted the snowball sampling approach. Snowballing is a technique in which the researcher identifies someone (study participant) who meets the criteria for inclusion in a study and then asks that person to recommend others that they may know who also meet the criteria (see Trochim, 2002). Participation was on a voluntary basis. Participants were requested, sometimes during the interviews or through informal conversations, to recommend other individuals (women with disabilities, students and university officers) who could be interviewed (Creswell, 2005; Trochim, 2002).

Although snowball sampling was an effective way to gain access to respondents, it often caused limitations in the diversity of the sample population. This limitation was largely due to the fact that a great percentage of the women referred by the other women had similar kinds of disabilities and were pursuing the same program of study. Specifically, women with visual impairments and those pursuing teaching degrees were disproportionately represented.

After interviewing the first six participants and realizing that they were all from the faculty of education, efforts were made to address this limitation by posting more recruitment flyers in the students' centers of the two universities, their libraries and offices of accommodation, places thought to be frequented by students. Participants were also requested for referrals to students from other faculties. Since these efforts did not yield positive results, I decided to rely on the snowballing approach. Despite these challenges, I sought to examine diversity among the participants in terms of age, ethnicity, class, geographical location and religion. In the data analysis, I draw attention to these aspects of difference and their implications for the experiences that the women narrated.

ACCESSING THE PARTICIPANTS AND RESEARCH SITES

Before entering the research site, I sought permission to carry out the study. This was a three step-process. First, at the Ontario Institute for Studies in Education, University of Toronto (where I was then enrolled as a doctoral student), the study was subjected to ethical review from the university (see www.research.utoronto.ca/ethics/eh_how_edu.html). In this respect, an ethics review proposal was submitted to the university research office and approved.

Second, in Kenya, the Ministry of Education requires that researchers get approval to conduct research in the country. An appropriate application to conduct research in the selected universities was submitted through the Kenyan Ministry of Education. Obtaining clearance from the Ministry of Education was important because, given that the study was targeting a vulnerable population, it was important for participants to get assurance that the study was officially sanctioned. The clearance acted as a "gate opener" during the conducting of the research. At the research sites,

60

university officials often wanted to know whether permission to conduct the study had been granted.

The research authorization from the Ministry of Education in Kenya was followed by negotiations with potential research participants (university officials and students) at the research sites. Despite the ministerial clearance, permission was still sought from faculty deans and other administrative officers in order to access study subjects.

THE RESEARCH SITES

Research participants were drawn from two public universities in Kenya (herein referenced using the pseudonyms University of Ongozi and University of Khafee), located in one large city in Kenya. Both universities offer graduate and undergraduate degrees. These universities were selected as part of the study partly because they could be easily accessed transport wise. In addition, I felt that these institutions, being among the largest public universities in Kenya, provided a good starting point to investigate public higher education institutions' commitment to widening access to university education for students from "non-traditional" groups (the poor, mature students who want to come back to university, women, the disabled etc.).

One limitation of these sites, however, was the lack of diversity in selection of disabled students. As noted above, most of the disabled students interviewed were often in one program of study/specialization, which made the experiences similar, to some degree. Although this may have also been a limitation of the snowball sampling approach, it is also important to note that even those participants that were referred by some professors coincidentally ended up being in the same areas of specialization as those of the snowballing participants. As discussed in chapters five and six, most disabled students are more likely to be enrolled in certain degree courses, predominantly Bachelor of Education and Bachelor of Arts programs due to, among other reasons, limited accommodations and modifications made by the universities. Nonetheless, the participants drawn from largely two focus areas (B.A. and B.Ed) ended up providing far richer and more critical insights into what was happening in their university lives, compared to the few that were drawn from the sciences.

Familiarity with the city in which these universities are located was an advantage when it came to recruiting participants and setting up interviews. For example, knowledge of the off peak hours when there was not a lot of traffic in the city helped in scheduling interviews to coincide with the much easier travel times. Moreover, in cases where a study participant was not able to meet at the university, as was the case for two participants, it was easy to select centrally located coffee places and libraries in the city that were comparatively "quiet and slow" for conducting the interviews.

Furthermore, being an alumna of a Kenyan public university provided familiarity with the dynamics of the university political culture in the country. This position gave me some degree of insider status while still remaining an outsider (not being a graduate of either of the universities which were research study sites). Even so, my knowledge of some students and faculty from the selected universities helped in getting leads during the recruitment of study participants. Insider status was advantageous in setting study participants at ease. Upon learning that I was an alumna of one of the Kenyan universities, participants became relaxed and willingly opened up and shared their experiences knowing that I had knowledge of some of the concerns and may have observed related experiences as a non-disabled student.

Interviews with university officials were more formal. The length of the interviews was generally shorter. The officials interviewed were willing to share their experiences especially when they learnt of the research authorization from the Ministry of Education or when they learnt of a referral by their colleagues, particularly when the referees were of the same level or their senior. This experience shows how questions of power operated even in recruiting study participants.

DESCRIPTION OF STUDY PARTICIPANTS

This study engaged disabled women students enrolled in two public universities in Kenya and four officers working in these institutions. To qualify for participation in the study, the students had to be female students with disabilities, and had to be enrolled in university. Although efforts were made to recruit participants with a range of visible and invisible disabilities, the sample ended up with all, except one, of the student participants having visible disabilities. The exception had an invisible disability, epilepsy. Visible disabilities are disabilities that can be readily observed, for example, deafness, stroke, paraplegia, amputation, etc. (Eisenberg, 1982). Invisible/hidden disabilities are disabilities that cannot be readily observed or identified, for example, dyslexia, attention deficit hyperactivity disorder (ADHD), etc. (Cavet, 2000; Harden, 2003).

With respect to officials working with the university, one had to have worked with the selected institutions for at least a year. In total, 24 respondents participated in the study (20 women students with disabilities and 4 officers). The age ranges of the study participants were from early 20s to late 50s.

Profiles of the disabled female students

All the study participants' names used here are aliases. Kiswahili names for minerals such as gold, iron, diamond etc. are used to represent the richness of the natural resources in the African continent or names representing selected attributes, such as grace, faith, kindness, hard work, unity etc., which the interviewees mentioned a lot in the course of our discussions.

1. *Afya* is a female mature student pursuing her master's degree in education. She is in her mid 40s and is married (but did not say whether she has children or not). Afya is totally blind. She is a teacher by profession. Afya started off as a primary school teacher[12] and later earned a diploma in special education. When discussing her schooling experiences, Afya noted that she had attended a special school for the blind during both her primary and secondary school years. Teachers' college was her first experience in a class setting with non-disabled students. Since graduating from a primary school teacher's college, Afya has been teaching in a school for visually impaired students. She is a self-sponsored student.[13]

2. *Aminia* is a single female in her early 20s. She has a physical disability which is a result of polio. She uses crutches for mobility. Aminia is currently an undergraduate student in education[14] at the University of Khafee. She attended a regular elementary and high school. She joined university as a regular student (admitted by the joint admissions board – JAB). Both of her parents are alive and are the ones who pay for her tuition fees and take care of her day-to-day upkeep.

3. *Aziza* is a 21-year old undergraduate student in education at the University of Ongozi. She is partially blind. Aziza indicated that she was born fully sighted but began losing her sight gradually when she was in grade three. When Aziza's parents took her to an optometrist, the optometrist diagnosed her with retinal pigmentation. Because her brother and sister had been diagnosed with a similar condition, it was deemed to be genetic. Aziza studied in a regular high school. Upon graduation, she applied for university in 2003 but was not admitted. She applied in each subsequent year. In 2006, she was admitted for the bachelor of education degree program at the University of Ongozi. She is a self-sponsored student.

4. *Dada* is a single female in her early 40s. She is a mature undergraduate student in education at the University of Ongozi. She has a physical disability and uses a wheelchair. Dada got polio when she was in grade six. Because of the polio infection, Dada left the regular school setting, and her parents enrolled her in a school for students with physical disabilities for rehabilitation. After rehabilitation, Dada returned to school to complete

her elementary and high school education. When she completed high school, Dada did not qualify to join university. She decided to join the teaching profession as an untrained teacher (UT) and was posted in one secondary school in the western parts of Kenya. She then began to apply to join various colleges. She was called for several interviews for college entry but, upon realization that she was disabled, the interviewers (who often happened to be college principals) turned her down on grounds that the college physical environment was not accessible. Dada stated that she realized that, because of discrimination and because of lack of understanding of challenges faced by persons with disability, she could not easily get admission into college. She continued teaching as a UT with an A-level certificate. Up until the year 2000, the government of Kenya had offered short-term in-service courses for untrained teachers in which Dada participated in order to get certification and promotion. With time, Dada decided to take a study leave of four years and enrolled at the University of Ongozi as a self-sponsored student to get a degree in teaching.

5. *Dhahabu* is a 23 year-old female student at the University of Ongozi. She is also a self-sponsored student, pursuing an undergraduate degree in education. Dhahabu was raised in a family which experienced significant financial challenges. Both of her parents are peasant farmers. She has five siblings and none of them has attended university, primarily due to financial limitations. She attended an integrated school for her primary and secondary education. Her dream is to work with children in a school setting or in a children's home.

6. *Faizah* is a 48 year-old single mature female student who had been living with multiple sclerosis (MS) for eight years at the time of interview. She is a self-sponsored student, pursuing an undergraduate degree in education at the University of Ongozi. Faizah was divorced and has two teenage daughters. Her MS was not diagnosed for more than a year because, as she indicated, it is a relatively rare condition in Kenya. Faizah was an elementary school teacher when she fell sick. She faced many challenges in her work place, including a lack of understanding from colleagues about the MS symptoms. Faizah also experienced problems with the administration because the management could not comprehend what was happening to her. She could not withstand cold and, therefore, was not able to make it to school on time especially during the rainy seasons. Faizah's optical nerves were affected and she started losing sight. Her spinal chord was also affected and she could neither stand nor walk a lot. She also had difficulty walking long distances but, due to lack of reliable public transportation, she often had to walk for 30 to 40 minutes to school each day. When she requested to be transferred to a closer school, she encountered resistance

from the district office and was only granted her request after sustained lobbying efforts by her principal. Faizah was placed in a school closer to her residence and worked with children who had mental disabilities. She enjoyed this work but continued to face challenges, not only because of her condition, but also due to lack of reasonable accommodation and understanding offered by her colleagues and the community. Eventually, these challenges compelled Faizah to return to university where she enrolled in a special education program, in order to develop skills related to increasing awareness of disability and with the aim of learning more about how to use tools, such as Braille, which would assist her in dealing with her own disability.

7. *Fedha* has a physical impairment, caused by a polio infection. She is an undergraduate student in sociology and joined university through JAB admissions. She has two other siblings. Her mother is a stay home mom. Her father works with one local NGO. Fedha attended a regular school for primary and secondary education. Her long-term goal is to work with an NGO, like her father, particularly one which focuses on issues of gender and poverty in rural communities.

8. *Feruzi* in the final year of her Bachelor of Commerce degree at the University of Khafee. She is 24 years old and single. Both of her parents are alive and are government employees. Feruzi has five siblings, three brothers and two sisters. She indicated that she became physically disabled during her early elementary years as a result of an unknown illness.

9. *Hawa* is a 23 year-old single female who is partially blind. She is an undergraduate student in education at the University of Ongozi. She is a parallel student (self-sponsored). Hawa was not born visually impaired, but lost her sight during her early childhood years, as a result of what she described as an unknown illness. Her illness began as a headache which caused her hospitalization and induced a coma that lasted for approximately two months. When she regained consciousness, her sight was partially gone. Hawa attended a regular mainstream school for both her elementary and high school education.

10. *Hereni* is a 24 year-old single female enrolled at the University of Khafee. She has epilepsy, a condition which with which she was diagnosed when she was 12. She is pursuing a Bachelor of Education degree. Her father passed away when she was three years old. She has two other younger siblings (a brother and sister). Her mother is alive and owns a retail business in on of the cities in Kenya. Hereni attended mainstream schools during both elementary and high school education. She indicated that, because her disability is often invisible, many people do not know that she is epileptic and, as such, she is subject to less stigmatization

than many other students with disabilities. Hereni joined the University of Khafee as a JAB (regular) student. She won a Ministry of Education scholarship during her second year.

11. *Jamila* is a single female in her mid 30s and is hard of hearing. She is pursuing a master's degree in sociology at the University of Khafee and works as an administrative assistant in the office of student affairs. Her job is to take care of the needs of students with disabilities. Jamila hails from the central province. She indicated that she is committed to making a difference in the lives of other students in the university. Her family and friends have been very instrumental in her efforts to attain higher education.

12. *Johari* is a 23-year old single female with a physical disability. She is in her final year of undergraduate study at the University of Khafee. Johari is doing a Bachelor of Arts degree. Johari became disabled at the age of two after a polio infection. She explained that she actually managed to go to school "because of her disability." This is because, when she was about 6 years old, her mother decided that the nature of nomadic life would be too difficult for her. As a result, her mother took her to live with her uncles in their home town so she could go to school. Johari has been living with her uncle since then and he is the one who took her to school. Thus far, Johari is the only one in her family who has gone to university. In spite of the numerous difficulties that she faced, Johari worked hard and joined university as a parallel student. At the time of interview, she was planning to enrol for a masters program in gender studies after completing her undergraduate degree.

13. *Karuli* is 22 years old and is a law student at the University of Khafee. Korali has a physical disability and is the second born in a family of four. She has three non-disabled siblings: two are undergraduate students and one is in high school. Her mother is a high school teacher and her father is a financial accountant. She joined university as a parallel student and is therefore self-sponsored.

14. *Lulu* is a mature female student at the University of Ongozi. She is 44 years old and is currently pursuing an undergraduate degree in education. Like Afya, Lulu is a primary school teacher. She took a four year study leave from the Teachers' Service Commission of Kenya (TSC) to do her undergraduate degree.[15] Lulu is totally blind in one eye. She indicated that she was born with no eye problems. However Lulu caught measles when she was about nine months old. She was taken to a hospital but one of her eyes had been badly affected and she lost sight in it completely. The other eye remained fine. Her parents took her to hospital and doctors recommended that she go to a school for the visually impaired. Lulu

went through the 7-4-2-3 education system. She attended a segregated school for the visually impaired from standard one to seven, after which she joined secondary school, which was also segregated. After form four, Lulu did not qualify for form five and six, and, therefore, decided to join a primary school teachers' training college in the early 80s [16]. Lulu taught at the primary school level for 14 years. In 2002, she decided to return to university for a degree program.

15. *Mkufu* is a 23 year-old female undergraduate student at the University of Ongozi. She has a physical disability and is pursuing an undergraduate degree in commerce. Mkufu became disabled at the age of five after falling sick and being hospitalized. She noted that she had been given an injection and became paralyzed. To this day, she does not know what happened. In terms of schooling, Mkufu went through the regular school for her nursery, primary and secondary education. She joined university as a joint admissions board (JAB) student and thus automatically qualified for government tuition subsidy and a HELB loan for university students. Her goal is to work in a financial organization and to further her education.

16. *Nadra* is a 24 year-old undergraduate student at the University of Ongozi. She is doing a bachelor of education degree. Nadra is partially blind. She began to develop sight problems during her early childhood years. When her parents noticed that she was having problems, they took her to an eye specialist and the physicians recommended that Nadra be enrolled in a special school for the blind. Following the doctors' advice, Nadra's parents took her to a special school where she spent her primary and secondary school years (from nursery school until form four). Nadra noted that when she was young, her sight problem was more severe; she could neither read well nor walk by herself, and had to have someone to guide her. However, over the years her sight has improved greatly and she can now read a little bit, and walks without assistance. Nadra has older and younger siblings, both of whom are non-disabled. Nadra plans to teach for a few years and, thereafter, to pursue a master's degree in early childhood studies or in psychology.

17. *Pete* is a 33 year-old female with a physical disability. When I interviewed Pete she had just completed her Bachelor of Arts degree from the University of Khafee. Pete indicated that her early childhood years had been very challenging. This is because, in the village where she grew up, she was the only person with a disability. The perceptions of the community created a challenge for her although the community was small enough such that she became well known and was often accommodated. Pete attended a regular school. She started going to school late at the age of

nine. Pete was a brilliant student and was always among the top students in her classes. She noted that although some teachers and students in the schools she went to were very accommodating, some were not. Some fellow students had negative attitudes towards her and this affected her both psychologically and academically. With time, Pete adjusted and chose to relate with those who appreciated her. Pete hopes to enroll for a graduate degree after working for a few years.

18. *Shani* is a 28 year-old graduate student at the University of Ongozi. She is completely blind. Shani lost her sight as a consequence of an illness she suffered when she was about four years old. Her parents enrolled her in a special school for the blind where she studied from nursery school until standard three.[17] After standard three, Shani transferred to an integrated school in one of the Kenyan cities and stayed there until she finished standard eight. After graduating from primary school (after standard eight), she joined an integrated[18] girls' high school in the same city where she did her elementary and high school, from which she graduated and went on to university. Shani is currently pursuing a graduate degree in education.

19. *Yakuti* is single female pursuing a Bachelor of Science (Nursing) degree at the University of Khafee. She is 22 years old and has a physical disability as a result of a polio infection at the age of five. She joined university as a JAB student. Yakuti was schooled in a mainstream primary and secondary school. She indicated that although her family was very supportive and loving, she encountered difficulties at school where some students made fun of her walking manner. Some teachers punished the students who made fun of Yakuti, but others did not. Yakuti's inspiration to continue her studies comes from a female nurse with a physical disability who she met in hospital in her home city. Her goal is to finish her undergraduate degree and enrol for a master's degree in public health.

20. *Zumaridi* is also in her early 20s and is a Bachelor of Arts student at the University of Khafee. She became physically disabled during her early primary school years as a result of polio and now uses crutches to increase her mobility. She is a self-sponsored student. Her parents are peasant farmers. Zumaridi noted that her limited mobility is one of the most serious problems she faces: "moving from one point in this campus to another is very tedious, the buildings are not accessible and the footpaths are terrible, especially during the rainy season." Zumaridi's dream is to secure a scholarship for graduate education outside of Kenya. In her words: "I wish to one day to get a scholarship to go to another country just for my masters and see how other people live and relate with people with disabilities."

Profiles of University Staff/Officials

1. *Akil* works in the department of student affairs at the University of Khafee as a students' counselor. Her job is to counsel students and staff as well as performing some administrative work. The department of Students Affairs is headed by the Dean of Students. Akil's office oversees everything pertaining to student life. Akil has worked as a counselor for three and half years. Prior to this job, she was head of a counselling department in another university. When asked why she chose to come into the University of Khafee as a counselor, Akil indicated that she loves working with students and has taught at virtually all levels of education (pre-primary to postgraduate levels): "... working with students is something I have done for most of my life. I have a background in education; I have a B.Ed degree and taught at every level of education pre-primary to post graduate students. So I am a teacher by profession..." Akil had no clear picture of the number of disabled students enrolled in the university. She noted that, when it comes to issues of disability, her office is more highly focused on students with mental disabilities than those with physical disabilities. Akil also indicated that, although she had no accurate statistics on the numbers of disabled students in the university, she is aware that the numbers have reduced considerably because of the curriculum (making reference to change from 7-4-2-3 to 8-4-4). The 8-4-4 system's emphasis on practicals, especially in science subjects makes it difficult for disabled students to excel in science courses. These difficulties are particularly acute for students with visual impairments. The university approach to teaching disabled students is also a challenge. Akil noted that the university does not have enough resources or facilities to take in students with disabilities.

2. *Amani* heads one of the departments at the University of Ongozi. He oversees a staff of 16 members. The department has various specializations. Amani's duty is to facilitate curriculum development and to make sure that academic/class work is done, and that faculty attend to students in a helpful way.

3. *Neema* works in the department of student affairs at the University of Ongozi. She also teaches at Ongozi University. Her office deals with non-academic aspects of student welfare. She deals primarily with non-academic personal matters, such as roommate problems, parent relations, student illness etc. Her office also liaises with personnel at the Higher Education Loans Board and assists students with their financial aid issues. Neema's office, as well, oversees the welfare of students with disabilities. They, for example, ensure that announcements sent out by the university reach visually impaired students by converting them into Braille; oversee

on campus transportation for disabled students; and also liaise with different bodies and groups that provide Braille paper for visually impaired students. The Kenya Society for the Blind is the group that usually helps with this. The office also liaises with other organizations in offering activities such as sporting, conferences etc. for disabled students. They also liaise with academic officers as well as faculty, organizations, which sponsors disabled students about funding and other forms of support.

4. *Sauda* once headed the department of student affairs at the University of Khafee. She is now a psychotherapist. As the head of student affairs, she was in charge of students' welfare from entry to graduation. She also oversaw other service providers such as counselling, advocacy, chaplaincy, students with disabilities, student organizations, entertainment, students' security, accommodation and sports and work placements. Like Akil, Sauda indicated that the number of disabled students enrolled in university has declined over the years because of curriculum changes but did not specify which years and the rate of decline. Sauda noted that during the period she worked in the office of student affairs (about 16 years), her biggest challenge was the lack of funding. She had to continuously lobby the administration and advocate for the needs of disabled students who were often unrepresented and for whom services were rarely targeted.

DATA COLLECTION PROCEDURES

Data collection took place over a three-month period, using three approaches: (i) document review (documentation) (ii) individual interviews and (iii) a supplementary data collection questionnaire. The use of more than one data collection method allowed for a more comprehensive understanding of the issues participants faced.

DOCUMENTATION

Marshall and Rossman (1999) define documentation review as qualitative research concerned with the examination and evaluation of written sources in order to extract data and to gain deeper understanding of the phenomena being explored (see also Creswell, 2005; Merriam, 1998). Information generated through document analysis can advance new categories and hypotheses, verify existing hypotheses, and add contextual richness to a qualitative investigation (Merriam, 1998). Marshall and Rossman (1999) suggested that documentation is most effective when it supplements participant observation and interviewing (p. 116). In this study, the documentation process involved a review of university policies on disability and the stated principles relating to admission and accommodations for disabled students in higher education. Institutional enrollment statistics were also to be considered, to determine the number of women with disabilities enrolled in the selected universities. Unfortunately, there were no accurate records of the numbers of disabled students enrolled in the selected universities. Findings from this document analysis framed the questions that were posed to participants and served as evidentiary support for the issues that study participants raised.

INTERVIEWS

In a semi-structured interview, the interviewer develops a list of questions and has a preconceived plan for proceeding (Bogdan & Biklen, 1998). Many researchers use such a guide and may modify it as needed (Lichtman, 2006, p. 113). In this study, the use of semi-structured interviews with open-ended questions was to give participants the space to express themselves in their own words, while at the same time giving direction to the interview process. I developed a list of questions prior to the interview as a guide. Even then, I allowed the study participants to talk freely and to explore the issues that were most important to them.

Two categories of participants were interviewed. The first group included 20 women students with disabilities who were enrolled at the two selected universities in Kenya. Each interview consisted of a discussion about the women's experiences in university. Its intent was to reveal the underlying barriers to education access and participation. The second group included four officers from the two universities (two from each). The intention in interviewing this group was to examine how they and their faculties viewed issues of disability, and to what degree they adhered to stated policies and practices. Discussions with university officers were, thus, intended to get a sense of the strategies put in place to assist women students with disabilities succeed in their higher education.

Marshall and Rossman (1999) noted that interviews involve personal interaction. These co-authors argue that cooperation is essential because interviewees may be initially unwilling to share all that the interviewer hopes to explore (p. 110). In conducting the interviews, it was vital that I develop trust with my participants. To build this trust, I conducted initial, informal, face-to-face conversations with potential participants individually. Where individual face-to-face meetings were not possible, this was done by phone. In these conversations, I gave potential participants information about myself and vice versa. I also informed the participants about the research purposes and provided details on what they would be asked. After the conversations, the potential participants were asked whether they were willing to participate in the research. Initially all agreed to participate. However, in the process of interview scheduling, two potential participants had to be replaced after several cancellations.

The interviewing process often began with small talk on topics ranging from current events, snapshots pulled from the week's news, or an inquiry about what the participant was planning to do for the day etc. The purpose of this chit-chat was to develop a rapport (see Bogdan & Bigden, 2006). I employed Holstein and Gubrium's (1995) method of the active interview. That is, the interviews began as one would begin a conversation, albeit a conversation with a "guided purpose or plan" (cited in Najarian, 2006, p. 16). This method enabled maintenance of some order in the interviews and facilitated asking similar questions to each respondent, while leaving room for the women to discuss their lives in their own way. Others who use feminist interviewing methods have done this, in an effort to resist imposing themselves and unduly affecting the ways in which the participants want to tell their stories (Reinharz, 1992 cited in Najarian, 2006, p. 16). This allows for more varied views about their experiences.

During the interviews, the women were encouraged to talk about their personal biographies in order for them to have some control over what was discussed. This approach also led to gaining a deeper and more comprehensive understanding of their lived experiences (see Vernon 1996). Encouraging women to tell their stories often spurred them to reflect on their experiences from elementary and high school and to consider them as their own stories. Additionally, telling their stories allowed these women not only to reflect on the societal forces that influence their experiences but also to acknowledge the experiences of their bodies and/or their impairments (see Morris, 1996, p. 13).

At the start of the interview, participants were, once again reminded about the purpose of the study and its structure (Creswell, 2005, p. 218; see also Bogdan & Biklen, 2006). The goal was to affirm understanding and consent to participation. Participants were encouraged to think about the research context and to describe and interpret their lived experiences as they saw them (see Zitzelberger, 2005, p. 392). This was to limit any negative power dynamics which might have made participants feel like they were being "studied" rather than giving voice to a study. This strategy also encouraged participants to develop as self-advocates, bringing their way of seeing things with them, so as to gain a better understanding of their lives. During the interviews, probes were used to elicit more information whenever participants raised points that seemed useful but needed further elaboration (Creswell, 2005, p. 218). Efforts were made to complete the questions within the time specified, although many of the participants took longer. This accommodation was due to the emphasis in the study that everyone needed to be able to have their story told and heard (see Morris, 1996).

To keep an ongoing track of the data collected, content logs of all the interviews were kept. All the interviews were tape-recorded to provide an accurate record of the conversation (Creswell, 2005, p. 217). Field notes were also written to augment the tape recording and as a reminder of any occurrences, body language etc. to be reflected on after the interviews. Writing field notes was also important as a backup in case of tape recorder malfunction.

SUPPLEMENTARY QUESTIONNAIRE

Although this study was intended to be predominantly qualitative, a brief questionnaire was used as a supplementary data collection strategy to collect demographic data about the study participants. The questions explored personal information such as the participants' age, number of siblings, year of study, type of disability (visible/invisible; congenital/ acquired), race/ethnicity, religious orientation, urban and rural demographics, etc. I gave this questionnaire to the interviewees at the interview meetings and collected it at the end of the interview.

DATA ANALYSIS

Glesne and Peshkin (1992) described data analysis as the organizing of what one had seen, heard and read to make sense of what is learnt. This is done by categorizing, synthesizing and searching for patterns and by interpreting the data collected (p. 27). It is about understanding how to make sense of text and images in order to develop answers to your research questions (Creswell, 2005, p. 230).

The research data was analyzed qualitatively, borrowing aspects of grounded theory advanced by Strauss and Cobin (1990). Grounded theory is an inductive and discovery based approach which allows the researcher to develop an account of the general features of a topic while simultaneously grounding that account in empirical observations or data (see Martin & Turner, 1986, p. 141). The theory aims at generating a descriptive and explanatory account of the phenomenon being examined (Martin & Turner, 1986). McMillan and Wergin (2006) assert that the purpose of a 'grounded' methodology is to discover or generate a theory, an abstract schema, or a set of propositions that pertains to a specific experience, situation or setting. According to McMillan and Wergin (2006) individual interviews are the primary method of collecting data in grounded theory. This is because theory is developed through a process of *constant comparison*, in which emerging ideas and themes are continually tested or recalibrated with new data (p. 95) and individual interviews provide for that opportunity.

In discussing data analysis using a grounded theory approach, Strauss and Corbin (1990) suggest that analysis begins with "open coding", i.e. by identifying the themes emerging from the raw data. In analysing data, this study also identified themes to guide interpretation and write up. The data analysis began the moment that the field research started. Effort was made to listen to each interview at the end of the day, and notes were made with the purpose of identifying significant ideas, concepts and themes that emerged from the data. The field notes were analyzed to identify any gaps or inconsistencies that needed further clarifications so as to map out a strategy for the next interview (Kamau, 1996, p. 101).

When all the interviews were done, verbatim transcription was immediately done, following the coding steps described by Creswell (2005). Transcriptions were initially read to get a general sense of the whole, while writing down in the margins some ideas as they came to mind. Segments of text and assigned code words or phrases that summarized the meaning of the text segment were then identified and marked. After coding the entire text, a list of all code words was made, grouping similar codes and looking for redundancies. The objective was to simplify the list by reducing the number of codes to a smaller, more manageable number (pp. 238-239). The data was then re-examined to see if new codes emerged. Specific quotes from participants that support the codes were circled. After this checking, a list of themes, which are discussed in chapter five, six, seven and eight, was generated (see Strauss & Corbin, 1990). These themes were identified by an examination of the codes that the study participants most frequently discussed. A decision was made to select only a few of the themes, as suggested by Creswell (2005), to allow for a more detailed write up, rather than providing general information about many themes (pp. 238-239). After this organization of data, the transcripts were re-read and a re-examination was made of the identified categories to determine how they were linked. Strauss and Cobin (1990) called this process of re-examining and determining links in themes as "axial coding". After this re-examination, there was a refocus on the literature for further analysis, which helped in the interpretation of the findings. Chapter four presents a discussion of findings relating to disabled female students' choices to attend university.

CHAPTER FOUR

Making Choices

In his book *Making choices: A recasting of decision theory*, Frederic Schick (1997) provided an excellent analogy relating to choice when he noted: "Life is a long trip in a cheap car. In *an unfamiliar terrain* [my addition] ... without a map and not knowing the roads, we must stop at each fork and make a decision ... (p. 1) ...We have to make choices, like it or not; and we often have reasons for the choices we are making ..." (p. 8). The disabled women students interviewed for this study made choices to go to university and to focus on a particular program of study. They had reasons for the choices they made. This chapter analyzes the choices the women made and the reasons why they made those choices. Central to the analysis are the factors that influenced the women to attend university and the choice of program of study once enrolled. The discussion of these factors also highlights the circumstances under which these women operated as they made the choices and the extent to which they exercised their agency. Referencing women's educational experiences in Kenya, Kiluva-Ndunda (2001) described agency as "the ability of women to critically examine their situations and to adopt strategies that will address their needs" (p. 173; see also Parker, 2005, p. 16). This chapter, therefore, looks at the ways in which the women negotiate the ableist, classed and gendered borders in the Kenyan universities and how they make various choices to enhance their success in university. In exploring these women's choices, the chapter looks at the various rationales offered by study participants for their decisions to attend university; the women's views about the universities they chose to attend and the factors which influenced their choice of programs of specialization.

DECISION TO ATTEND UNIVERSITY

Education plays an important role in any country's socio-economic development by cultivating a stronger workforce as well as guiding a country's cultural, social, economic and political dynamics (Amutabi, 2003, p. 127). As demonstrated earlier, most Kenyans see university education as an important bridge to accessing employment and as a pathway to personal prosperity. The government formally recognizes university education as key to human development and as a crucial exit route from poverty (Republic of Kenya, 2005). For women, education is not only attributed to improving their earning capacities but also society's general health and well-being (see Bunyi, 2004b; Onsongo, 2006; Psacharopoulos, 1994; Psacharopoulos & Patrinos, 2004; Shultz, 2002).

Consequently, since independence in 1963, the Kenya government has made efforts to expand university education in order to support and accommodate the increasing enrollments in public universities. This movement is also in recognition of the increasing educational expectations of the workforce (Chege & Sifuna, 2006). More students in Kenya choose to attend post-secondary education in order to be better able to compete for the limited job opportunities available. However, despite the wide-spread recognition of education's importance, students with disabilities remain underrepresented at universities.

In discussions with the female students with disabilities in this study, many made comments that brought back memories of an excerpt from a popular Kenyan song of the 1980s:

> *Someni vijana, muongeze pia bidii, mwisho wa kusoma, mtapata kazi nzuri sana.* (Go to school young people, work hard, when you are done with your education, you will get good jobs).

The above excerpt is a signature tune that was played by the Kenya Broadcasting Corporation[19] in the 1980s at the introduction and conclusion of primary school radio programs. The goal of the tune was to urge Kenya's youth to take education seriously, emphasizing that education was the best path to a good job (see Shikwati, 2007). Reflecting this belief, all the disabled female students interviewed talked about the desire to secure a job as a significant factor in their decisions to attend university. The women saw university education as a necessary preparation for the job market. They also perceived university education as a process through which they could undermine the ableist and gendered oppression they experience in society (see also Merrill, 1999; Pascal & Cox, 1993). Some participants indicated that entering university was a 'dream' they had held from their early childhood years. Others talked about individual and collective advancement (e.g. wanting to have a career and become self-reliant in the future and support their families) while still others pointed out that their friends, peers, family and other disabled persons in society inspired them to pursue a university degree. These factors are explored further below:

Economic independence

All the twenty disabled women held university education in high regard and linked it to individual and familial economic success (see Wotherspoon,

2004). The women saw coming to university as a huge step to attaining economic independence and hence being able to sustain themselves and their families in the future (see also Goode, 2007). They believed that university education would enable them realize their career ambitions and open doors to the job market thus allowing them to throw off the marginality characterizing their everyday lives. For example, Hawa, a 23 year-old visually impaired Bachelor of Education undergraduate student at the University of Ongozi, explained how the notion of achieving economic independence motivated her to come to university:

> With my disability, it is a bit expensive. I need to work hard so that I can sustain myself in the future. Instead of relying on my parents I can start living on my own somehow.
>
> _Interviewer:_ I see, expensive how?
>
> _Hawa_: I need extra stuff that other people who are not blind do not need and they are more expensive. Things like Braille papers, readers and even seeing the doctor at least once or twice a year.

For Hawa the economic costs of her disability became a motivation to attend university. She expressed a desire to lead an independent life in the future. Also implicit in Hawa's response is the role of higher education in equipping individuals with skills and tools that will enable them to become self-reliant. Mero (n.d.) described self-reliance as doing things for oneself. Mero added that self-reliance does not, however, imply that one does not need others in his/her life but rather that independence is an important step between dependence and interdependence. In Hawa's case, self-reliance is not about rejecting her parent's help but rather ceasing to have to rely on them for financial support. In her remarks she provided examples of the extra disability-related expenses her parents incur to ensure that she receive essential services such as education and healthcare. This insight reveals the everyday additional costs associated with some disabilities which must be met in order to maintain standards of living comparable to those of non-disabled people (see Jarbrink & Knapp, 2001; Zaidi & Burchardt, 2005). Hawa sees this additional spending as a "financial burden" on her parents. She chose to come to university so as to work towards economic self-sufficiency and also to relieve her parents of future financial burdens.

Zumaridi, who is physically disabled and is an undergraduate student at the University of Khafee, shared another perspective relating to support in a slightly different familial context. When asked why she chose to come to university, Zumaridi responded: "What motivated me to pursue university education is the poverty that my family has languished in and I wanted to change things for the better." In their examination of the determinants of poverty in Kenya, Geda, de Jong, Kimenyi and Mwabu (2005) found that poverty is concentrated in rural areas in general and in the agricultural sector in particular. Geda et al. indicated that to a greater extent, people employed in the agricultural sector in Kenya tended to be generally poorer (p. 14). The authors observed that educational attainment of the head of the household, particularly high school and university education was also a significant determinant of a household's poverty level. A lack of education accounted for a higher probability of poverty (pp. 14-15). Also noticeable in their findings was the fact that female education was correlated with reductions in poverty. However, Geda et al. also noted that female-headed households were more likely to be poor than households of which the heads were men. Although the authors did not provide a theory to explain this differential, it is possible that males had better opportunities to access higher education, compared to women and thus had greater chances of accessing salaried employment. Geda et al. recommended that promoting female education be given priority in poverty reduction policies in Kenya.

Zumaridi's parents are subsistent farmers in rural Kenya.[20] Literature has shown that subsistent farmers in Kenya are among the poorest in the world (Nyakundi 2005). They not only have limited access to land but also suffer economic exploitation by global market actors, by the state and by the ruling elite who offer them very low prices for their agricultural products and charge high prices for the manufactured products they buy. Consequently, these farmers rarely have money available for investment (Nyakundi, 2005). This means that most people who rely on subsistent farming in Kenya can barely make ends meet. Taking into account her family's living standards, Zumaridi decided to further her education so that she would be able to improve her life and that of her family. When asked to elaborate on the notion of "making things better for her family" Zumaridi observed: "If I finish my degree and get a job, I can earn some money and support myself and my family. That is what I am hoping for."

Johari, a physically disabled Bachelor of Arts student at the University of Khafee, likewise, indicated that she was motivated to come to university because of the prevailing poverty in her family. She remarked:

> Because of the kind of life my parents are leading, they are living a very hard life. I wanted to improve their lives in one way or another. I have not yet done something to improve their lives but I want to build a house for them in town [name of town] so that they don't move from one place to another anymore.

Johari is from a pastoral farming community in Kenya. Pastoralists form more than 10 percent of Kenya's population. They rely on livestock as their means of livelihood and often move from place to place depending on the season, generally in search of water and pasture for their animals. Although pastoralists constitute a significant economic grouping in Kenya, they are not always reflected in the country's economic data or acknowledged in economic policy discussions (see Odhiambo, 2006, p. 4). This economic marginalization of pastoralists has roots in colonization whereby the British colonialists chose to develop particular regions of the country at the expense of others. Unfortunately, even after independence, North Eastern and Eastern parts of Kenya remain "have-not" provinces and this has consequences on resource distribution and service provision. Therefore, most pastoral communities, majority of whom live in these "have-not" provinces, remain a neglected group and majority are languishing in poverty. As in other Kenyan communities the majority of women in many pastoral communities remain particularly disadvantaged. They have limited direct access to finances, education and power and decision making (Al-Haji, n.d.) and this is true of disabled women.

In the above narratives, Zumaridi and Johari bring to our minds the notions of communalism and mutual interdependence, ideas common among many indigenous African societies. These participants point to how parents invest in their children believing that these children will also support them (parents) in old age (see Nathani, 1996). In African indigenous settings, sharing and interdependence are part and parcel of community and humane living (Nnaemeka, 1998, p. 11). Children have the duty to respect; honour and take care of their parents when they are old (Ingstad, 2007; Mbiti, 1990/1991; Nathani, 1996). Zumaridi and Johari are cognizant that they have a social responsibility for their families. They are also cognizant of the fact that acquiring higher education is not only for their own good but for the good of their families and their communities as well. Their narratives reveal the conviction that university education is an important force in ameliorating poverty. This idea is consistent with UNESCO's (1999) observation that investments in education, health and nutrition and other social services are mutually reinforcing and will benefit both the individual and family. Zumaridi and Johari are hopeful that a university education will enable them to secure a good job with good pay, a condition that will enable them to liberate their parents from poverty.

Overall, the above narratives show that the women's agency, to some degree, lies in the enactment of familial relationships (see Parker, 2005, p. 10). The women's efforts and choices to attend university are defined by the way their communities are structured and the conditions and expectations within their families. They are constantly reflecting on how to make things better not only for themselves but also for their families. The women are acting because they know that "something is at stake" in their families and that the outcome of their actions matters (see Hay, 2005, p. 38), hence their decisions to attend university.

Realizing personal dreams

Disabled women students also talked about realizing their dreams and ambitions as an important motivator for their higher education pursuits. Shani, a 28-year-old blind graduate student at the University of Ongozi, observed:

> It had always been my dream to pursue a university education, though actually the courses I really wanted to pursue were quite different. I wanted to pursue Law and not Special Education. But when I finished [high school] and I didn't make the grade for Law, I was called for something else. I was called for Special Education. I do not regret to have done Special Education because it also taught me a lot. I think I learnt much about myself and may be how those teachers [referring to elementary and secondary teachers] should have been trained. You know you learn something that at least will enable you to help others coming after you.

Shani observes that joining university is a goal she had set for herself in her early years and reveals the inextricable link between grades and program choice. One's ability to meet the aggregate grade required for a particular program of study is a crucial determinant for the disabled women students' career-related choices as they transition from high school to university (see Ainley, Robinson, Harvey-Beavis, Elsworth & Fleming, 1994; Shah, 2005). Shani wanted to study law but failed to meet the entry requirements for law school and instead chose to pursue a degree in special education. Initially Shani did not offer any particular explanation for failing to meet the requirements for law school, but during the later interviews, she and other study participants noted that the curriculum was unfavourable to disabled students (see also Ainley, et al., 1994; Shah, 2005). She explained that the elementary and high school curricula are rarely adapted to meet the learning needs of disabled students and this mismatch leads to lower success rates for disabled students in the Kenyan school system. This, in turn, affects career decisions regarding post-secondary education.

The structure of the curriculum (8-4-4) limits disabled students' subject choices which impacts on their final grades when they sit for the

Grade 12 national examinations, which serve as a bridge to university. The 8-4-4 education system emphasizes practical subjects and not all disabled students are provided with the required accommodations to engage in these practical aspects successfully (these limitations are analyzed in chapters six and seven). Nonetheless, Shani does not regret having gone on to a degree program in Special Education. She indicated that the special education program has enabled her to better understand herself. She is also now able to reflect on some of the gaps evident in the training of the teachers who taught her over the years, particularly the teachers' pedagogical techniques. Following both her educational and lived experiences, Shani looks forward to engaging in some form of activism in order to improve curriculum design for future students. Shani's excerpt above points to ways agency could be bolstered through activism. The respondent has a vision on how to rupture the oppressive structures in the future using the knowledge and skills she has acquired. She hopes to challenge the status quo in the future and claim a space for disabled people in the curriculum.

Expounding on dreams, Nadra, a visually impaired Bachelor of Education student at the University of Ongozi, explained that she was determined to go to university since high school because she wanted to acquire more knowledge: "Okay, since high school, I always had that ambition to clear my Fourth Form and come to university because I wanted to be more knowledgeable." Fedha, a physically disabled female undergraduate student at the University of Khafee, added: "I guess it [university] is one of those things that your heart has already set out for you. I like reading a lot ... to gain knowledge. ..." Both Nadra and Fedha decided they wanted to attend university in their earlier days. They had ambition and the determination to come to university to acquire more knowledge. This perspective is also shared by Dada, a physically disabled mature Bachelor of Education student at the University of Ongozi. Dada affirmed that she was not stopping at the undergraduate level but will continue with her education until she becomes an academic:

> ... I don't want to just study for a degree, I want to move on and even make my career move further and I think by the time I am through I will even continue with my master's. I want to be a don actually ...

Nadra's, Fedha's and Dada's stories indicate that, contrary to the biased assumptions that people with disabilities are passive individuals who rely on charity (see Brisenden, 1986; Linton, 2006; Shakespeare, 1994); these women have goals and aspirations for higher education and strive to realize those goals (see Burchardt, 2005). Shani and Nadra envisioned going to university from their early years while Dada is already looking past the undergraduate level; she is determined to continue with her education until she becomes an academic. These women thus effectively complicate agency by challenging the everyday stereotypical representations of disabled people, particularly as regards academic success.

Education as a better option

The notion of education as a "better option" was another theme that the respondents alluded to in their discussions of university education. Aminia, is a 20 year-old female Bachelor of Arts student at the University of Khafee. She has a physical disability. When I asked Aminia what motivated her to come to university she replied: "Considering my disability, I thought that it was wise to get education, because there is nothing I can do physically. So education was the better option. ..."

Dhahabu, who is totally blind and is an undergraduate student at the University of Ongozi, also described how she was motivated to come to university because of her disability rather than despite of it:

> I am blind and so I knew that the only thing I can do is education because there is nothing else I could do comfortably. Because if it was me starting a business, I cannot run the business alone I have to look for someone to help me so I knew the only thing I could do comfortably and alone is just education.

Both Aminia and Dhahabu acknowledge that although they cannot perform manual tasks well, they see education as a source of empowerment for coping with social, political and economic challenges. Aminia's and Dhahabu's assertions of university education as a 'better' option are largely congruent with the existing literature on this aspect of post-secondary education and persons with disabilities. That is, post-secondary education increases the number of opportunities for people with disabilities to participate in salaried employment (see Frieden, 2003), which in turn improves their quality of life (Frieden, 2003). For Aminia and Dhahabu, therefore, university education offers possibilities of an alternative means of survival that will allow them to lead a better life.

Becoming a "somebody"

From the interviews, it became evident that the study participants not only "wanted something", but also they wanted to become a "somebody" out of their decision to go to university. Talking about the need to obtain "something", Johari, who has already been introduced, noted: "... I just had this mentality that I need "something", I need education ... I don't know how to put it. ..." Likewise, Aziza, a partially blind undergraduate student in education at the University of Ongozi captured her inspiration to come to university as follows:

> I knew I have to work hard so that I could at least achieve *something*. Because I cannot sit there, back at home, and like becoming a farmer would be cumbersome. So it is like it is only education that can make me be a *somebody*....that is what motivated me and I decided to work hard.

Aziza recognizes that some occupations such as farming[21] can be challenging for persons with disabilities. She employs the words "somebody" and "something" to emphasize on the importance of higher education in not only her social mobility and empowerment (see Oanda, 2005, p. 91) but also in generating her self-worth. Robert Hattam (2000) describes the notion of "becoming somebody" as follows:

> ... "Becoming somebody" might be understood as "the daily project of establishing a social identity" or the "construction of the self" ... Becoming somebody might also be thought of in terms of a "desire for recognition, and protection over time and in space and always under circumstances not of their own choosing."

Aziza perceives university education as a pathway to acquiring a particular form of identity or recognition (e.g. career-related identity). She believes that higher education can empower her to experience a sense of personhood and hence feel *worth* in a society that denigrates people with disabilities and projects them as passive non-persons (see Charlton, 1998; Nicolaisen, 1995; Willett & Deegan, 2001). The respondent looks at university education as a means to realizing her life plans and wishes. From her response, we get the sense of how people with disabilities continue to be marginalized persons in society (Turner, 1967 cited in Willet & Deegan, 2001, p. 140). We also get the sense of the struggles that people with disabilities have to endure in order to gain recognition. A further reading of Johari's and Aziza's use of the analogies of "something" and "somebody" draws attention to the many ways in which people with disabilities are often accorded low social status or, as Fine and Asch (1985) noted, rendered "roleless". The respondents believe that university education can accord them social status or power and recognition.

Self-determination

The disabled women students also talked about self determination and having principles as fundamental attributes that drove their choices to attend university. As Johari noted: "I think my own principles made me to come to university". Principled people often hold strong convictions about certain values. Johari valued university and worked towards being there.

Another participant, Dhahabu, also remarked: "the motivation to come to university that was really high was within me". Here Dhahabu is pointing to intrinsic motivation. Deci and Ryan (1985) defined intrinsic motivation as the energy source that is central to the active nature of the organism (p. 11). It is the motivation that derives from within the person (see Deci & Ryan, 2000). Ray Andrew (2008) calls it a real self motivation. That is, a person has real interest in what he or she is doing. Dhahabu had an interest in education; she knew the benefits of university education and how it could help improve her life, hence her desire to attend university. This awareness of the importance of education prompts her to act. Awareness thus can enable agency.

Similarly, Pete, a Bachelor of Arts female student at the University if Khafee, who has a physical disability, noted that self-determination and believing in oneself contributed toward her decision to go to university. She explained:

> Deep down in me, even if I didn't make the grade to join university, I knew that I was bright and was university material and, therefore whatever happens in one way or the other, I will get there and I believed in God that I will do it ...

In spite of the low societal expectations of the academic abilities of individuals with disabilities, Pete held a deep conviction that she was capable of completing a university education and worked hard to achieve this goal. Her narrative shows that a strong sense of confidence in one's abilities has effects on academic success. Pete's response reveals the importance of believing in oneself, listening to one's inner voice and engaging in personal reflection as important pillars of motivation (see Wane, 2007). Pete also shows how spirituality can be a source of agency. This theme of spirituality is further explored in chapter seven wherein the women explain how they tapped into their spirituality/religiosity as a coping strategy. In that sense, spirituality as a source of agency "transforms into a coping/resistance strategy but is deployed more as a self-serving and pragmatic strategy" (Parker, 2005, p. 87).

Confronting prejudice

Negative stereotyping of disabled people also accounts for the disabled women students' choices to attend university. The women view attending university education as a way of confronting societal prejudices against disability and people with disabilities. Yakuti, a Bachelor of Science (nursing) student at the University of Khafee who has a physical disability, wanted to prove society wrong:

> You know back there in the village people think children with disabilities cannot do or achieve much; which is not actually true. ..This is one of the things that made me work hard in school. I wanted to do something that will allow me meet many people out there and show them that I can also make it academically and also serve them in some way.

Yakuti shows how society continues to perceive people with disabilities as "unable" and for her, joining university proved that disability is not inability.

Likewise, Mkufu, a Bachelor of Commerce student at the University of Ongozi who is physically disabled, wanted to come to university to prove her parents and neighbours wrong because they believed that she could not make it to higher education. She also wanted to have a good life in the future:

> *Interviewer:* What motivated you to come to university?
>
> *Mkufu:* hey I really wanted to come to university. You know it was like my parents used to worry about me a lot [laughs]. They were like, now the way she is how is she going to make it in life, how is she going to survive? They thought I could not even make it in high school. Sometimes you could hear them talk, "may be we should take her to some course where she could use her hands and do things like *shona* (knit) sweaters"... and I was like, you mean I cannot make it? ... I said to myself, no I can make it. I wanted to prove them wrong. So, I had that vision of coming to university. I wanted to prove my parents and even my neighbors wrong. You know like in my village, I am the only one with a physical disability; and I could not go or walk long distance and interact with many people. I also wanted to have a good future life.

In this narrative Mkufu shows the kinds of worries that parents of children with disabilities go through. Society remains unfriendly to people with disabilities and has not been structured to accommodate this population. In Kenya, the colonial tendency to train persons with disabilities for craft courses such as knitting, tailoring etc. still lingers and many parents, including Mkufu's, are caught up in this trap. This is particularly true of parents who live in rural areas or in small towns where in most cases there are not enough resources to support the education of all the family's children. Mkufu's parents thought that she was not capable of earning a high school diploma let alone a university degree.

They often contemplated taking Mkufu to pursue craft courses and when Mkufu heard of these plans, she sought to show her parents that her "disability might not actually be a 'problem' in the way that they viewed it" (Linton, 2006, p. 63).

Faizah, a physically disabled undergraduate student in the faculty of education at the University of Ongozi, reiterated Yakuti's, Aziza's and Mkufu's discussions of the marginal experiences of people with disabilities in society in her narrative which focused on the challenges she experienced in her own community when she became disabled:

> One thing, our community, it is like they don't know what they can do with people with 'problems'. They only appreciate people who are "able", even the most educated. When talking about where I was working, even the district office could not understand why they should transfer me from a regular primary school to a special school that was near my home. They could not understand at all. They could only assume that it (her impairment) is just a condition. No matter how you try to explain to them that it is almost a permanent condition they could not understand. There is a problem down there in the community. Even the local people, when they see you on wheelchair they cannot understand what you are going through, there is no support they can give you, very little. ... after going through those problems with administration at my place of work, I just decided to go back to school at least to get educated to know how I can handle children with disability; to know how I can help the community back there. That is why I decided to come back to university and specifically I decided to tackle special education to have knowledge on Braille so that even if I become blind I can be able to communicate. I can also be able to go on with my work.

Faizah draws attention to the various manifestations of ableism in her community. She indicates that society continues to see disability and/or people with disabilities as a 'problem' (Michalko, 2002; Titchkosky, 2003; 2007). Her narrative demonstrates that society's failure to understand and accept disabled people is one of the most challenging aspects of having a disability. This finding indicates that much of the barriers and limitations disabled people experience are not a result of their impairments, but a result societal reactions to disabled people (see Michalko, 2002; Oliver, 1990; Titchkosky, 2003; 2008). According to Faizah, the limitations people with disabilities face occur in part because society lacks understanding on what accommodations to provide for a disabled person. As she remarks, "society doesn't know what to do with people with "problems" ... there is little support they can give you." There is a lack of understanding and awareness of disability in not only Faizah's community but the Kenyan society in general. As her story illustrates, even those with education in society hold the same prejudiced views about disability and disabled persons – they valorize "normalcy" and only appreciate the non-disabled. Faizah reiterates that even in her teaching job, other teachers failed to make efforts to better understand her MS condition.

Faizah's experiences show that not every educated person is aware of what disability involves and what it means to be disabled. This finding suggests that disability awareness campaigns in Kenya are not only to be targeted at those without an education but also the educated or elite. Moreover, it is possible that there is a problem with the kind of education the "educated" are getting. The foundation upon which Kenya's contemporary education is grounded often contributes to the alienation and marginality of people with disabilities in the country.

The missionaries put up separate schools for those with disabilities, a practice that set them apart from the larger society. This colonial legacy persists today in spite of increased advocacy for inclusive education. Disabled people are seen as people who cannot contribute much to societal development. This reinforces the socialization of people with disabilities as the "other" in society. How a particular community views disability has implications for the manner in which its members will act toward disabled persons. Perhaps this is an area that will need further examination so as to better understand the role formal education can play in enhancing the integration of disabled persons into the mainstream society in Kenya.

Credentialism and job mobility

Following the challenges raised by Faizah above, some of the study participants acknowledged that transgressing societal prejudices is complex. This complexity is evidenced in the women's explanations of how they felt they had to continuously prove themselves, far more than their non-disabled counterparts, before being "fully acknowledged" as "capable" contributing members of society. Dada, a physically disabled Bachelor of Education student at the University of Ongozi, pointed to this situation in her description of the importance of having a degree or diploma in order for society to accept that she can be a "good" teacher:

> Well, it is not really nice not to have "those papers", it is not. And sometimes, okay when you have a disability you really need to prove so many things, you need to prove yourself really. And one thing for me is just that, because we used to work very hard in

our department, (name of the subject she taught) would be done
very well otherwise there are so many nasty comments; even in
teachers' teachings there is a lot of tension between diploma and
the graduates teachers. So they will just throw comments, so
you can imagine that kind of scenario and you, you are actually
untrained. But just because students were doing well in my subject,
I think I didn't go through so much of that. Because, even if there
is someone who is a graduate teacher, how were they showing it
in students' performance? ... I think that one shielded me a lot...
So that one worked for me, but otherwise, I also felt like, surely,
if I was good, if I keep on saying I was good throughout my school
life, then there are things that should show. I mean, I believe I am
quite bright but you see that one is like a stigma, but it is now like
stigma times two. I felt I needed to come and read. I also felt like I
want to advance myself.

Recollecting her teaching experiences, Dada demonstrates how in,
contemporary society, individuals with disabilities have to pay a high price
to earn acknowledgement as being capable of doing something (see Maskos
& Siebert, 2006). Dada provides us with a picture of the competitive and
hierarchical working environment in her school. She reveals the culture
of "teaching excellence" her department laid out for itself and how she
had to work hard to prove herself as an "excellent teacher." Even so,
Dada feels that her authority remained incomplete without credentials to
backup her assertions of excellence. This finding speaks to a prevailing
trend in contemporary neo-liberal societies, which dictates that expertise
and professionalism be substantiated with training and credentials.
Dada chose to return to university to get her degree, not only in order to
enhance her expertise, earnings, and professionalism but also as a means
of self-advancement.

Pete also seemed to be in agreement with Dada's assertion that the
contemporary world is indeed about credentialism when she remarked:

I realized that the current world is a paper world, as in documentation;
are you trained in this? Have you reached university? And then I
knew, fine I can work towards that. So I asked myself, what is it
that is in this paper that I cannot get? And I have to say this paper
comes with hard work. I have completed this degree.

Pete thinks of the increasing trend toward credentialism as a means
of not only facilitating institutional hiring and promotion processes but
also as a way of increasing her professionalism. In modern societies,

diplomas/degrees are more than ever a power phenomenon. Diplomas/ degrees are indeed "scaling tools" (see Goffman, 1963). They are used to measure performance and often determine who gets the job and who does not. Consequently more and more employers are now demanding postsecondary diplomas and degrees for employment positions (see Walters, 2004). Individual competence and ability are weighed in terms of one's level of training.

What does this trend mean for individuals with disabilities? Credentialism has been cited by some commentators as one of the biggest problems facing people with disabilities (Walters, 2004). This is because most job applications list post-secondary education as an important requirement, a practice that shuts out the majority of applicants with disabilities even if they posses work experience that may be relevant and valuable (see Center for Curriculum Transfer and Technology & British Columbia Ministry of Advanced Education, 2002).

Are governments addressing the limitations that the emphasis on credentials poses to those with disabilities? In what ways is the Kenyan government assisting people with disabilities to obtain these credentials? As pointed out in chapter eight, the government may be expressing or may have expressed commitment to addressing the plight of people with disabilities but as Okeke (2006) notes in relation to women, "in most cases such commitments remain on paper, failing to address the structural and ideological barriers that militate against disabled people's societal well-being" (p. 82).

Closely tied to the theme of credentialism is the notion of upward mobility in the work place. Some of the study participants, especially those who had already entered the work force and attended university on study leave, were at university in order to move up the employment ladder and improve their social status. This was evidenced when Afya, a visually impaired graduate student at the University of Ongozi, remarked:

> I felt that I needed to study so that I could improve my status. The very thing that made me to go for a diploma course was that I wanted to be promoted and by then those people who were being promoted were those who had worked for longer years than I had worked. They wanted people with more experience like maybe ten years or more and I had worked for only five years. So I was not able to be promoted on merit. I said the best thing to do is to go and work hard in school so that I get a degree and knowledge. That is what made me to go for higher learning, to better my life. So now from the time I got my diploma, I got a promotion, when I got a

degree, I got a promotion. From that I feel that I have added myself value and some knowledge which those people who were promoted on merit may not have. I feel good and I cannot never regret.

Afya wanted to improve her status and also to facilitate potential promotions in her teaching career. Some details about the Kenyan teaching profession and its various categories and levels of teachers are provided, in order to better understand Afya's story on promotions.

Teachers in Kenya are employed by a national commission of teachers called the Teachers Service Commission of Kenya (TSC) [which could be roughly equated to the Ontario College of Teachers in the context of Ontario]. The TSC was established under the TSC Act of 1967 (CAP 212) and is mandated to: (i) establish and keep a register of teachers; (ii) establish and maintain a teachers' service adequate to the needs of public schools in Kenya; (iii) recruit and employ registered teachers, assign teachers for service in any public school and pay remuneration of such teachers; (iv) promote teachers at various professional grades; (v) transfer teachers; discipline teachers; (vi) compile, publish and amend the code of regulations for teachers which applies to all teachers employed by the Commission; (vii) establish and periodically review standards of education and training for teachers; (viii) exercise the powers conferred on the Commission by the code of regulations and delegate functions with the consent of the Minister and subject to such conditions as may be imposed; (ix) keep under review the standards of education and training; and refuse to register an unsuitable person as a teacher (www.education. go.ke; ww.tsc.go.ke).

The TSC maintains three schemes of service for teachers namely: (i) graduate teachers; (ii) non-graduate teachers and (iii) teachers for technical subjects. Graduate teachers are required to hold either: a bachelor's degree from a recognized university with at least two teaching subjects as majors or; a bachelor's degree in education from a recognized university or; a post-graduate diploma in education from a recognized institution or; a master's degree in education from a recognized university (www.tsc.go.ke). Graduate teachers are also graded into job groups J to R with R being the highest. Job group J is for untrained graduate teacher; K is for Graduate teacher II; L is for Graduate teacher I; M is for Senior graduate teacher; N for Principal graduate teacher II; P for Principal graduate teacher I; Q for Senior principal graduate teacher; and R for Chief principal graduate teacher (www.tsc.go.ke).

Non-graduate teachers, on the other hand, possess either of the following qualifications: (i) a Kenya Certificate of Primary Education (KCPE) or equivalent recognized qualifications; (ii) a Kenya Certificate of Secondary Education (KCSE) mean grade D and above or equivalent recognized qualifications; (iii) a P3, P2,or P1 certificate in education offered by the Kenya National Examinations Council (KNEC) or any other recognized institution; or (iv) Diploma in education from an approved teachers' training college; or (iv) Diploma in Special Education from an approved institution. (www.tsc.go.ke). Holders of the first three levels of certification (KCPE, KCSE; P3, P2, P1) can teach at the primary school levels while holders of the latter two (diploma) can teach either in primary or secondary school levels. The schemes of service for non-graduate teachers include: (i) P3 Teacher; P2 Teacher; (ii) P1 Teacher; Approved Teacher IV; (iii) Diploma Teacher/Diploma Teacher in Special Education; (iv) Approved Teacher II; Approved Teacher I; (v) Senior Approved Teacher; (vi) Principal Approved Teacher. Non-graduate teachers can acquire a degree or a relevant technical qualification from a recognized institution and join the Scheme of Service for Graduate Teachers or the Scheme of Service for Technical Teachers/Lecturers as appropriate subject to availability of vacancies (www.tsc.go.ke).

Afya started off as P1 (non-graduate) primary school teacher. She went for further training and obtained a diploma and degree respectively. She is now working toward a master's in education. Her narrative illustrates that in Kenyan contexts, like anywhere else, educational attainment is a central factor in gauging one's upward professional mobility. This is why Dada and Pete kept emphasizing the importance of having "those papers". For these women, earning a degree establishes a quantifiable benchmark that ensures recognition of their expertise and knowledge. The other point Afya makes is that university education has not only enabled her to obtain certification and promotion but also contributed positively to her personal and professional development. These are all benefits she would not have gotten had she chosen to stay in her job as a P1 teacher and relied on promotion through work experience.

Influences from significant others

Family members, peers, friends and people with disabilities in the wider society also played a significant role in motivating the disabled women students to attend university. For example, speaking of her husband, Lulu explained how he has been instrumental in her decision to do a degree in teaching:

> With him (referring to her husband), he was for it, he really encouraged me, … he was the one who was telling me to apply. … when I told him that I want to go for further studies, he just

> accepted. He is the one who even made the effort of looking for the forms, brought them for me to fill. Even when I came for the interview, he has been supportive [laughs].
>
> *Interviewer*: Did he also go to university?
>
> *Lulu*: No with him he is still with his primary teaching diploma. Maybe this is the time I will try and encourage him to go because I have children and he is the one who remained home with the children. May be when I finish, he can even go for parallel, yeah. Even if he won't go for special education, he can just go for a general education degree.

Lulu explains how her husband has taken the initiative of caring for their children as she pursues her undergraduate degree. Lulu's husband is committed to supporting her as she strives to move up the education ladder. Lulu's observations offer an example of the need to remain reflective in our criticisms of the overburdening and oppression of the African woman. It is an example that reminds us to contextualize this oppression, since women in Africa are not a homogenous group and may not have homogenous experiences (see also Oyewumi, 2003).

Zumaridi, the physically disabled Bachelor of Arts student, affirmed that family was a key factor in her decision to go to university. Not only did her parents encourage her to work hard, but she was also encouraged to follow the footsteps of her uncle who was at the university. Zumaridi observed:

> I have an uncle who also passed through here (referring to the University of Khafee) so they (family members) used to tell me, "you just work hard and if you work hard like your uncle did, you shall see the doors of university." So, I got motivated through that and I used to work very hard and God answered my prayers.

Dhahabu shares similar views in her comments: "The motivation I got from the parents was that they were supporting me, they told me to always go to school ..." Zumaridi's and Dhahabu's responses point to the ways in which material support and positive encouragement from parents and other family members can allow children to further their education (see also Cabrera & Padilla, 2004; Ceballo, 2004; Rhamie & Hallam, 2002). Positive support gave these women students a sense of hope and assurance that they were capable of academic success.

Aminia of the University Khafee, was not only pushed by her parents to go for higher education but she also wanted to become a role model to other people with disabilities:

I got motivation from my parents. They always encouraged me to work hard. Also, because in our village there are some people in our area who are disabled but they have not achieved much in terms of education; ... I just wanted me to be like a role model to them [laughs] ...

Aminia's response demonstrates the centrality of family members in motivating these women to further their education. In her case, parents instilled the expectation of attending university in her and provided the encouragement and emotional support that enabled her to meet these expectations (see Dennis et al, 2005; Rodriguez, Mira, Myers, Morris & Cardoza, 2003). Aminia's story also lends support to the theme that people with disabilities often remain an invisible group in their communities. In Aminia's case this invisibility motivated her to pursue university education so that she could serve as role a model to other people with disabilities.

For Aziza, of Ongozi University, other students with disabilities motivated her to go for university education. She indicated that her interactions with these students inspired her to pursue higher education:

Interviewer: And did you have motivation from other people?

Aziza: Okay I have interacted with other visually impaired persons and they have been a source of motivation.

Aziza's narrative reveals that peers are important influences in the career pursuits and decisions of the women students with disabilities. This finding resonates with Hurtado et al's (1996) report about the role of peers in Latino college students' lives in the U.S.A. Hurtado and colleagues found that peers were key in students' social adjustment in college. For Aziza, interactions with disabled peers boosted her self-esteem and confidence. This theme of peers and friends is further explored in chapter seven when analyzing success factors for disabled women students.

SELECTING UNIVERSITIES

In selecting the university they planned to attend respondents weighed various factors. These factors included the university's reputation for accommodating disabled students, the programs offered and the proximity of the institution to medical facilities. More often, however, participants made choices based on geographical or the university's reputation within their particular social circle.

Information access and university reputation

The women noted how thy explored provisions available in terms of courses and university reputation when deciding what university to apply to (see also Goode, 2007, p. 44). Commenting on how the history of the University of Ongozi, with regard to students with disabilities influenced her decision to come to Ongozi, Hawa remarked:

> I only knew about the University of Ongozi. It is the one that takes disabled students. Most of those who were with me in high school came here for higher education. But for (name of another public university), I don't know so much about it, but I had an idea of the University of Ongozi.

Johari and Lulu also noted that they did not know enough about the range of public

> universities in the country to make completely informed choices:
> Johari: Well let me say I didn't know the differences between the universities in Kenya really.

Lulu: Okay ... the person who told me just told me it was the University of

> Ongozi. So when I came here it is when I heard that even special education is in (name of another public university), but at first I just knew it was the University of Ongozi. So, I knew it was either the (name of institution) for diploma or the University of Ongozi for a degree. I had not known about (name of another university). You know sometimes when you are in the interior inside there it is not easy to know some of these things especially in special education.

Johari came to the University of Khafee because she was not aware of differences between the various public universities in Kenya. Lulu chose the University of Ongozi because it was the only university she had gathered information about from friends. Hawa picked the University of Ongozi because it was the only university she was aware of which had enrolled disabled students in the past. These narratives demonstrate how the women's decisions were highly influenced by university reputation and availability of information (Goode, 2007; Osoro, Amundson & Borgen, 2000). Information is key for successful decision-making. Lack of sufficient information limits the choices of disabled students and incorrect decision making. In order to realize the goal of increasing the enrollment of this marginalized group (Republic of Kenya, 2005), it is important that post-secondary institutions in Kenya find alternative ways of disseminating information to disabled people. It is possible that many people with disabilities, particularly in rural areas, may be interested in furthering their education but have no information or may become interested if provided with additional information about their opportunities. Geographical location thus seemed to be an important determinant when it came to accessing information. Persons living in rural areas tended to be disadvantaged compared to those in urban areas.

Facilities and programs of specialization

Other students, especially those who had information about the various public universities in Kenya, took into account the facilities available in their respective universities and programs of specialization. As Aziza remarked:

> Actually what made me choose the University of Ongozi is limitations, because these other universities always talk of not having facilities, skills programs and so forth. Facilities actually are the main problem so they cannot accommodate, for example, the visually impaired students in their colleges. So I had no option.

Aziza reveals the determinants of universities' limited enrollment of disabled students in their programs. Lack of facilities and trained personnel to work with students with disabilities is one of the reasons. Aziza noted that she had no option but to go to the University of Ongozi because it had resources and was more physically accessible compared to the other universities. This shows that students with disabilities tend to avoid universities that do not have the facilities and support systems that they require in order to realize academic success.

Expounding on facilities and access, Aminia added that she chose the University of Ongozi because the University's halls of residence are accessible and because it offers transportation services to disabled students.

> The University of Ongozi provides special services for disabled students like they spare lower ground rooms for students with disabilities in the hostels. The also have a three wheeler which helps us in terms of transport to lecture halls, yeah. But I understand that in other universities, they don't have such services.

Similarly, Afya came to the University of Ongozi because of the academic adaptations and accommodations and support the university offers.

> Because the University of Ongozi was the only one giving chances to visually impaired students, the rest of the universities had not yet

95

started. Otherwise the University of Ongozi started and then they followed. So by the time I was coming here, the other universities had not yet admitted students with special needs and more so the visually impaired because of the technicality ...; they need Braille material, they need the work to be transcribed, yeah and it was the University of Ongozi that had such facilities.

Aziza, Aminia and Afya preferred the University of Ongozi because of the programming and accommodations the university provides. The participants' narratives reveal that educational services, supports, and programs available to students with disabilities in Kenyan universities vary from university to university. This finding echoes Stodden et al.'s (2001) observations of the American situation indicating that postsecondary educational services, supports, and programs available to students with disabilities vary widely across states and campuses.

University's geographical location

As I continued my discussions with the disabled women students, Yakuti, a physically disabled nursing student at the University of Khafee, explained that she did not want to travel to distant cities to do a nursing degree there, hence her choice of the University of Khafee:

I wanted to do nursing and nursing degrees were mostly offered at the University of Khafee then. Although (name of another public university) offers it, I really didn't want to travel that far. I understand it is a good university but, this was my choice and I am pretty happy with it.

For Shani, her decision to do special education at the University of Ongozi was a result of failure to secure admission for a law degree:

You know when you are so green, you don't know which university is the best. Actually, when we were filling the clusters I had selected Law. And when I failed to get into Law School, I applied for, okay, the University of Ongozi. It was the only one that was offering Special Education then, there was no other doing that.

Shani notes that she was 'green', implying that she had limited knowledge about which university might be the best choice. In her case Ongozi ended up being the only option because it was the only institution that offered her second choice of program.

In the case of study participants whose impairments required medical attention on a regular basis, it was necessary that they be in a city where they could easily access medical care. This was true of Faizah, a physically disabled student at the University of Ongozi. In addition to program specialization, Faizah took into account proximity to medical services when making decisions about which university to attend.

> I decided to choose the University of Ongozi because it is only (name of other public universities in Kenya) which offers Special Education. But of late we have got (name of private university in Kenya), which is starting. We used to have the only two universities. Then I found the University of Ongozi to be a little bit central because with my MS condition, I need to visit the doctor now and again. So I found (name of university) a little bit far. From here (University of Ongozi). I can actually go for treatment now and then at the (name of hospital). So, on medical grounds, I decided to go to the University of Ongozi so I can be near medical facilities.

Employer influences

Dada chose the University of Ongozi because of her employer, the Teachers' Service Commission (TSC) (the employer for teachers in Kenya). This decision was also affected by TSC's policies over study leave. Dada is an untrained teacher and had to take leave from her job (under TSC) to pursue her education degree.

> I chose the University of Ongozi because the TSC told me to ... I needed the study leave... At the beginning I thought I couldn't make it to the University of Ongozi so I thought of going to a private university (name of private university). I went to view it and I talked to the people there. They said they had never had any person with a physical disability ...but they assured me that I could make it. ... However TSC told me that they don't give study leave to that college and so I had to apply to the University of Ongozi. So I started to find out more about the University of Ongozi and realized that they take care of the disabled ... and that is how I ended up here. So after I got admitted, TSC gave me study leave and by the way by the time I was getting it they had stopped giving study leave to undergraduates but I appealed because of having asked in 2004 and they gave me.

Here Dada alludes to the fact that university choice is sometimes constrained by factors which are entirely external to disability or program specialty. In her case, TSC policy had a huge impact on her decision and presumably on the decisions of others employed by the TSC. The TSC has set rules as to which universities and programs teachers can go for further studies, pointing to Foucault's idea of how structures are used to regulate subjects. The TSC policy stipulates that teachers must pursue a degree program in the field of education. The rationale behind such a policy is to limit the number of people using teaching as a stepping stone for other professions and thus keep as many teachers as possible within the teaching profession or at least with the field of education. If they don't comply they will not get paid for their leave and there is no guarantee that they will be allowed to return to their jobs after completing their program.

Other factors

Other participants could not offer explicit reasons for selecting the universities they attended; all they knew was that they wanted to be in that university. Mkufu is an example:

> I just wanted to be in the University of Ongozi; I have no specific reason but I just wanted to be in here. I prayed to God, please help me to be in the University of Ongozi and not any other university. I even didn't know anybody in the University of Ongozi from my area.

Nadra, on the other hand, had no specific preferences and was prepared to go to any university. When she got admission at the University of Ongozi she accepted it:

> Actually, I was prepared to go anywhere, so I cannot really tell why I chose this university. I just got a letter from the University of Ongozi that I had been admitted and I decided to come. Maybe for my masters I can decide to go somewhere else.

For Jamila, she was impressed with the University of Khafee when she visited it during her high school years and thus decided to apply there: "I loved its environment when I first visited it in my fourth year in secondary school and when I finished high school I decided to come here".

From the above narratives it is clear that most respondents' university choices were influenced by the impressions they had about the university, impressions which were the combined result of the information they got from friends and relatives or following prior visits to the institution; the programs the university offered; the location of the university and influences from sponsors or employers. Other participants had no specific preferences and were open to admissions from any of the universities.

SELECTING PROGRAMS OF STUDY

Individuals choose educational programs in order to develop specialized skills and experiences that will enable them to have more opportunities socially and economically. But what informs a person's choice to specialize in a particular discipline? A majority of the participants in this study were drawn from the faculties of education (12 participants). Four were in the arts, two from commerce, one from law and one from nursing. When asked why they chose these programs, the respondents pointed to factors such as their own skills set and the influence of family and friends, as well as the desire to become a role model, or to debunk societal prejudices about disability. For example, Aziza noted that she selected teaching because she loves the profession and would like to be a role model to students with disabilities:

> I feel I like it (teaching). I feel that is what I like doing. I want to be a teacher and I feel I should be a teacher. *Why?* Okay, in most cases, I would like to teach, even in a school where I can teach my fellow visually impaired students and maybe, be a role model. Otherwise I like teaching. ...

Zumaridi chose to do a Bachelor of Arts because of her love for arts subjects, in particular sociology. She was also attracted by the various opportunities the degree could expose her to when she finished:

> I don't know, I just love the courses in the B.A. program and especially sociology. Also anthropology, even though but not as much as sociology, I find. And then when I graduate I think I will not limited to one particular area, hopefully, I can go into various fields, either into government or go for a masters degree, something like that.

Karuli's decision to go to law school was inspired by disabled role models in her life, and by her desire to engage in social activism and bring about change. She noted:

> I was looking forward to this for a long time, like from high school. I just saw, for example when ... Josephine Sinyo, she is a lawyer and she is blind. She has been involved in many things like the constitution reform process, things like that, and they help people with disabilities - which is good. I don't think she could have done so without the training she has, you know, as a lawyer. I also want to be involved in bringing about change some day and I thought a law degree would be good for that.

Dhahabu selected the Special Education program because she wanted to better understand herself as a person with a visual impairment. She also wanted to be a role model and make a difference in her rural village where many visually impaired people remain neglected:

> I selected special education, especially for visually impaired, because, myself, I am visually impaired and I wanted to know more about myself. I also wanted to, okay, because where I come from there are many visually impaired people who have been neglected, I wanted to learn more about them and about myself so that I learn how to take care of them and also come out as a visually impaired teacher and be an example to them.

Evident in the above response is the need to understand oneself better when choosing special education as a specialty. Dhahabu is interested in gaining more knowledge about her disability. She wants to understand herself more thoroughly so that she is able to better reach other students with disabilities. Dhahabu wants to 'come out' (Linton, 1998) as a visually impaired teacher and be a role model to other disabled students. Her response provides support for Alder's (2002) observation that novice teachers tend to frequently cite caring for students as their dominant rationale for entering the teaching profession.

Hawa is also focusing on special education and identified with Dhahabu's desire to understand herself better. Hawa was also attracted to special education because of the level of support provided by faculty in that department:

> ... I prefer special education because I am fall in that category, and it will help me understand myself more. And then the lecturers will take care of us better than those who have no experience of special education.

Hawa believed that the faculty members in special education were likely to be more "caring", compared to professors from the other departments. When asked to elaborate further on this notion of caring, Hawa replied:

> Well, at least they understand us; they know our needs. Some of them are just disabled like us. And have you found this to be the case? Yeah, there are some (faculty) who are visually impaired like us so they identify with our experiences. How about in other departments? Okay, there are some who don't care; they just write things on the chalkboard and don't care whether you are there. For special education, at least even when they are giving the course outline they bring in Braille and during exams they take care of

us. But in these other departments sometimes you go to an exam room and unless you follow up they don't remember that there is a student they were supposed to give an exam in Braille.

From the above responses it is clear that identity is key in Hawa's selection of special education. Besides wanting to be more aware of herself, Hawa points out that a similar awareness also mediates the relationships between professors and students. She noted that she could identify with some of the professors in her department because they have disabilities too. Hawa considers these relations as key to creating an atmosphere conducive to learning. She believes that, compared to other specializations or departments, the faculty in the special education program are more cognizant of the needs and challenges of disabled students and will therefore strive harder to provide accommodations for them. This shows that support and care from the part of professors has significant implications on the learning experiences of disabled women students at the university and many disabled students perceive this as being extremely important.

For Shani, pursuing special education was both a personal choice and also a product of parental encouragement: "... I just decided by myself because, okay it (special education) was my second choice, after law. So I decided by myself and also my parents motivated me to go to university and do special education". Shani explained her parents' preference for special education as follows:

They gave me a choice to decide what I wanted to do. Now that I could not go for law why couldn't I go for special education? Anyway, after all, I was going to get a degree. And for them since it was my second choice, since I couldn't get the first one, why not go for the second choice? The other reasoning was that, since I have seen the problems that have been there especially in integrated settings, maybe after my schooling I may go back there and give some input, contribute, make a difference, you know.

Shani's narrative is another illustration of how academic grades or performance have implications for one's career choice (see Osoro et al. 2000). Shani did not meet the subject cluster requirements for a law degree and thus went for an education degree. Her narrative also shows that parents play an important role in disabled people's career choices. She explained that her parents took the initiative to discuss with her what she could do with a degree in special education emphasizing the opportunities to make a difference in the lives of other disabled people.

Johari, also like Shani, was interested in pursuing a law degree but did not make the grade. Instead she chose to enroll in a Bachelor of Arts degree program in economics and sociology: "For the case of taking a Bachelor of Arts (B.A.), okay I wanted to do law first, but I didn't make it; so I was admitted to do a B.A." In this case, grades limit disabled women's agency when it comes to choosing programs of specialization.

Jamila of the University of Khafee attributes her decision to do a B.A. and Master of Arts program to lack of information: "I had no idea which program was good for me and no one adviced me. In fact it was my last choice." Jamila's observation points to gaps in career counseling for students with disabilities in Kenya particularly at high school levels in preparation for transition to post-secondary institutions (Kithyo & Petrina, 2002; Kotlik & Harrison, 1989; Osoro et al., 2000).

Other study participants looked at what skills they possessed and which careers they were interested in when choosing programs of study. Mkufu, who is doing a Bachelor of Commerce degree in Accounting, pointed to her love of math and the desire to work in the financial field: "I love playing with numbers and I have always wished to be a financial manager in some organization at some point." Yakuti indicated that she chose nursing because she is good in sciences. She also wanted to debunk prevailing prejudices about employment of disabled people in the healthcare field.

> I chose nursing because I am good at biology and chemistry. I felt nursing would be a good thing for me. Also, you know, sometimes people think that we, people with disabilities, cannot work in the hospitals - become doctors or nurses. I wanted to show that this is possible.

Lulu, on the other hand, wanted to realize her long held dream of attending post-secondary education and doing special education. She noted that after finishing form four (grade 12), her brother was allowed to go for form five and six (equivalent of grades 13 and 14) while she was enrolled for a primary school teacher's college:

> First when I did my form four, actually I passed and got the second division. You know that was good for girls those days. But I didn't make it to join form five and six. We were two in the family, I and my brother and they (parents0 preferred to take my brother for further education A levels and I was just left there [laughs]. So ... at least I had that feeling that one time I could go for higher education and especially do special education. So that is why ... I decided to apply to the University of Ongozi. I applied, they called me for interview and I went through.

This narrative offers a firsthand example of some of the obstacles discussed in chapter one, discrimination faced by women with disabilities in obtaining education. Lulu feels that her parents, influenced by feminine and masculine societal expectations, favoured her brother and preferred to have him go for his form five and six while Lulu had to leave at form four and join a primary school teacher's training college against her wish. She notes that this decision de-motivated her but that she retained a desire to attend university at one point in her life.

CONCLUSION

This chapter has demonstrated that disabled women students in Kenya see higher education as a tool for economic empowerment and also as a vital stepping stone toward success in life (Okeke, 2006; Paul, 1999). They hoped that completing a degree program will improve their chances of securing a job (Thompson & Dickey, 1994). In many African nations, "higher education is seen as the basic mechanism for equipping ...women with the skills for participation in the public sphere" (Okeke, 2006, p. 83). All the women interviewed noted that a university degree would provide them with credentials that would equip them for a career (Okeke, 2006). They saw education as important for resisting and challenging the marginality they experience (Kabira & Nzioki, 1993).

Even so, the women were also cognizant of the fact that disabled people remain a stigmatized group in society. They were aware that negative attitudes toward disabled people have an impact on their efforts to secure meaningful employment (Thompson & Dickey, 1994). This feeling of being underestimated motivated the study respondents to pursue university education.

The women were uniformly aware of the challenges they faced, and mostly the need to overcome the myth that disabled people cannot succeed academically. This awareness enabled them to take a lead in confronting societal prejudices by engaging in self-advocacy and through acquisition of a university degree.

Other factors that encouraged the study participants in their decision to seek higher education included the under representation of disabled students in Kenyan universities (see also Paul, 1999). Some study participants indicated that their decision was also influenced by significant others - family, friends etc.

As for program specializations, respondents selected programs based on their academic performance and their personal goals. The women also selected their programs based on their subject interest, that is, what they were good at and what they liked the most. Some found themselves with limited options after they failed to get into their intended programs and, therefore, settled for other alternatives. Some selected their programs because of the influence of parents and other family members, friends, and disabled role models etc.

Lacking from the participants' narratives, however, was sufficient information about existing universities and programs offered, a factor that limited the disabled women from exercising agency in making informed decisions about higher education. These information gaps suggest a need for career counselors, particularly in high schools and even university to assist the students. The disabled women students seem not to be getting sufficient counseling and advice on what programs or specializations they are interested in and where they can pursue those programs. This situation limits their choices because they are not sure if they are eligible to apply for university education and particular programs or not (see Tinklin & Hall, 1999). Borland and James (1999) observed that information, housing, equipment, social facilities and access to affordable transport have a crucial effect on the degree of independence and choice afforded to students with disabilities (p. 97). The disabled women students pointed out problems relating to accessing information, accommodation and support, all of which as Borland and James (1999) observed "undermined their feelings of independence or deprived them of choice" (p. 97). These problems are particularly acute for women who live in rural areas. The women's narratives show that the Ministry of Education, as well as schools and universities, all have a role in disseminating information as well as perhaps creating transition programs for high school students, particularly those with disabilities. It would be important to examine the extent to which this lack of information also applies to non-disabled students. Such information would allow for a more accurate understanding of the degree to which disability plays a role in the individuals' decision to pursue university education.

CHAPTER FIVE

The Lived Experiences of Women Students with Disabilities in University

This chapter discusses the experiences of the women students with disabilities that I interviewed. Particular attention is paid to the women's experiences with the curriculum, interpersonal relationships, and physical access in the university. A focus on these issues is not meant to be a conclusive representation of the vast lived experiences of the study participants but serves as a guide to the varied discussions that emerged. The themes discussed herein are a useful beginning to bringing to light the silenced experiences of women students with disabilities in post-secondary education contexts in Kenya. This information is lacking as much of the existing research studies on gender and higher education present women as a homogenous group and thus fail to account for the diversities in women. From the analysis, it is evident that positive experiences with the curriculum, physical access and interpersonal relationships contributed to disabled women students' positive learning outcomes at the university while negative experiences were associated with limitations to participation in university education and their lives in general.

CURRICULUM EXPERIENCES

The concept curriculum remains a contested term with multiple interpretations among different people (Burton & McDonald, 2001, p. 190; Kelly 2004, p. 2). This chapter does not examine these multiple understandings of curriculum but highlights how the disabled women students perceived and interpreted their experiences with the curriculum offered in Kenyan educational institutions. The study adopts the aspects of curriculum advanced by Colin Marsh (1997) in his book *Planning, management and ideology: Key concepts for understanding curriculum*. Marsh describes curriculum as the vast aspects and dimensions of the educational experiences that students have during any formal education and their underlying principles and rationale (see also Kelly, 2004, p. 8). Marsh provided eight selections of curriculum definitions in his explanation of the different meanings attached to curriculum: "(i) what is taught in school; (ii) a set of subjects; (iii) content; (iv) a set of materials; (v) a set of performance objectives; (vii) what is taught outside and inside of school and is directed by the school; (viii) what an individual learner experiences as a result of schooling; (ix) and curriculum as everything that is planned by the school personnel" (p. 3). In this analysis I employ the term curriculum to reference what is learnt or experienced inside and outside of the classroom both overtly and covertly. I use the terms "in-class" and "out of class" curriculum to frame my discussions of the women's curriculum experiences.

In-class curriculum experiences

When discussing in-class curriculum experiences study participants talked about what was taught, how it was taught, and the extent to which disabled students were involved in the overall learning process. During the interviews, some of the women reflected on their primary (elementary) and secondary (high school) curriculum experiences and linked them to what they experienced at the universities. Some participants rated the curriculum favorably while others expressed complete dissatisfaction with the general education curriculum, especially at primary and high school levels. The majority of respondents felt that the curriculum is used as a form of control, which propagates the exclusion and disenfranchisement of disabled students. For example, pointing to primary and secondary schools, study participants noted that the curriculum at these levels of education remains unfavorable to many disabled students and serves as what is effectively a "gate-keeper" to disabled students' transition to higher education. Some of the curriculum-related aspects that the women described as contributing to their academic disenfranchisement include:

- content, instructional approaches and assessment and evaluation methods
- peer and faculty perceptions and attitudes
- inclusion practices
- scheduling and locations of classes
- resources and accommodation strategies and
- class size

These aspects are examined in the following sections:

Curriculum content and instructional approaches

Speaking about what is taught and how it is taught, study participants explained that the curriculum content and pedagogical approaches posed challenges to disabled students' successful participation in the learning process. Faizah, a blind undergraduate student at the University of Ongozi, had the following to say about the primary school curriculum:

In the primary school curriculum there is nowhere that it includes a person with a disability. Like children with visual impairments, and those with mental challenges they have no room in primary.

Interviewer: How about in secondary and university?

Faizah: Same thing. When you think of those Tom and Mary books we used to read in primary, those are all pictures of the so-called "normal" children. In secondary school, all the texts we use, the novels and plays we read mostly "normal" characters are presented except for a few. So it is like the students who have disabilities don't see themselves anywhere. Not even here in university (laughs). May be when we are learning those special education courses.

Here, Faizah is talking about representation. Disabled students are invisible in the primary school curriculum. They can neither see themselves in the curriculum nor identify with what is taught because much of the content represents and speaks to non-disabled people. This is also true of high school and university curriculum. Faizah's comments leave us with the questions: Who are the rightful/legitimate students as depicted in the curriculum? Whose knowledge and voices are privileged in this curriculum? What does this mean for those students who are not represented? What does this tell us about the people who are developing these curricular?

Faizah's narrative provides a picture of how power plays out in a hidden way in the Kenyan education system from policy planning levels to the classroom itself. Her narrative draws attention to the fact that knowledge production and dissemination in Kenya as in other parts of the globe, remains pervasively ableist. Non-disabled students are privileged at the expense of disabled students, both in theory and practice.

Curriculum limitations occur not only in terms of representation but also in the manner of its delivery. When asked about teachers'/faculty's instructional approaches, Pete, a physically disabled undergraduate student at the University of Khafee, replied:

> I think the teachers need refresher courses. There is no need of bringing students who have disabilities to be integrated into the regular classroom and the teachers in there are not prepared to teach them. They don't know how to teach them. They need to be retrained.

Faizah, who has already been introduced, reiterated:

> Actually those who handle those children have no knowledge at all, they don't have the resources and they don't know how to handle a person with a disability.

Pete and Faizah acknowledged that the teachers implementing and delivering the curriculum lacked adequate skills, knowledge, techniques and resources to teach disabled students. This has implications for the quality of inclusion practiced in mainstream classrooms. Pete and Faizah's observations point to gaps in teacher preparation, professional development and resource provision in Kenya, which need to be addressed.

Hawa and Lulu, both undergraduate students from Ongozi, seemed to be in agreement with Pete and Faizah when they added that curriculum in secondary schools is a major impediment to disabled students:

> The secondary curriculum is not favorable to disabled students because most of the time there are no qualified teachers. I was in an integrated school and we didn't learn much in math from form one to four (grades nine to twelve). There were no qualified teachers and facilities. (Hawa)

> Secondary school students are supposed to do mathematics, chemistry and physics. Actually with mathematics they are supposed to do it up to form four (grade 12) and then for chemistry and physics at least do it up to form one and two (grades nine and ten). But the way the curriculum is set, it is like it does not suit disabled students. (Lulu)

For Jamila, a hearing impaired graduate student at the University of Khafee, the university curriculum is challenging for deaf students because there are no sign language interpreters:

> The curriculum is not suited to students with hearing impairments because it doesn't include sign language as language of instruction in deaf education. Making some subjects compulsory such as subjects requiring use of sound impedes success for hearing impaired children.

In the narratives above, Hawa, Jamila and Lulu showed how lack of resources and qualified teachers impacted on disabled students' learning. Hawa felt that the secondary curriculum is unfavorable and disadvantages disabled students who may not be able to learn particular subjects because of lack adequate resources and skilled teachers. Lulu reiterated that although high school students are required to do math and sciences, the standard curriculum is a major barrier to disabled students' learning of these subjects. Teachers lack the knowledge and skills when it comes to modifying the existing general education curricular materials to enable disabled students access this standard curriculum. These curriculum limitations have consequences on disabled students' future enrollments in science programs in higher education. Studies have shown that disabled student continue to be underrepresented in science and engineering courses at the universities because of problems of accessing the curriculum and the learning environment (see Borland & James, 1999). It is likely to be even more difficult for disabled women students considering the fact that women, in general, have traditionally been a minority in science programs in higher education (Erwin & Maurutto, 1998; Logan & Beoku-Betts, 1996; Papadimitriou, 2004).

Unfortunately, the challenge of teaching the standard curriculum to disabled students is not only an issue in Kenya but also across the world. For example, research in North America has shown that students with disabilities face tremendous challenges having their educational needs met. These challenges are attributed to the "lack of knowledge about disability, a dearth of teacher training in the area of modifications and accommodations, insufficient collaboration between general and special educators, and persistent attitudinal barriers" (Lunsford & Bargerhuff 2006, p. 407). Many teachers do not know how to modify the curriculum to better reach all of their students. Lunsford and Bargerhuff (2006) argue that teachers need to be equipped with skills and knowledge that will enable them to involve disabled students in the learning of science and math more effectively.

Afya, a visually impaired graduate student, also from Ongozi, pointed out that although faculty in general tried to provide accommodations in their teaching, there were some who often forgot that there were disabled students in their classes/lectures:

> There was not much problem in the teaching except for a few who would write on the chalkboard and forget that we are there. They would write if it is spelling and forget to spell it back to us. And sometimes they could use overhead projectors and when the projector is up there the rest can read and write notes, but us we could not. ... Then some lecturers could talk so fast and forget that we are also supposed to be writing. So if they become too fast we stop writing and just listen then look for notes later from those who wrote from the projector. ...

Afya explained the limitations of using technology in large classrooms with students with diverse learning needs. Her observations prompt us to carefully assess the effectiveness of using such teaching tools with disabled students. As Riddell, Tinklin and Wilson (2002) observed, sometimes the use of technology and other teaching aids may end up further increasing the exclusion of disabled students in the learning process rather than aiding their learning if not well thought out.

Jamila, a hearing impaired graduate student at the University of Khafee, concurred with Afya and was critical of the lecture method of teaching that faculty often employ:

> Mostly in the university they use the lecture method yet here we are mixed up, we have all kinds of people. ... Like for those hearing impairment, they do not have the interpreters and that is a major problem.

Faizah also commenting on the challenge of interpreters remarked:

> When you come here (referring to the University of Ongozi) and you have a hearing impairment you must look for an interpreter for yourself. ... The department has no interpreter or the college has not employed one. So we have lecturers teaching sign language but we do not have interpreters [laughs]. You know even when teaching sign language there are parts you will not be able to explain with signs so this person with hearing impairment needs an interpreter.

Afya, Jamila and Faizah's narratives show that although there are efforts being made to promote successful learning for disabled students, there are also challenges posed by the instructional strategies used by professors which cannot be easily negated; for example, in both universities (Khafee and Ongozi) there are no full-time sign language interpreters for hearing impaired students. In fact, when I wanted to conduct an interview with Jamila, the one sign language interpreter at Khafee (who also happens to be a part-time employee) was not available. I ended up requesting Jamila to write down the answers to the questions, an approach that was limiting especially in topics where elaboration would have been helpful.

In spite of the challenges presented above, participants also pointed to the positive experiences they had with the curriculum. Shani, a blind graduate student from Ongozi University noted that she had good experiences with some aspects of the curriculum especially at the university level and provided examples of the modifications and accommodations that were made to facilitate disabled students successful learning:

> In (name of course), there is a unit on neuropsychology where we learn about the brain, the nerves and other things and for the person who can see, they will draw on the board and you will see what is being talked about. For me as a blind person they have to put it Braille. So they draw it, label it and give us to study and understand. So that is one of the adaptations they make. Other than

that, actually others didn't need that much adaptation because it is just verbalizing everything. And if it is handouts, there are some courses they gave handouts, they just take them to the resource center where they are brailed and then distributed to us.

Shani noted that in some courses adaptations and modifications were made to enhance disabled students' learning. Perhaps more could be done in other courses if the university and government had more clearly spelt out policies on the education of disabled students in higher education. As shown in chapter two, although the Disability Act 2003 in Kenya prohibits discrimination against disabled people in education provision, it only does so in a generalized manner pointing to admissions, curriculum, examinations, auxiliary services, use of school facilities, class schedules, physical education requirements and other similar considerations (Kenya Law Reports, n.d). There are no tangible provisions on what exactly higher education institutions are to do to enhance the learning of disabled students. My concern here is that with these blanket statements about disability, it becomes difficult to identify the roles faculty, the administration, fellow students, support staff, government, parents and society as whole should play in enhancing success of disabled students in higher education.

Aziza also felt that the teaching approaches of her professors were all right: "I think they are okay so far; those whom I have attended their classes they are aware ... at the moment I would say I haven't seen much, they are doing their best." Yakuti added that she liked the teaching approaches of her teachers and professors and that she did not experience any major challenges going through the education system:

I liked almost every bit of my experiences with the teachers and professors although I cannot deny that there were challenges. But overall, I would say I was lucky to have met supportive people who helped me with the curriculum.

From the foregoing narratives, we can see that the majority of the study participants faced significant challenges in accessing the curriculum and that this affected their overall academic achievement. On the other hand, participants also appreciated the support they got from their teachers and faculty which was crucial to their university experiences and achievements.

Faculty and student prejudices about disability and disabled people

The other issue that disabled women students raised and which had implications on their curriculum experiences is that of negative attitudes towards disabled students. The women spoke of the tendency to "judge a book by its cover" or what Hughes (2002, pp. 61-62) described as "visual

111

materialism", that is, how stereotypical assumptions about disability create rationalizations of the exclusions that disabled students experience in higher education. The women indicated that they often experienced veiled discrimination. For example, Johari, a physically disabled undergraduate student at the University of Khafee, remarked:

> I think in the current world, discrimination is not so much but even if they discriminate they can't tell you or show you directly. It is there but I wasn't shown openly.

Johari's observation is consistent with what existing research says about the pervasiveness of discrimination, particularly toward minority students and female students in higher education contexts (see Allan & Madden, 2006; Hurtado, 1994; Nora & Cabrera, 1996; Suarez-Balcazar, Orellana-Damacela, Portillo, Rowan & Andrews-Guillen, 2003). Johari suggested that disabled students experience discrimination expressed in a subtle manner. Other respondents confirmed these masked discriminations and offered examples of events, contexts and actors of the discriminations. For instance, Shani of the University of Ongozi illustrated how disabled students are "read off from physical appearance reinforcing perceptions that the deprivation of disabled persons is located within individuals and their impairments and not in the wider socio-political, cultural and economic environment" (Hughes, 2002, p. 62; see also Oliver, 1990) when she remarked:

> There are many courses I would have liked to do but as a blind person I cannot be allowed to take them because they believe they don't know how to teach us as they say [laughs]. The lecturers say so. When you take (name of specialty) you also take one teaching subject. I wanted to take English and they really refused because there is a small section in phonetics where you do a bit of drawing on pronunciation *sijui* (I don't know) what, so they really refused. But the funny thing is that the French department used to allow the visually impaired students to take French. So we used to sit down and wonder, why can't English and Kiswahili take students and yet French is taking students? Some of us were really bitter and we really fought until the people who came after us were allowed to take the languages they wanted.

When asked why she thinks visually impaired students were barred from taking English and Kiswahili but the French department allowed them to take French, Shani noted:

> I have no idea why this was so, maybe the people in the department, I don't know. But anyways now they allow us to take the English

and Kiswahili. The phonetics part, I don't know how they do it but somehow they go through it.

Shani eventually decided to take another teaching subject other than English or Kiswahili language:

The only subjects they were allowing us to do were either History or Religious Education, so I did Religious Education. And also if I want to do a course like in math or business I won't be allowed to do it. ... I can't blame them (lecturers) because I remember even in high school my math teacher refused to teach me and said that he was not taught to teach visually impaired learners on mathematics [laughs] so I don't actually blame them. I think what they need is to be informed and there should be training for lecturers and even teachers in high school on how to teach visually impaired learners.

Shani describes the covert forms of discrimination disabled students face when choosing courses of specialization. Visually impaired students are limited to particular courses because faculty feel that they "do not know" how to teach disabled students. Shani had the same experiences during high school where her math teacher refused to teach her arguing that "he had not been trained to teach visually impaired students". Some professors and teachers tend to perceive disability as "something beyond their means"; that disabled students are not the "type of students" they have been trained to teach. In high school, Shani's teacher did not know how to teach her math while at the university level, some faculty could not fathom visually impaired students studying English and Kiswahili languages, particularly phonetics, as they presumed it to be beyond disabled students' capability (Boxall et al, 2004). Here, disability is constructed as "a reserve for professional specialists"; a typical characterization of the medical approach to disability. Shani's experiences illustrate how society has effectively socialized its members to view disabled people as "other", perceptions which continue to structure the marginal experiences of people with disabilities. Her narrative points to the negative attitudes and stigma disabled students have to deal with in educational contexts (see Stone & Colella, 1996). It also shows how the education system serves to reproduce societal inequalities based on individuals' identities. Disabled students continue to be discredited and constructed as defective individuals and are, consequently, discriminated against in the learning process (Longmore, 2003).

Shani's responses also demonstrate some differences in levels of activism and resistance among disabled students at various levels of education.

At high school, Shani did not contest her teacher's ableist attitudes and comments. However, at the university, Shani and other disabled students regularly engaged in collective action challenging the discriminatory practices carried on by their department and they were eventually allowed to take the courses they wanted (English and Kiswahili).

Dhahabu, a visually impaired undergraduate student at the University of Ongozi, also showed how stigmatization of disabled people drives the inequities they experience in society:

> One day I was in a bus from my rural coming to college and the bus conductor came around collecting the bus fare. When he got closer to me he said to this guy sitted next to me, *sasa huyu hata ako na pesa kweli, nitawezaje kumwomba pesa?*" (now this one, does she even have the money, how can I ask her for the fare). I was very upset and I told him that even if the eyes are not there the mouth and ears are there *tena* (again) very sharp ones. People in the bus *walicheka* (all laughed). Don't think people who have disabilities don't have money who said that? The man went on saying, *eh, ni mwerevu, tena anaongea kizungu ingine hapo inaonekana amesoma sana* (eh she is very smart and she speaks very good English). I gave him the fare and he went. When I got to the station where I was alighting, I think he was ashamed and he came and apologized to me. Then we started talking and I told him I was going to college. You know we became good friends and some days I could take that bus and he doesn't charge me any fare. But again had I kept quiet he would not have learnt to respect people with disabilities.

Dhahabu's narrative points to ways disability stigma operates in society. Schur (1983) writing about stigma and deviance observed:

> Reactions to perceived deviance emerge through a process of "typing" ... the individual is responded to, first and foremost, in terms of his or her presumed membership in the devalued category. Furthermore, once this categorical label is applied, people tend to impute to the individual various "auxillary traits" they believe (however erroneously) to be characteristic of anyone bearing the label (p. 24).

In Dhahabu's case, the bus conductor singled out her "blindness" and used it to create a mental map of what or who Dhahabu is – someone poor, uneducated etc. He used the biased attributes he held about visually impaired persons to draw conclusions about Dhahabu's identity and/

or ability. As Goffman (1963) remarked, bodily signs that deviate from ordinary are discrediting and that a discredited person is a discounted person:

> While the stranger is present before us, evidence can arise of his possessing an attribute that makes him different from us ... of a less desirable kind ... He is thus reduced in our minds from a whole and usual person to a tainted, discounted one (p. 12).

Society discredits and makes prejudiced judgments against disabled people (see Corrigan, 1998). Non-disabled societal members see disabled people as "poor and lacking". Dhahabu's response shows how a disabled person's impairment is taken up as the key defining characteristic of the individual obscuring all other characteristics, skills and abilities that the individual may have (Stone, 1995). It also shows how "visible disabilities" draw instant negative evaluations and perceptions of a disabled person (Taleporos & McCabe, 2002, p. 972).

Literature on societal perceptions of disabled people (Oliver, 1990; Onken & Slaten, 2000; Stone, 1999) show that a lot of times disabled people are seen as a "burden" to society and helpless. Perhaps these are the underlying perceptions that came to the bus conductor's mind when he saw Dhahabu, hence his demeaning comments. On the whole, the examples provided by the women in the foregoing narratives depict the kinds of discriminatory activities and behaviors that contribute to their feelings of marginalization in education.

Problematizing inclusion

Participants also commented about the practice of inclusion and its failures in their discussions of curriculum experiences. The women felt that inclusion was more of a theoretical construct that a practical one. As Faizah, who has already been introduced, stated:

> No one is bothered here whether you have a disability or not, whether you are able to reach the class or not that is your own problem. When you reach there you do what others are doing. There is a problem and I don't know what can be done to make it total inclusion because we claim that we have inclusion but it is not there. It is just by name that it is there but practically it is not.

Pete too talked about how the quality of inclusion is affected by lack of resources:

> You have integrated schools as they say but the things that are taught can be out of context. The ideas are tailored to non-disabled

people. The curriculum is adapted, let me say there is that universalism in terms of what is happening in the society which is okay. But when it comes to us the disabled we have special needs that need to be addressed. They have to find a better way of teaching disabled children in those classrooms.

Faizah and Pete are critical of the ways in which inclusion is put into effect in the Kenyan education system. The respondents feel that "full inclusion" remains primarily superficial, as it is largely articulated in theory but is lacking in practice (see also Slee, 2001). Although the university talks about equality for all students, in reality, much is lacking. There are significant challenges in terms of translating theoretical policies into practice. For example, Faizah remarked that in her university "nobody cares whether a student is disabled or not". Pete likewise observes that integrated classrooms are not serving disabled students well. This shows that there is a problem in the degree to which teachers embrace inclusive pedagogical practices. The respondent report that all students are subjected to same teaching approaches with limited modifications, adaptations and accommodations for disabled students. The women feel that faculty and teachers have not yet recognized that equity and inclusion is not necessarily about diverse student populations getting the same treatment but rather about getting what they need to ensure opportunities for their successful learning (Chassels, 2007).

The other important finding relates to some of the women's recognition that the challenges of inclusion are not only in educational settings but also at home. Mkufu noted:

Inclusion starts sometimes also at home. My parents doubted my ability to finish high school and that was a challenge in itself. Not that they didn't love me but they had fear because I think, of the way disability is seen. And in school it was the same, some teachers you could tell they did expect much from students with disabilities. Like for those children who are blind study, sometimes things are just done and teachers don't know they are leaving them out or even what to do with such kids. I don't know, it is hard, there is no real inclusion. But for me I also insisted and knew that I can make it. So I worked hard and here I am [laughs].

Mkufu draws on her experiences to show how parental actions and perceptions can contribute to the marginal experiences of disabled students. She further demonstrates how inadequate teacher skills impacts on the learning of visually impaired students. Nonetheless, Mkufu reports that she worked hard and made it to university. Of importance here is that exclusion of disabled people can be a by-product of both school and home factors. It is more challenging when parents/family members of disabled children fail to support them which make it hard for them to be grounded and fight oppression in the school system.

Resources

Teachers and students need additional resources to facilitate teaching and student learning. In this study, the participants noted that at times the curriculum was a challenge because of lack of sufficient resources to support learning. Jamila provided an example of the hearing impaired students:

> The curriculum is not suited to students with hearing impairments because it doesn't include sign language as language of instruction in deaf education. Making some subjects compulsory for example subjects requiring use of sound impedes success for hearing impaired children.

According to Jamila, the curriculum is especially challenging to many hearing impaired students because they are not able to comprehend what is being taught when there are no sign language interpreters to interpret the information being presented to them.

Other study participants highlighted resource-related limitations, particularly Braille machines and computers:

> Even the facilities - they do not have them. You will hardly ever see a machine like that one there (points to Braille machine). You will never even see a stylus which is just a simple gadget. And even if they were there, who is going to train these children to use them? The teachers do not have the knowledge; they do not know what those dots mean (laughs); they cannot interpret them. There is a lot to be done. There is a lack of facilities; we do not have trained teachers. Even the curriculum itself, they don't include people with mental impairments, because these people need to be taught systematically, slowly. (Faizah)

> One thing in this university, in terms of computers and library there is a gap. You know e-learning is a great source of information and they need to embrace that. But they don't have that developed very well. Yes we have computers to help us search for books in the library and such like but that is not enough. Sometimes you are forced to go out and pay to look for articles and other reports,

117

which is very expensive. For me I can go to (names of places and organizations) and browse but for other students like the blind who didn't have the facilities it was hard. (Karuli)

When it comes to technology; like in integrated settings, very few schools actually I don't know of any that has fitted their computers with job access with speech (JAWS); the speech software they install into the computer. Most schools have not done that and even when they do, they don't have teachers who are trained in teaching that. For instance, now I cannot do a course in IT because such things have not been put in place. There is a unit in computer that was made compulsory for all Ongozi students but there was no way we could do it until they bought that soft ware, and they have not yet upgraded it. The one that is there cannot access the internet because it is still using the 3.7 version I think the latest one then which was the 6.2. (Shani)

The quotations above show that upgraded computer systems/programs and resources are lacking at their universities, in spite of their centrality in research activities and information dissemination. Computer technology is touted as a beneficial tool in enhancing both teaching and learning for disabled students. These technologies are useful in connecting disabled people with non-disabled and disabled counterparts and also living and functioning more independently (Hasselbring & Glaser, 2000; Margalit, 1990; Ray & Warden, 1995). However, in many low income countries where computer and technological advancements are not yet established, people with disabilities remain disadvantaged. As Karuli and Shani reveal, their universities are making efforts to introduce students to this technology and integrate them into it, but their services are not up to date. Moreover, priority is often given to non-disabled students, reinforcing their advantaging.

In addition to computer technology, the university libraries also have no current editions for many required books. There is a dearth of Braille and audio-taped books and readers, which limits disabled students' ability to experience successful learning, particularly those who are blind. Aziza explained:

Like the University of Ongozi library mainly has, unless they have updated it of late, it has ancient books; if you want new books you can hardly get them; there are no new versions.

What the voices presented in the above section demonstrate is that one of the biggest challenges facing the two universities studied entails updating their resources and keeping them in line with current global trends.

Scheduling and class size

Scheduling was another issue that disabled women students raised when discussing their curriculum experiences. The women noted that, at times, classes were scheduled in distant locations or in inaccessible buildings which made it difficult for them to get there on time. For example, Feruzi of the University of Khafee, remarked:

> You can imagine when you have one class here (referring to the building where we were) and the next class across the other side of campus. These other guys will, of course, run and get there earlier, and you will be struggling. When you get there you are late. And you know some lecturers just turn you away when you are late. They can't allow you to come in because you are late for their class. You try explaining to them that you have no break between the classes, they don't understand. So you sometimes end up dropping some of those classes because you can't make it going back and forth from one end of the campus to the other.

Dada, a physically disabled undergraduate student at the University of Ongozi, also added that lectures are scheduled in distant buildings, which makes it hard for disabled students to move from one corner of the university to another within the short period of time available:

> I don't think they even think of disabled people that much. For example, when it comes to the timetable, they just expect you to go from point A to B; unless they knew a disabled person would be there. Like this semester, I have classes down the other end then after that I have classes across the university on the other zone then back down and it is not changeable, it is not easy to change. We complained to the lecturer, he said he will look into it but it is not changeable ... I think there we might not blame them so much. Because unless they knew so as to make the time table to suit. But again, they assume that everybody will be able to reach there. ... Because even the professor was saying, well we can get you transport, but I think, he also didn't know, there is nothing much we can do. So we just run with the wheelchair all the way. There is no break in between; the classes just follow each other.

Johari added that having lectures that follow each other too closely in time limits disabled students' ability to get to lecture halls before they start:

> Sometimes you have a class in the morning from 8 am to 10 am and then another one from 10 am to 11 am or 12 pm. So you see there is no break in between. And then may be that class is on the fifth floor of a building and then the next one is in (name of the building) which is at the other end and there is no time within the classes so I have to be late for the second class always and that means relying on friends' notes to get going ...

I can attest to the participants' concerns relating to undergraduate program scheduling which I, as well, found problematic when studying in Kenya. Dada and Johari's claims that lecture schedules can aggravate the limitations that disabled students face bring out a fundamental problem. The quotations above explain the struggles respondents encounter in terms of moving from one lecture location to another, especially when they do not have any breaks in between their lectures. This is because many buildings in the selected universities are not only far apart but also inaccessible, making it difficult for severely disabled students to get into and out of lecture rooms. Inaccessibility is, thus, in itself a stressor that can discourage disabled students in their academic pursuits.

Dada brought up another important point that deserves further examination. She started off neutral, noting that the staff responsible for scheduling lectures cannot be "blamed" because they do not have the information available to them (about disabled students) when scheduling classes. However, she later challenges her stance, saying that "they (those who schedule) assume that everybody will be able to reach there." In scheduling, it is presumed that all students will be able to move from one point to another without any problems. This assumption negates the reality of those living with disability. This finding confirms critical disability scholars' observations that the environment is rarely structured or planned with disabled people in mind (see Imrie, 2005; Imrie, 2000; Titchkosky, 2008). Dada's narrative reveals the kinds of assumptions schedulers make – the general expectations of enrolled students is that they are non-disabled. These are ableist assumptions which validate normalizing scheduling, and this ultimately privileges non-disabled students. The notion of "not knowing" is used to rationalize exclusionary practices, insensitivities and lack of accountability in university settings. It is a clear indication of a lack of critical thoughts, discussions, and planning in the inclusion of disability in the everyday curriculum and general planning on the part of those charged with "ordering" university life (see Erevelles,

2005). This "not knowing" stance leaves access unproblematized and such unproblematization leaves unresolved negative consequences for the lives and experiences of disabled students.

Participants in this study also reported that, in addition to scheduling, large class sizes posed significant challenges to disabled students' successful experiences with the curriculum. Pointing to class size at the primary school level, Faizah remarked:

> In our schools, even the teachers are overloaded. Children are so many such that even teachers are not able to handle each child individually or to look into an individual's problem specifically. You generalize and you only teach the average child. So the extremes are not dealt with, the very low ones and the very intelligent ones. Something has to be done about it.

Most elementary classrooms in Kenya are overcrowded, and there is a limit to what teachers can do with the students. The problem of overcrowding was exacerbated with the introduction of Free Primary Education[22] in 2003. Primary school enrollments doubled or even tripled in some areas and schools reported class sizes ranging from 30 up to 100 students in one classroom. Since the Free Primary Education policy was adopted, only limited efforts have been made to put up new classrooms and to hire additional teachers to deal with the increased enrollments. As a result, the quality of education has suffered and teacher fatigue has become a serious occupational concern. Hence, Sifuna's (2005) observation that the challenges of the Free Primary Education program have been primarily to compromise the quality of education:

"...the situation of the teaching force in most of the districts is generally bad. ... Many primary schools are understaffed ... This does not augur well for the quality of education being delivered ..." (http://africa.peacelink. org/wajibu/articles/art_6901.html)

Congested classrooms have resulted in increased competition for the limited resources available, and teachers have had to make sacrifices in their teaching. In this context, students with specific learning challenges who require dedication of time and resources are particularly likely to suffer.

At the university levels, the women noted that the large number of students in the common courses made it hard to secure seats in positions where they could hear the lecturers well and take notes. As Lulu commented:

> Some lectures, especially these common units, are big classes over 1,000 students and some of the lecturers don't care whether

121

you hear what they are saying or not and they don't want even to repeat. Even the students themselves when you come to such a class, maybe you had a class on the other side of campus, when you reach there you find that the room is full; no place to sit. These other students are not willing to give you the front seats because when you are at the front that is when you can hear. So you will be forced to sit behind there and sometimes you won't even hear. If the room does not have a public address system you waste your time there, seated, and later look for a friend to read for you the notes.

Literature on disabled students and academic achievement especially in the U.K. and North America shows that class size has an influence on the achievement levels of students (Finn & Achilles, 1999; Odden, 1990) and disabled students in particular. In Lulu's narrative above, the large class sizes in her university compels students to adopt "survival of the fittest" strategies when they are in common courses. The earlier one gets to class, the better chances he/she has to secure front seats where they can hear their lecturers more clearly. In such situations, disabled students have to rely on friends and peers for notes.

Out of class curriculum (extracurricular activities)

Respondents also described their experiences with extracurricular activities in the university. Existing literature documents various merits and demerits of extracurricular activities in the lives of students. Kuhn (1995) indicated that extracurricular activities influence students' learning and personal development and the development of skills such as decision making, group process and team work (p. 147). Other studies have linked participation in extracurricular activities to development of positive self-concept and improved/increased high school grade point averages (GPA), enhanced school engagement and educational aspirations (Lamborn, Brown, Mounts, & Steinberg, 1992). On the other hand, extracurricular activities also have the potential to promote negative peer influences and school deviance (Lamborn et al., 1992).

This study examined the extent to which participants were involved in extracurricular activities. Some of the disabled women students noted that they were actively involved in extracurricular activities, while others were not. Facilities; environmental adaptations; lack awareness of activities available at the university; interest and motivation; high school experiences and gender were some of the factors that influenced the women students' choice of whether or not to engage in extracurricular activities.

Facilities, awareness and environmental adaptations

Availability of facilities for extracurricular activities available in the university had a significant impact on the degree to which disabled women students participated in games and sports. Pete reported that she was not involved in extracurricular activities because there were no facilities and no sports that disabled students could engage in at her university:

> I am not involved in any extracurricular activities and especially sports. There are really no facilities for us. Usually they have like netball and football. They did not have any indoors, any table tennis. If you want to play you go to the community facilities and that becomes a whole different story...

Johari indicated that she would like to participate in swimming but there are no facilities which accommodate her religious needs:

> The only thing I can do is swimming. I can swim and I would like to, but there is only one swimming pool and that one is for both men and women. And for me as a Muslim I cannot swim where men are. So I have never used it. But I have to keep paying the KShs. 2,000 every year for extracurricular activities even when the facilities are not there.

Johari raises an important point in terms of facilities, pointing to intersections between gender, religion and sports. She points to her dilemma around engaging in games and sports at the university as a Muslim woman. Muslims have a particular dressing code and it is wrong for women to expose their bodies in public, as will happen when one is in sports attire. If Johari has to participate in swimming, it has to be in a female only pool but the university has no such accommodations.

Shani, on the other hand, is rarely involved in extracurricular activities because she does not know what sorts of activities are available at her university:

> Most of the time we are not involved in some of those things like clubs and games. ... we are not aware which games we can be involved in or which clubs we can participate in. One needs information relating to most of these things, and we don't have it, so most people are not involved. Recently is when they have started some games for the disabled. Like in Ongozi I know there is a game called goal ball. That is the game most visually impaired students are involved in and it is doing very well. Others are also involved in groups like the Red Cross, some small, small clubs like that.

Shani notes that disabled students are not involved in games and sports because they do not know what is available for them at the university. But why are disabled students unaware of what sports and games are available in their universities? What are the universities doing to address this information gap? The major limitation, especially for blind students, is related to poor information dissemination. This is why Nadra is critical of the ways in which information is disseminated to disabled students within the university, as demonstrated in the narrative below:

> And even when there is information, they will put it in handbooks and those handbooks are not in Braille. Even the way they put them on notice boards, I do not see. Unless someone reads for me or someone thinks that Nadra needs to know such and such information and tells me, I don't get it. Unless someone reads and comes and tells me, I won't know, even when it is there. I might be passing that notice board everyday but I won't know that it is there [laughs].

Nadra indicates that, even when the information is made available to students, it is often simply printed in handbooks which are difficult for visually impaired students to read. She shows how most disabled students rely on the good will of other students to get information passed along to them. Most activities are advertised in print and visually impaired students are at a disadvantage with respect to using such information. This demonstrates a failure on the part of the university administration, especially in terms of institutional policies relating to communications with students.

Jamila is not involved in sports because there is no interpreter for hearing impaired students. She believes that this lack of resources is primarily responsible for disabled students' limited engagement in sports:

> No, I do not get involved in extra-curricular activities because interpreter services are not available. And I also do think that this is why few students with disabilities engage in extra-curricular activities in our university anyways.

For Afya, lack of sports variety and family commitments impact on her participation in extracurricular activities:

> I am not involved in many activities outside of my regular class work. I am married and have a family. You know, sometimes it is hard to be in college over the weekends away from your family. Plus, as a blind woman, there is not a lot for me to be involved in, not many games. And since I don't come from far, I make it a

point visiting my kids and husband every weekend, unless I have an exam. So I don't get time to go playing some of these games. It is not nice because you don't get to integrate with other students and to share, but there is nothing much one can do when it comes to family issues.

Afya has limited time for extracurricular activities, as she has to juggle, balancing her academics and taking care of her family. Her comments draw attention to some of the challenges mature students face when they return to college to further their education. They have to balance family and academic work. The respondent acknowledges that, not being on campus all the time, especially during the weekends, has disadvantages, but again she has to support her family.

Interest in extracurricular activities

Some study participants identified lack of interest in sports as the cause of their limited involvement in extracurricular activities. Mkufu is not involved in sports because she does not like sports:

No and it is not really because of facilities, I just don't like sports that much, that is why I am not involved.

Interviewer: Why?

Mkufu: No big reason but I just don't like sports.

Other women also reported having limited interest in games and sports, but being actively involved in academic clubs and religious organizations:

I don't do any sports, but I belong to the French club. I am not a sports fun; I just dislike it, even in primary and high school I was just forced to do it, I didn't like sports. (Nadra)

I have no interest in sports really, but I am very active in our religious group. May be that is how I compensate with sports. (Yakuti)

When I hear of sports I am so afraid. *Why?* Because I got badly injured at one time in my Form Four. We were out in the field playing and I slipped and fell on my back, I even have some mark here on my head. That made me dislike sports because the fields are not meant for us anyways. Like if you are on wheelchair you can't even run around the tracks. I lost interest in sports since then. (Fedha)

The narratives above reveal participants' reasons for not engaging in sports and games. Nadra and Yakuti acknowledge that games and sports are important but they do not like to be involved. These respondents do not provide further explanations as to why they are not interested. Is it that they just don't like sports or something happened? Could be a socialization effect or culturally influenced? Fedha is fearful of being hurt following her high school experiences which made her lose interest in games and sports. These comments indicate women's preferences for particular kinds of extracurricular activities compared to others. The narratives show that some of the women either just do not like sports or are de-motivated by the lack of variety or by fear of getting injuries, since facilities have not been adapted for persons with disabilities. These findings provide a glimpse of the factors behind the marginal experiences of disabled women students in extracurricular activities at university levels.

High school influences

Other disabled women students indicated that their choices to engage in extracurricular activities were based on what they did during high school. Hawa, who is visually impaired, is an active member of the environmental club and of the Christian Union evangelistic team at her university. She also plays goal ball. Hawa decided to join the environmental club because in high school she was a member of a somewhat related club: "I was in wildlife club when I was in high so I wanted to join a related club ..." In other words, Hawa made connections between her prior knowledge and experiences and the current ones, as she moved up the education ladder.

Aziza pointed to the question of numbers when explaining disabled students' involvement in extracurricular activities:

> When it comes to sports for the disabled students in an integrated school, I can say that it is not favorable. May be you are like four of you in the whole school, so you know they cannot consider you as much as those other teams because you are like competing with nobody.

Because disabled students were fewer in number and generally required extra expenditures to be accommodated, their sporting options were limited. It is possible that such preferences may have influenced many disabled persons' perceptions of games and sports.

Dada was not involved in any extracurricular activities in high school and is not involved in any at the university: "I was not into any sporting activities in high school, and right now I don't do any, either."

Hereni also is not doing any games or sports:

> I never participated in any sports really even from my high school years. But I was in the Young Christian Union club. In university, I don't play any competitive games. As for clubs, I may consider joining one but I haven't decided which one.

When asked whether she is involved in any out of class activities, Karuli feels that it may be another new world for her to start venturing into sports:

> In my high school I was very much into the historical club. When I came to university, I don't belong to any club yet, but I am connected to several organizations out there which do various things for people with disabilities. Sports no, I haven't been to that field for long it will be like starting something new for me. But I like watching sports, not participating.

What the study participants have shown in their voices above is that even though they are not into games and sports, they do engage in other social activities. It is also possible that the lack of appropriate facilities, like of variety of games and sports, and lack of motivation from an early age may have contributed to the women's shunning these extracurricular activities.

Gender and extracurricular activities

Study findings revealed significant gender differences in extracurricular involvement, particularly games and sports. More disabled male students than disabled women students were found to be actively involved in games and sports in the university. However, more disabled female students were involved in other social activities especially religious organizations and academic clubs. This confirms what some existing studies have shown, that men are more likely than women to be active participants in sports (Canadian Heritage Report, 2007). But why is this so?

In explaining these gender differences in sports participation, Martin and Martin (1995) posit that for a long time sports have been constructed as a male domain (see also Lenskyj, 2003). Koivula (1999) suggests that these constructions of sport as a largely male activity influences the way in which men and women perceive sports. These perceptions are likely to influence the benefits men and women attribute to sports and the amount of time they will dedicate to sporting activities (see also Salminen, 1990 cited by Koivula, 1999, p. 363). Elsewhere, Koivula (1999) pointed out that "body-related and social factors are stronger motives for women's participation in sports while competition and competence motives are more valued by men and are likely to have emerged due to expectations of society of proper behavior for men and women" (p. 362). Men are depicted as competitive, and women are expected to be yielding and concerned about their physical fitness, not competing with others (Bem, 1974, 1981a, cited by Koivula, 1999, p. 362).

Participants in this study cited reasons such as dislike of sport on the part of women, or a general shying away from sports and lack of motivation as some of the factors influencing their participation in sports at the university. Hawa remarked:

> Men are determined to participate, but ladies are reluctant. Like we are only four who participate in goal ball and the men are almost 20 who are willing to participate. When we tell the women to come and join us they are not willing I don't know why. ...We have tried but they don't come. I think they just see it as waste of time and they are busy with their reading and updating notes and other personal issues. Like me, I have now to plan my timetable on how to go for goal ball, do my assignments, etc.

Hawa notes that disabled women students were more reluctant to participate in sports than disabled men. She attributes this limited participation of disabled women to time constraints especially for the blind women who dedicate their after school hours to finding readers to help them with notes or books etc.

Nadra and Faizah also acknowledged that more disabled men than disabled women were involved in extracurricular activities, and cited shying off and lack of motivation as the contributing factors:

> I don't know why, they could be shying away, and disliking it. May be they like doing other things not really sports. (Nadra)

> Not really, I don't know whether the women are shying away or they don't like it, not many are involved. They are not involved like the men. May be they are not motivated or something? They need to be motivated; they need to be encouraged. (Faizah)

Nadra, who, as we saw earlier, is critical of the way information about sports and games is disseminated to visually impaired students, together with Faizah speculate that shying off and lack of motivation are the other possible reasons behind the limited number of disabled women engage in sports and games. The respondents do not, however, explain what caused this shying off.

Dhahabu, on the other hand, remarked that the low enrollment of disabled women students in the university contributes to the low numbers of their participation in extracurricular activities:

> The ladies are not so much involved because, for one, we are few. And then most ladies, like those who are direct from school and those who are teachers from the field, are not always interested, because they feel they are old and feel out of place. Those of us who are direct from school are very few, so we also feel out of place because most of the people who are there are men. So, we don't also like to be involved.

In this response Dhahabu raises the question of belongingness and influences of gender and age on mature disabled women students' perceptions of "fitting in" when it comes to sports participation.

Hawa, Nadra, Faizah and Dhahabu agree that more disabled male students are involved in sports than disabled female students. The most common reasons given by these participants for choosing not to participate included shyness, their small numbers, other responsibilities and lack of awareness or interest. Resources and access are also a challenge. But could this be all that bars them from getting more involved in sports? Further investigations into disabled women's involvement in sports at the postsecondary levels in Kenya would be useful in understanding the challenges and barriers they face.

Of concern here, though, is the respondents' lack of critical interrogations of the discourse of gender and sports participation that they articulate. They acknowledge that disabled men are more involved in sports compared to disabled women but fail to interrogate the ideology informing this biased representation of women and femininity and men and masculinity in games and sports in our societies (Pirinen, 2002). For example, what social structures sanction male superiority in sports? In the media, men are often stereotypically represented as the "strong," "courageous," "competitive," "committed," "aggressive," sport "excellers" while women's excellence in sports is down played. Men's determination and participation in sports is presented as an "acceptable" characteristic of their masculinity (Pirinen, 2002) while women continue to struggle for recognition (Lenskyj, 2003). In my view, the women's failure to look critically into their marginal participation in extra-curricular activities shows how biased valorizations of men as the "sporty" subjects have become so normalized and continue to be perpetuated from one generation to another in our societies in spite of feminist struggles for equality and change.

Conversely, this silencing of gender on the part of the disabled women students could also be conceptualized in another way. It is possible that there were differences in terms of the priorities these disabled women have when it comes to naming and challenging oppression. Indeed, Nnaemeka (1998) pointing to differences between African feminism and Western feminism especially when priorities are taken into account noted:

> The much bandied about intersection of race, class, sexual orientation etc in Western feminist discourse does not ring with the same urgency for most African women for whom other basic issues of everyday life are intersecting in most oppressive ways. This is not to say that issues of race and class are not important to African women in the continent ... rather ... African women see and address such issues first as they configure in and relate to their own lives and immediate sorroundings ... (p. 6)

Probably the women look at addressing ableism as the bigger project and issues of intersectionality are to come later once the project has taken root. On the other hand, it is also possible that the inclusive nature of African feminism has implications on the women's reluctance to trouble gender thinking that they could be creating male/female dichotomies, which might affect a collaborative approach to challenging ableism. Thus, the women could be feeling that "united we stand" while "divided" we fall, and want to address the challenge of ableism together, without being seen as divisive. Further research is needed to explicate why these women did not analyze gender as an ideology in their extra-curricular experiences.

INTERPERSONAL RELATIONS

In their narrations of curriculum experiences above, the women remained dissatisfied with their representation and participation in the curriculum. They felt that disabled students are devalued, stigmatized and neglected in knowledge construction and knowledge dissemination across all levels of education. Participants pointed to lack of serious commitment on the part of teachers, faculty, curriculum designers, policy makers, government and society in addressing the question of inclusion. To gain further insights into the women's descriptions of their marginalization, this section explores their relations with people disabled women students interact with in the university.

Scholars studying the social aspects of schooling have argued that non-academic factors, such as interpersonal relations, influence students' academic adjustments and learning outcomes (Crosnoe, Johnson & Elder, 2004). This implies that students' relationships with other students, teachers and faculty are important variables in the learning process (Baker, 1999; Crosnoe et. al, 2004). Research shows that positive, caring teacher-student relations are correlated with better student integration into the school system and positive learning outcomes (Crosnoe, 2002; Crosnoe et al., 2004) while poor student-teacher relationships are linked to students' feelings of alienation and negative learning outcomes (see Coleman, 1988). Certainly the principle of caring has become a central tenet in teaching (see Acker, 1995; 1999; Noddings, 1992) although not to a great extent in higher education. Noddings (1992) emphasizes that schools have to be moral places that educate the heart as well as the head and teachers need to model caring behavior. Educators are thus increasingly working on, and advocating for the incorporation of the principle of care into the curriculum – formal and informal (Darling-Hammond, 2000).

As for relationships with peer and friends, studies have shown that friends and peers have important impacts on students' schooling experiences. This is also true of disabled students' learning experiences. In an exploration of the views of disabled and non-disabled college students on the inclusion of peers, Ash, Bellew, Davies, Newman & Richardson (1997) found that poor relationships with other students, poor resourcing and poor planning were among the factors that discouraged disabled students from pursuing college education. Stage and Milne (1996) in their study on the experiences of students with learning disabilities and their adjustment to college, indicated that "successful programming for learning disabled students requires cooperative endeavours among students, peers tutors, and faculty" (p. 429) and that such efforts require mutual understanding and supporting attitudes (Aune & Johnston, 1992 cited by Stage & Miles, 1996, p. 429).

Research findings demonstrate that faculty's and friends' attributes and relationships have important influences on disabled students' higher education experiences and on their lives in general. Positive relationship between faculty and the study participants meant better adjustments at the university and increased possibilities of positive in-class curriculum experiences. Likewise, positive relations with peers and friends correlated with disabled women students' positive experiences both inside and outside of class. On the converse, negative experiences with faculty, friend and peers turned out to have negative influences on participants' educational experiences and reinforced prevailing stigmatizing societal attitudes about disabled people.

Relations with faculty

Although all the respondents indicated that they had positive relationships and experiences with their professors, they also agreed that not all faculty had good relationships with disabled students. Respondents appreciated the support they received from faculty, which enhanced their success in university. They also pointed to incidents depicting negative student-teacher/faculty relations that culminated in discrimination, frustrations and feelings of "lesser than" on the part of disabled students. The women gauged their relationships with the professors based on approachability and faculty actions and interactions with disabled students.

Approachability and support

What caused faculty to be characterized as supportive or unsupportive?

Most faculty are receptive, a few are indifferent, but not that much. (Mkufu)

> Not all lecturers are supportive, but I will say most of them are supportive, especially in my department, Christian Religious Education (C.R.E), we had very good lecturers. (Lulu)

Study participants pointed to behaviors such as accommodations of disabled students' needs, approachability and basic attitude in their descriptions of supportive and non-supportive faculty. Pete provided an example of the positive support she got from faculty:

> I was lucky to have met very supportive faculty ... they were able to listen to me. When I had health issues they assisted and proposed where I should go and seek medical attention...

Hereni added:

> I have never had any problem with lecturers ... Most of them are very good, very cooperative and always ready to help where there is need...

Hawa on the other hand showed that some lecturers were great but others could at times be mean and unsupportive:

> Professors are supportive but not all. ... Like when I came here during my first year, there is one who told me never to go to his class with a Braille machine because it was making a lot of noise in the class and disrupting other students. So some are good and others are not.
>
> *Interviewer:* And what did you do?
>
> *Hawa:* I didn't know what to do, I came to know it later, I just stopped going with it (Braille machine). So I could just go to class sit, listen and then ask other students to read for me notes later. I

did not do anything. I just came to know about things I could have done when the semester was over, but he gave me handouts after the class, although they were not in Braille. I just had to persevere and get help from other students. But I passed the course. But now, looking back, I look back I feel bad I wish another student does not have to go through such an experience. I don't know - it is just bad. Some of these lecturers can be so mean but may be they don't know or see it that way.

Mkufu, Lulu, Hereni and Hawa appreciate faculty who are receptive, accommodating and who listen to their students when they are faced with difficulties. They, however, dislike faculty that are insensitive to the needs of disabled students. For example, Hawa's professor had stopped her from going to class with a Braille machine, an essential tool equivalent to non-disabled students' notebooks, arguing that it was a disruption to others' learning process. Even though the professor provided her with handouts, they were in print and she had to look for readers to help her out. This leaves one wondering which assistive devices belong and which ones do not? What can disabled students bring to class and what can't they? Are faculty prepared for the inevitable reality of diversity in contemporary higher education, particularly in Kenya?

The participants' responses above show that supportive faculty are accommodating, approachable and responsive of students' needs. Unsupportive faculty are insensitive and hesitant to accommodate disabled students' learning needs as illustrated in Hawa's example. Dhahabu provided another example of attributes that characterize unsupportive faculty:

> There are those lecturers who take us like any other students and, you know, with us disabled students we have some special needs... Like when they are teaching...those (topics) that involve calculations, we may not get them accurately, so we need some extra assistance. There are some who are really nice and accommodating, but there are those who don't bother, so we don't know if they really know or they don't care and just assume.

Dhahabu confirms that not every faculty member is accommodating but acknowledges that there are those who take the initiative to assist disabled students. Nonetheless, other faculty (the unsupportive group) treat all students the same without taking into account the diversity among students and their learning differences.

Actions and interactions with disabled students

All disabled women talked about how faulty interacted with disabled students. Aziza pointed out that she had good experiences with her professors:

> I will say I have not seen anything bad with them (professors). They are good, social and when you go to them on one to one basis, actually they help. I have never approached one and been let down. Even the administration, when you go there with a problem and you approach them, they are very friendly, they help out.

According to Aziza, the professors she had interacted with, thus far, were very personable and helpful. She had never been turned down by any professor she had approached for assistance. She made similar observations about the administration staff who she indicated were friendly and helpful. Johari, too, had a very positive relationship with faculty:

> Many of them were very friendly to me, I had good relations with them and we are still very good friends. They even encouraged me to go for my master's degree because they saw I am capable of doing it. So I am thinking of coming back after I graduate.

Reflecting on her high school experiences, Karuli noted that her teachers were understanding and friendly:

> With teachers, I had a good relationship. In fact most of them were my friends and even those who were not teaching me. I found that most of them were understanding and friendly. But at the university, not so much.

Karuli acknowledges that she had good relations with faculty and teachers but also draws comparisons between her experiences in high school and universities, indicating that faculty at university level were more friendly and understanding than at her high school.

Other respondents indicated that faculty were good with disabled students but others held prejudiced perceptions toward disabled students and this affected the latter's experiences in the university. As Yakuti explained:

> I haven't experienced anything that extraordinary so far, but you can notice some differences in the way the professors relate to disabled students and those who are not. Sometimes it is evident that some think of you as not being able to do something, but then you can't judge them before they utter it out, you know what I mean?

Aminia added:

> ... people will not, for example, tell you that you can't take this
> course because you are blind, or something like that, but when you
> go to register, they will tell you it is full and you come to hear from
> friends who went to that office later that there are still spaces and
> they got registered. I have experienced that and I think it is some
> kind of indirect discrimination as you said. What do you do, do you
> demand to see the list? How do you see it when you can't even see
> [laughs]?

As noted earlier, disabled women students experienced both overt
and covert discrimination. Yakuti and Aminia point to some examples of
concealed discrimination against disabled students. It is evident that, in
spite of the efforts made to address issues impacting disabled persons, such
as improving physical access to public facilities; providing employment
opportunities; and the enactment of laws against discrimination of disabled
people (see Deal, 2007), there still persist many hidden prejudices, as
demonstrated in Aminia's story above. In borrowing from the anti-racist
analysis, I argue that Aminia's accounts are an example of covert ableism.
Covert ableisms, like covert racisms, "are subtle, subversive, and deliberate
informal and formal mechanisms that allow differential access to rewards,
prestige, sanctions, status, and privileges based on ablest hierarchies"
(see Coates, 2008, pp. 211-212). Racism as a form of social control is
used to restrict and regulate the behavior of particular racial groups to the
advantage of specified racial group (see Coates, 2008). Similarly, ableism
is used as a form of social control to the benefit of the non-disabled. In
this case, Aminia's being denied registration in a course she wanted is
indicative of a covert policy of the university which encouraged disabled
students to register in particular courses that the department deemed they
could do better, while simultaneously reserving spaces for non-disabled
students that the department deemed more capable of success.

In general, the narratives above show that good student-teacher/faculty
relations are paramount for students' positive academic experiences
and for their overall success. The women reveal that supportive faculty
and administrators provide a sense of confidence, which leads to better
university experiences.

Relations with friends and peers

Positive influences from peers and friends

All the disabled women students affirmed that they had friends both within and outside of the university. These friends and peers are an important support system in their higher education experiences. Faizah, who has friends inside and outside of university, explained their importance as follows:

> I have a variety of friends, the young ladies, the JABs, people of my age; they keep on coming to visit; and outside the university the same way. I have very supportive friends who have been encouraging me to continue with my studies. Friends from outside visit me, we share and when I am out there at home we also talk. They tell me "you have been a big challenge to us. ... Even some of them actually have gone back to school. I have a lady friend who joined diploma course and she has finished because that takes two to three. She graduated last year. I have another taking the same course and there are others willing to join university only that now study leaves have been halted a bit. Teachers' Service Commission will not give study leaves again till some other time.

Faizah's friends offer her positive support and encouragement. She has not only benefited from their encouragement, but has also inspired some of them (especially her workmates) to further their education too.

Other disabled women students noted that friends have influenced their academic achievements and university through study group supports/ discussions, informal counseling, acceptance and helping out with their day to day activities:

> We always discuss some issues about education and advice one another on what we should do ... like in choosing our careers and such kind of things. So they have been really encouraging me to continue working hard. For those who did not get a chance to go to university and they would really have liked to come we always advice one another that even if they didn't get a chance to come to university, they should pursue what they can like in college or wherever and then go to university after. (Nadra)

> My friends are important; their support has been very important, especially when it comes to movement from one place to another within and outside campus, they give me a ride...borrowing books, photocopying etc. (Pete)

There are friends who are very helpful, they have influenced me a lot because when you use them, they are the ones they will pay you some hours to go read for you or even try to help you; read for you things you missed in class or may be try to teach you that thing that was hard or that was being done on the board and you could not seeing. They are the ones that will help you in the rooms. (Dhahabu)

Sometimes ... some courses are difficult, especially those that need illustrations and elaborations ... I have friends, we used to be in a discussion group; most of the time they used to come to my room, we sit down, we discuss and make sure each one of us has understood. Actually that really helped me in my academic achievements ... And also in reading books they are always there. There was one who used to come and find out if there is anything that needed to be read and she would read for me. ... (Shani)

As the above quotes suggest, friends serve different purposes and continue to positively influence disabled women students' lives. For Nadra, friends are a crucial sources of motivation, assurance and advice. Pete asserts that her friends and peers are critical supports when it comes to mobility and accessing learning materials. Dhahabu and Shani, on the other hand, speak of friends and peer support when it comes to readers and study groups. These findings are consistent with some of the existing literature which has shown that friends and peers influence students' school adjustment levels and academic success across educational levels (Berndt, 1999; Wentzel & Caldwell, 1997).

Challenging experiences with friends and peers

In spite of the many positive things, the women talked about peers and friends, the participants also revealed that some friends and peers were not supportive. When I asked Aziza of the University of Ongozi about her experiences with peers within the university she said:

Some are friendly, just friendly, but others, once they realize that you have a weakness, they just keep off from you. They would not like to be associated with you. That is what I have realized.

Aziza, who is partially blind, narrates that some peers are friendly but when they realize that she has visual challenges, they tend to withdraw and try not to associate with her. Her narrative suggests differences in reactions when it comes to visible and invisible disabilities. Aziza's disability is not overtly evident, unless one gets to interact with her closely. Her comment reminds us of Jones et al.'s (1984) idea of concealability of stigma. In their book *Social stigma: The psychologies of marker relationships, Jones et al.* identify six dimensions of stigma namely: concealability, course, disruptiveness, aesthetic qualities, origin and peril. The dimension of concealability takes into account the question of whether the condition being stigmatized is hidden or obvious and to what extent its visibility controllable. Since Aziza's partial blindness is somehow concealed, she does not get instant negative social reactions from her peers until they interact with her closely and realize that she has a visual impairment. Visibility of a disability thus plays a central role in producing negative social reactions and thereby affecting interpersonal relationships (Jones et al. 1984).

Hereni added that, although many of her friends have been instrumental in her life, there are also friends who have been unsupportive and unaccepting at times:

> For students not all of them are friendly. I would say not all of them; you know some of them wouldn't even mind saying hi. And some of them you could ask for assistance and they are like I am busy, they are not willing to help.
>
> *Interviewer:* Why do you think this is so?
>
> *Hereni:* I think it is a lack of awareness. Yeah may be they don't understand that you with disability there is no difference between me and them. You know may be they see you, you are there disabled and may be you don't deserve anything than what you are, they never appreciate you. Some were however very good, understanding and they treated me well. They don't treat me in a special way to show that I am disabled; they interact with me ordinarily and they understood me.

Elaborating on friends and their impact on one's academics, Nadra remarked that some friends may have negative influences on disabled students' academic endeavours and therefore cautioned that one has to be careful when it comes to choosing friends:

> There are different kinds of friends; there are those who can make you move up or those who can let you down. Like some of the friends I had in first year were those who used to like spending their time may be moving up and down, go to town, walking and some other funny, funny things, ... they didn't like reading. So sometimes if you don't watch or choose friends carefully, you can easily be trapped and not do what you really want to do.

Mature students revealed that age and gender influenced friendship relations for disabled women students. For example, Dada, who is physically disabled and is a mature student, stated:

> I have friends, but you see the only problem is that people of your same age-set are not many. I have friends mostly like boys and of course they were my students. And even my students, I told you it is those ones that came later that seem to want to associate with me.

Dada is alluding to some of the challenges mature students encounter as they go back to school to further their education. She shows how these students have to negotiate space in social relationships, especially with younger students. Dada observes that some of the students she knows are reluctant to associate with her. It is possible that this reluctance is a result of the younger students shying away from their former teacher (since some of the students Dada is referring to her former students); or it could be that negative perceptions toward disability and disabled people influences non-disabled students' limited interactions with disabled students. In spite of these challenges, Dada acknowledged that friends have been instrumental to her academic achievement and overall life experience at the university:

> Well, of course we share ... like in literature we share books. In fact there, (referring to her literature course). I have a bit more girls and even the young girls they associate with me a bit more than in (name of other subject specialization). If I come to think of it, and some of them, we were doing courses together from last semester. ... in terms of sharing material we do. There are some ladies, lady not even ladies who got in this year, we are becoming friendly, and I think I feel at home with her.

Here Dada recognizes that there are gender differences in her relations and interactions with peers and friends. These differences vary with situations or social positioning such that when she is in a particular class/ lecture, she has more or less female students interacting with her.

Dada's remarks demonstrate that older students encounter not only academic challenges but also relationships. Writing about ageism in academic contexts, Carpenter (1996) observed that older people are likely to be discriminated against in favor of youth in higher education. This has implications, particularly for disabled students, who tend to return to postsecondary institutions when they are older as exemplified by Dada (see also Opini, 2008).

EXPERIENCES WITH PHYSICAL ACCESS

Writing about disabled people in Britain and the movement towards independent living, Barnes (1990) remarked that "independent living for disabled people necessitates a physical environment that does not disable them" (p. 149). Barnes went on to say that, because disabled people have traditionally been excluded from the mainstream economic and social life of the community, the physical environment has been created in a manner which disables them. Barnes concluded that institutional discrimination towards disabled people has never been more blatant than it is in the context of the physical environment (p. 149). Barnes' observations are very relevant to the Kenyan context. The physical environments, buildings, transportation media are explicitly "out of bounds" to disabled people. The majority of buildings, buses, and trains in Kenya are built without considering the needs of disabled people (see Barnes, 1990). In a recent conversation with one of my friends in Kenya, she described the condition of the roads in some parts of the country as a "nightmare" to disabled people and pregnant women (Mrs. X, 2008).

This "nightmare" extends to physical access in the university. During my research at the sites, in 2006, I found the washrooms in one of the universities too tiny even for a non-disabled person to navigate. There were no latches where one could hang up his/her bags (not even signs that they might have been there before and had since been torn off). In one building, the washrooms were located in the basement and could only be accessed by stairs. I wondered how disabled students using wheelchairs accessed many washrooms, and, when they did, how they went in and out, because they were too tiny, let alone for wheelchair use. In fact one of the officers interviewed acknowledged that the washrooms were inaccessible to disabled students, particularly those who use wheelchairs, although, the officer did not provide any strategies on how this problem of access was being addressed (see chapter eight in the book).

In this study, disabled women students spoke about their experiences with physical access within the university. Particular attention was paid to the general environment and to buildings. Sometimes the women also reflected on their experiences in other public areas such as transportation within the cities. They made general and specific comments about physical access, some noting that the environment was fairly accessible, while others indicated that physical access remained a major barrier to disabled students' movement in the university.

General observations about physical access

In her discussion of physical access at the University of Ongozi, Hawa felt that some places within the university's physical environment were actually accessible, and disabled students could get through with some minor challenges:

> I can say in some places like the classes on that building (points to the location of the building) like we have the ramps, so you can move at least a bit. Then in the library at least they give us some assistance, you just go with a specific topic or book and the librarians will assist you in finding the book. And then we are allowed to go in with readers to read for us.

Dada similarly noted:

> Some places at the University of Ongozi are flat, that is one thing, and then of course we have all kinds of hostels but for the disabled, their hostels are quite adapted. But of course the infrastructure is a bit scattered all over the place. But from what I can see they (the university) are trying to work on it from that other side, hopefully they will reach this other place. Because when you are in a wheelchair and you are in a tattered place, of course it affects you physically.

Nonetheless, Dhahabu of the University of Ongozi challenged Hawa and Dada's observations in her illustration of how visually impaired students, for example, struggle to navigate the unfriendly physical environment around campus:

> There are posts all over; there are so many potholes around too. For the physically disabled students there are no ramps into some places so it is hard for them to move. Also for the blind students you find that the roads are not so well defined so sometimes you get lost on the way and there are pot holes you go into them. When it has rained there is so much mud to some areas and there is also stagnant water so you can go into the water. You find that at certain places there are posts and you bump into them and you get hurt at times. In some places there are may be these cemented blockages along the sidewalks and sometimes you knock yourself against them and you are hurt. And even there are holes, I mean big holes (laughs), maybe they don't know that they are there you just go and find yourself inside there.

Pete commented the following about physical access at the University of Khafee:

> The environment is not accessible at all. As I said, there are no ramps, no elevators - so you have to keep climbing up and down the stairs, which takes a lot of your energy. I think they didn't consider that they might have disabled students coming here. Maybe because most disabled students don't even finish high school and, for the few who finish, very few institutions will take them. They don't get any sponsorship, and, you know, you need money for accommodation, fees and food, and when you sum it up, you can't afford. In the first place you are struggling down there so how do you start to talk about university education when you can't even feed yourself?

Here, Pete is contemplating why the university remains inaccessible. Most probably, she thinks, it is because many disabled students do not make it to university and therefore universities do not invest much in physical access and structures.

In more specific terms, the women talked about accessibility in areas such as the administration buildings, the library, lecture halls and halls of residence (hostels). According to the participants, accessibility varied across buildings and campuses.

Administrative offices

Some participants felt that the administrative buildings were accessible while others indicated that they were not. Dada, pointing to the administrative block at Ongozi, remarked:

> The old block is inaccessible. The new one has some ramps and I have gone there alone when I was trying to change the courses. There is this other *ghorofa* (highrise) place that has no ramp but the others have. But then again when it comes to offices upstairs, I am told you have to be carried up there with your wheelchair or somebody comes down, which of course is not nice [laughs]. There is no elevator. But I have not had a reason to go and see someone up there, but I have imagined how you can go there.

Afya added:

> The administration block where you are supposed to do various things you can't go there alone because it is very far and the roads leading there are not defined. They are confusing. So you need some help, may be somebody, to take you there or the tuk-tuks...

Even these other offices are very far apart and in different locations, and you cannot make your way there.

Referencing the challenge of accessing the administrative buildings at the University of Khafee, Hereni, who is physically disabled and uses a wheelchair, said:

The administration is completely inaccessible to people with disabilities. When it comes to entering the main offices there are stairs all over. I have to look for someone to help me up the stairs when going there. But again some of those stairs not everybody can be able to push a wheelchair up. So, if you have something to do, you have to, I have to send someone to do it for you. There should be some pavements which are accessible or ramps to allow someone on wheelchair to use.

Shani added the challenge of organization when talking about the administration block: "Firstly, it (the administrative block) is very far from the hostels, and then the offices are not in an organized manner so that you cannot access them easily". When I asked her to explain further what she means by offices not being organized she replied:

You know sometime you go there and you even don't know which office is which, so you waste some good time trying to figure out the place and rely on people to tell you the office you want. If they would put those offices in an organized manner, may be arrange them alphabetically so that when you go to the academic office maybe that will be the first one, then the next one like the office of finance, it will be less confusing. Yeah just have them in an alphabetic manner so it is easy to access them.

Dada, Afya, Hereni and Shani present their perceptions about accessibility of their universities' administrative buildings. Dada feels that the place is fairly navigable, especially "the new administration block", but when it comes to offices located upstairs, it is hard to access them. Afya adds that the administration block is not only inaccessible but it is also distantly situated from the residential halls, while Hereni shows how lack of ramps in the administrative buildings make it difficult to access offices. Dada and Hereni comment that one has to be carried upstairs when he/ she wants to see an administrator, which is a very risky endeavor. What happens if, by accident, when being carried upstairs one tumbles and comes rolling down the stairs? The universities have not clearly addressed the challenge of designing their buildings for "diversity" when it comes to physical access.

The university library

The women noted that the library, which they saw as a central place in the university, was both accessible and inaccessible to some degree. Talking about its accessibility, Hawa of the University of Ongozi observed:

> The library is also okay although I have not gone there much because I normally read in the room, unless when I want something there.

For Mkufu, the library is not that "okay":

> The library, it is not really accessible. We are told there are special people who cater for challenged people, but personally I don't see them. Maybe they are referring to support for those who are blind. Like for me I find that when I go there and I have to look for a book, you know, I get tired; I have to *zunguka* (go round) all over in the library. Sometimes I end up giving up. So they are not that efficient, I look for a book, I don't get it, I am tired, or I get a book it is very big, carrying it is a problem.

Mkufu, who is physically disabled, raised an important point regarding the experiences of physically disabled students in the library. It seems more effort is made to address the needs of visually impaired students at Ongozi than those with other forms of disability. Validating Mkufu's concerns, I found that the officers, from the University of Ongozi who participated in the study, emphasized the services provided for visually impaired students more than for students with other kinds of disabilities. There is a need for the university to balance their support services so as to address the learning needs of all disabled students in their universities equitably.

Nadra, on the other hand, was quick to note that the library was not only about books but there are other places in there that disabled students may want to use. Hence her observation about the washrooms in the library:

> The washrooms there are accessible; I think if those kinds of washrooms were also in the hostels and some of the lecture halls, it will be great.

Although Nadra noted that the washrooms were accessible, during one of the interview days I observed that, even though washrooms at Ongozi were spacious, they still fell short of required standards of wheelchair accessible washrooms, particularly as they lacked grab bars, coat hooks, switches and water basins, which were placed high up at an inaccessible height.

The challenges of an inaccessible library were also evident at the University of Khafee, as illustrated by Fedha:

> That library is not accessible. There are elevators but they stalled God knows when [laughs]. When I come for books, I have to get a friend to get them for me as   climbing those   s t a i r s is so tiring.

Aziza from Ongozi however likes the library because:

> To some extent it is accessible and I like it. Like I can go to the library and be given reference books but the problem is they are not in Braille. So you have to ask the librarian to assist you to get the printed one then come look for someone to read for you. But I think they should try and have the books in Braille or talking books.

The women's observations above give cause for concern, not only in terms of physical access, but also in terms of whether the information contained in those libraries is provided in accessible formats. In terms of physical access, the libraries in both universities are located in buildings that have no functioning elevators. This means that disabled students face difficulties using stairs to go to look for books. In terms of accessibility of materials, Aziza observed that there were no Braille books in the university library. In an era in which much of the information is digitized, one would expect that perhaps libraries would offer alternative ways of accessing information in addition to print material. Unfortunately, as noted earlier, the selected universities fall behind, technologically. Disabled students are affected the most because much of the technology they need to use is not available in these universities.

Halls of residence

Comments about the halls of residence ranged from participants finding them quite accessible to not very accessible. In fact, at the University of Ongozi, the halls of residence/hostels scored the most highly in terms of accessibility. As Shani explained:

> I will say that the hostels are okay, they are at least accessible; I think that is the best thing they considered.

Dhahabu added: "... the hostels are the ones that are accessible because the hostels in which disabled students stay don't have a lot of barriers. You can, at least, make your way through." Mkufu agreed with Shani and

Dhahabu about the hostels:

> Hostels, I think they are very fair; I find it very fair because you see like us guys we are located in (name of hostels), not like in other hostels where there is climbing of stairs. Then the tuk-tuks are just out there it is not far. And our washrooms are better, because like if you want to wash you can sit somewhere and fetch water and wash. So I find the hostels fair, they are not that bad. And like here in my room there is a balcony - I can wash, I can hang, they are fair.

Dada remarked: "... the hostels are okay too. There is ramp on the door in some of these places." Nadra, however, expressed some reservations about accessibility in the halls of residence at Ongozi noting:

> I can say that not all the halls of residence are easily accessible for disabled students. Some have no ramps and have only stairs. And, you know, someone on wheelchair cannot easily go up the stairs. I think they should consider and have some things like ramps to cater for their needs. And also, with regard to toilets, the physically impaired cannot use these regular washrooms; they need at least spacious and raised washrooms. So I think the university should also look into such issues to enable the disabled students to enjoy their movement here.

Unlike at the University of Ongozi, where the majority of the women acknowledged that their halls of residence were fairly accessible, participants from the University of Khafee expressed serious concerns about their residences. For example, Johari and Fedha noted that there was no guarantee that disabled students could get ground floor rooms reserved for them. Johari commented:

> Halls of residence can be tricky. You don't have any reservations really as a disabled person. I think this is something they need to look into. (Johari)

Fedha added:

> When you read the university handbook, they say that the university can provide single rooms but when you get here it is different. Okay, there are single rooms but they are all politically allocated. ... Like since my first year I have been applying and requesting them to refer to their own booklet that says we can get single rooms, and they say no. You see, that booklet was printed I don't when; the rooms are there but they are located to some other

people. They just say in the booklet that they are there but on the opening day when you come, you have to hassle with the other students, there are pushing to find a place to stay.

Fedha further pointed out that sometimes those allocating rooms allocate disabled students rooms on upper floors without considering the challenge of climbing up and down the stairs:

They can sometimes decide to give you a room on the fourth floor and there is no elevator there and there is nothing you can do. So you really have to make your case and explain to them that it is not practical for them to put you on the fourth floor. But they can only put you on this floor.

This is a challenge not just for disabled students, but also for the disabled staff who work at the university. As Aminia explained:

Actually, the main office of the unit for accommodation is in the hostel where I live, and the accountant uses a wheel chair. What he does is that when he comes to work in the morning, he has to leave his wheelchair outside and then he is carried up the stairs to his office. When he is going for lunch they carry him down and same thing all the time.

There are clear differences between what the Universities of Khafee and Ongozi offer in terms of students' residences. Khafee students are critical of the ways their hostels are designed and of the allocation of rooms, while Ongozi students reveal that efforts are made to address their needs, even though more needs to be done. The narratives above point to what the existing literature has shown in terms of housing. As Imrie and Hall (2001) observed, most dwellings are designed and constructed as "types" that comprise standard fixtures and fittings that are not sensitive to variations in bodily forms, capabilities and needs (cited by Imrie 2005, p. 13). Such designs reveal a disabling and disablist society (Imrie, 2005) that fails to recognize the needs of disabled people, as also demonstrated in the participants' narratives.

Lecture halls

As for the lecture halls, all the study participants agreed that there were problems with accessing the lecture halls in both institutions. Hereni of the University of Khafee noted:

You are coming from up there, the place has no ramp, someone has to help you. If there was a ramp, at least I could go through easily. So

I rush from there, then after the lesson I rush back to the (name of building) because most of my lectures are there.

Hereni observes that often their lectures follow each other closely in time and they have to keep rushing from one class to another, a practice that is very tiring and, for some, impossible. These findings confirm Losinsky, Levi, Saffey, and Jelsma's (2003) observations in their study, which investigated the ease of accessibility[23] for students who use wheelchairs in one campus of a large institution of higher education in South Africa. Losinsky et al. found that most buildings in the campus under investigation dated back to the early 1900s and the majority were only partly accessible. Many facilities in the buildings, such as the toilet cubicles, lecture theatres, library and sports centers etc., were totally inaccessible to wheelchair users (p. 307). The problem of physical inaccessibility caused students who use wheelchairs to consistently fail to reach their lecture venues within the 10 minutes between class periods allocated by the university (p. 307). In addition, these students' choices of fields of study were also limited as some faculties were far and less accessible than others (see also Borland & James, 1999 and Titchkosky, 2008 for analyses of accessibility in the U.K. and Canada respectively).

Johari added that the location of classes was also unfriendly to disabled students, mainly those with mobility challenges:

A lot of the class venues are inaccessible; they are not user friendly. Some are on the fourth or fifth and there are no ramps, no elevators.

Lulu described access to lecture rooms at the University of Ongozi as follows:

We didn't find many problems but people with wheelchairs, it was a problem especially if the classes are upstairs and they had to be carried up. There are no elevators and they are not modified in any way you know like you could find a stair and a ramp on the sides, there is nothing like that. And so most lecturers when they find someone who cannot reach up there they tend to change the venue at least for that person to be able to access the class.

Shani reiterated:

In the classrooms, the arrangement could be the same, although us we used to make sure we sit in the front so that at least we can hear the lecturer and especially in classes, you know most of the halls used to have microphones, but where there are no microphones we used to make sure we sit in front. The washrooms there, they had no problems, they were okay I would say; they are spacious enough and easily accessible to people who use wheelchair.

Johari, Lulu and Shani's narratives reveal that the built environment at the Universities of Khafee and Ongozi prevent disabled students from "doing what others take for granted" that is "moving around from place to place and gaining access into buildings" (Imrie & Kumar, 1998, p. 371) within the university without hitches.

CONCLUSION

This chapter has outlined the positive and negative experiences that the women students with disabilities had in relation to the curriculum, interpersonal relations and physical access. It has revealed how sometimes the Kenyan education system operates as "an aperture of continued surveillance" (Foucault, 1995, p. 172) and control, rendering disabled students invisible across all levels of education. The curriculum content, instructional and assessment approaches; faculty's/teachers' skills, knowledge and attitudes; resources; physical environment etc serve as disciplinary technologies through which continued "Othering" of disabled students in the education system manifests itself. Cannella (1999) defined disciplinary technologies as "objectifying practices in a culture that would produce docile bodies, the formal techniques and operations that create human bodies as objects to be molded" (p. 40). Cannella further noted that the disciplining techniques link various forms of power, creating an invisible colonization. This colonization is evidenced inside and outside of the classroom. Inside the classroom, teachers predominantly drew on teaching approaches that spoke to the needs of the non-disabled students. Outside of the classroom, extracurricular facilities and the physical environment were structured to address the needs of non-disabled students. The domination of curriculum by interests of non-disabled students and a physical environment that creates invisible yet visible colonizing and disciplining mechanisms over disabled students demonstrates the pervasiveness of ableist attitudes and practices in the Kenyan education system. Foucault (1995) remarked that disciplinary powers are "humble modalities, minor procedures, as compared to majestic rituals of sovereignty or great apparatuses of the state ... The success of disciplinary power derives from the use of simple instruments, hierarchical observation, normalizing judgment and their combination in a procedure that is specific to it, the examination" (p. 170). The women's narratives reveal that the rendering invisible of disabled students in higher education contexts is not necessarily done through overt state policies but through subtle acts within the institution that create "chilly in-class and out-of class climates" (Allan & Madden, 2006; Hall & Sandler, 1982) that privilege non-disabled students which disadvantages disabled students.

The curriculum was a huge concern for the study participants. The structure, content and implementation of curriculum for subjects such as science and mathematics in which limited accommodations are provided for disabled students particularly those with visual impairments is one worrisome example. To use Morris' (1991) words, the curriculum invalidates disabled students by ignoring them (p. 85) and excluding them from the mainstream curriculum. While there have been changes in the education system in Kenya for various reasons since independence, much of these have been in terms of curriculum content and less attention has been paid to the process by which the curriculum is delivered, hence the women's critical observations about the curriculum content and the pedagogical approaches teachers use. Although the study participants acknowledged and appreciated the various steps that faculty take to enhance their successful learning, they also identified serious drawbacks that need to be addressed. Participants cautioned against assuming that equitable access had already been achieved (Hibbs & Pothier, 2006). Needless to say that, and as Hibbs and Pothier (2006) rightly observed, balanced against these efforts to accommodate are the interests of the universities in protecting academic (and other) standards; in managing resources and restricted budgets and recognition of the potentially high costs associated with provision of some accommodations or modifications (p. 195) for disabled students.

The national examination was another challenge that the women expressed serious concerns about. The women saw the examinations as a sieving instrument designed to sort the disabled students from the non-disabled, and allowing for observations and calibrations of the "model product" the education system wants (Foucault, 1995, p. 172). Although one cannot deny that the exams gauge students' understanding of the curriculum, they are also avenues through which disabled students are "punished." Hence, Foucault's remarks that examinations are a normalizing gaze, a surveillance that makes it possible to qualify, classify and punish. Exams establish over individuals a visibility through which one differentiates them and judges them (p. 184). Disabled students are judged and admitted to university, courses, programs of specialization based on "standard exams" that benefit non-disabled students. Afya, Lulu and Shani's calls for the Kenya National Examination Council and the Ministry of Education to provide accommodations particularly in the math and science curriculum and examinations illustrates the pervasiveness of this privileging of non-disabled students. Consequently, disabled students often find themselves treated harshly by the prevailing academic climate/ conditions, which are unwelcoming. Many students subsequently leave the learning spaces without completing their education. These unwelcoming conditions include the curriculum, which does not speak to them, and the lack of skilled educators to modify existing curriculum and provide accommodations. This shows that when it comes to disability in higher education institutions in Kenya, instead of being instruments of change, these schools are caught up in the processes of generating, preserving and disseminating ableist cultures and practices, wittingly and unwittingly. There is a lack of a critical discussion of disability in curriculum theory and implementation (Erevelles, 2005, p. 421). Such an absence calls for urgent discussions that transcend the "normalized" curriculum to include critical disability studies. There is a need to reinvigorate the study and understanding of disability in a way that neither reduces disability to an individual medical problem nor ignores the predicament of bodily limitation and difference (Shakespeare, 2006, p. 2). That is to say de-medicalize disability but at the same time promote social change to enable and include disabled people (Shakespeare, 2006, p. 2). Higher education institutions should be part of the process of change and lead by example.

In terms of interpersonal relations, study participants provide examples pointing to stereotypical experiences both within and outside university. The women show how they are bombarded with overt and covert stigmatizing meanings including "lack", "unable", "incompetent", "problematic", and "unfitting", mappings which are framed by prejudiced readings of disability in the wider society. The presence of disabled students in a classroom or lecture hall, for instance, is seen as disrupting what the "normal classroom" ought to look like, hence some faculty's insistence that blind students should not enroll in their courses. This is because disabled people have historically been categorized as "outsiders", "not normal" or people to be controlled through special measures (Imrie & Hall, 2001); thus explaining the claims of "not knowing how to teach disabled students" offered by teachers and faculty and, which regulate these students' enrollment in particular programs or subject specializations. Such exclusionary arguments demonstrate how equal access to all remains *a theoretical mantra* far from being translated into practice.

Noteworthy also is the fact that the mapping of disabled students and privileging of non-disabled perspectives, experiences and ways of knowing in the curriculum is not only happening in university contexts but also in primary and secondary schools. As Foucault argued, power is not static at one particular point, but flows in all directions. Ableist privileging has historically been handed down from one generation to another, from one institution to another, from one political regime to another. Furthermore, power works through relationships and everyone is an active player (Foucault, 1982). Relations are rooted in social networks and builds on existing power mechanisms, extending them and transforming them (Foucault, 1982). The participants' experiences with the curriculum, physical access and interpersonal relations are shaped by relationships with players inside and outside of the university – curriculum experts, university officers, faculty, peers and friends, policy makers etc. and therefore discrimination against disabled people are shaped in all these spheres.

It is also clear that the women's feeling of interconnectedness with others inside and outside of the university gave them a sense of belonging to the university culture and enhanced their participation in academic and non-academic activities. Similar findings have been reported by scholars such as Goodenow and Grady (1992) and Wentzel (1994) who indicated that student perceptions of interpersonal connectedness to others at school and "belonging" to the school culture are associated with academic engagement and psychological well-being. Social variables thus play a crucial role in the academic and affective out-comes of schooling. However, participants also experienced stigmatization and invisibility in their interactions with other players in the university. Satisfactory learning experiences seemed to have been influenced by positive student-faculty relations (see Baker, 1999) while negative relations affected these students' academic experiences and engagement at the university (see Duquette, 2000a).

Study participants also revealed how their interactions with peers and friends are driven by intersectionalities of gender, age and disability. Mature students encountered barriers interacting with younger students but were capable of developing effective and elaborative ways of dealing with them. As Richardson and King (1998) pointed out, when it comes to dealing with challenges, mature students are likely to be far more adept at examining and exploiting their prior experiences in order to make sense of their situations (p. 69). Indeed in this study, Faizah showed how mature students were able to study and understand the minds and needs of younger students and in that way bridged the age rifts that were emerging between the two groups.

As for the professors and the university in general, it is evident that they largely address disabled students' requests for accommodation when the students press them with particular concerns. They do not see themselves as having a positive obligation to initiate proactive solutions or to create equitable access to the curriculum. This understanding places students in an "adversarial position vis-à-vis the university such that their objective of completing their program/degree/course is thwarted if they are unable to ... reach an agreement with an instructor over an accommodation" (Hibbs & Pothier, 2006, p. 197).

The physical environment also poses challenges to disabled students' participation in academic and social activities within the university. The women reveal that it takes time, energy and skill to access some of the inaccessible places within the university which unfortunately they have to use frequently or on a daily basis. Buildings such as the administrative buildings, library, halls of residence, washrooms and lecture halls remain inaccessible. Long distances to classrooms, poor schedules, classrooms without public address systems are identified as some of the limitations which make physical access a challenge. These findings support Imrie and Hall's (2001) observation that societal structures are put up in a manner that is insensitive to and ignorant about disabled people (p. 69).

Overall, disabled students continue to be rendered marginal in Kenyan universities. This marginality combined with inadequate resources, poor pedagogical approaches and physical inaccessibility creates troubling situations for many disabled women students at Kenyan universities, and calls for a problematization of five major aspects of Kenya's education system: the educational institutions; the knowledge forms taught and disseminated in these institutions; the educators themselves; the policy formulators; and the government (see Apple, 2004, p. 3). Chapter eight presents further analysis and recommendations to reinforce the need for these problematizations.

Additionally, the voices above show that ableism, like sexism and racism, is expressed in institutional and interpersonal levels (Barnes & Mercer, 2003). Disabled students are rendered subordinate in education because of the stigma attached to having impairment. Barnes and Mercer (2003) noted that disabled people are categorized and "marked as part of a distinct social group on grounds of their perceived bodily deficiency or abnormality and treated differently" (Barnes & Mercer, 2003, p. 20). Disabled people's bodies are thus sites of oppression, both in form and in what is done with them (Abberly, 1984, p. 14 cited in Barnes & Mercer, 2003, p. 20).

CHAPTER SIX

Success Factors, Barriers and Resistance/Coping Strategies

This chapter provides further analysis of the factors that facilitate and/ or hinder disabled women students' success in university. The chapter also examines the women's resistance/coping strategies. It is evident that mentorship and support of family and friends, the presence of disabled role models as well as self-determination and financial stability are important some of the key factors informing disabled women students' success in university. The common obstacles to success which the women identified included discrimination, negative attitudes, financial constraints, risks of sexual abuse and harassment, lack of sufficient learning resources, and restrictions to physical access. The women's stories demonstrate that they are aware of their marginalization within the university and have adopted a variety of approaches to challenge this aspect of their experience. These strategies are not simply about surviving in university. They are also a vital means of resisting oppression in the wider society. What follows is a discussion of the success factors that the women talked about.

SUCCESS FACTORS

The women talked about the various factors that enabled them to succeed in the university. These factors included family and friends; mentorship; individuals factors; finances and institutional supports.

Supports from family and friends

Family

Research shows that family members' engagement in their children's education enhances academic success. In a study examining facilitators of children's performance across family, school and community, Christenson and Peterson (1998) found that when adults give support and regular feedback and advice to youth about their academic work, the chances of success in school are improved (cited by Christenson & Havsy, 2004, p. 66). Similarly, in a study examining the institutional and interpersonal factors which contributed to the retention and graduation of Mexican American students in a predominantly White Bachelor of Science (Nursing) program in the U.S.A, Taxis (2006) reported that ongoing supportive family relationships and financial assistance were crucial factors in promoting these students' academic success. However, existing studies do not offer an adequate and specific analysis of the ways in which family members exert this influence on disabled students' success rates. This study addresses this area through the narratives of the study participants. The students interviewed sometimes had family members accompany them to university to offer support during their first year at the institution. Family members providing love, assurance, encouragement and financial resources were also important in helping them attain success. Shani, of the University of Ongozi, explains how she tapped into her family for assistance during her first year at Ongozi:

> During the orientation week, I stayed with my sister on campus. I asked her to come and stay with me for one week ... She came and taught me how to approach some places like the mess (dining hall) and lecture halls. And there is also that resource centre where we get our materials from, like Braille machine and such...how to go to such places. So, during the first week, she was the one who was there to help me with orientation. After that she had to leave for school.

She further added:

> When I needed books ... I used to ask my sister to borrow them for me from their library (name of the university) ... I read and then she returned them.

In these excerpts, Shani shows how her siblings contributed to her success in the university. They helped her to make the transition to campus life and to get acquainted with the university environment, as well as, providing her with access to reference books that were not accessible at Ongozi library.

For other participants like Hereni, from the University of Khafee and Hawa and Jamila, both of Ongozi University, family support came in the form of encouragement, financial support, love, appreciation and assurance:

> I will say that one of my success factors is that my parents encourage me all the time and they also support me with fees, which is a good thing. (Hereni)

> My parents are very good, they are very loving and helpful... and that is what has made me successful. Also, the entire family is very supportive. There are moments when they sit down with me and

advice and encourage me, stating that I am capable of succeeding, and that helps. (Hawa)

...my father knew I hated school because of ridicule and loneliness, so he kept on supporting and encouraging me to work hard. (Jamila)

Hereni, Hawa and Jamila point to the different ways in which parents contribute to their success. Parental support is important, not only in providing resources, but also in mitigating some of the challenges these students face. For example, Jamila, a student at the University of Khafee, talks about experiencing ridicule and loneliness, which had an impact on her success, but which she was able to endure because her family members supported, valued and validated her. Hawa narrated a similar story when she talked about parental love, and so did Hereni, who pointed to the encouragement and financial support of her family as key factors in her success.

Friends and peers

Study findings also demonstrate that friends and peers influence disabled women's success in their university education. Participants talk about support systems that include study groups and groups that assist in increasing students' mobility around campus, as well as those that provide advice, encouragement and financial assistance:

I have been successful also because of friends who have assisted me to get what I need, for example financially. In my first degree I had to do some fundraising to be able to meet the costs of university, and I feel that people around me have made me successful. (Afya)

... my pusher comes around and students in my class will say to him 'no, no, no, we will push her'. And they were saying that surely it would be sad to be in class with me for a whole semester and not learn to operate a wheelchair. (Dada)

Friends have been helpful, especially reading and discussion groups which help when you don't understand stuff taught in the lecture, for example the statistics course I told you about. (Shani)

These narrations are largely consistent with findings of North American studies on minority students and schooling. For example, in their study of academic success among Black students living in the U.S.A, Hovart and Lewis (2003) observed that support from peers and friends contributed to these students' success in their academic pursuits. These co-authors remarked that supportive peer groups were often particularly important in providing minority students with the energy and emotional support they needed to persevere (p. 277). This was also true of the participants in this research project. Afya, Dada and Shani's comments indicated that positive friendship, care, support and collegiality created a sense of belonging which contributed to their success.

Mentorship from other disabled students

A review of the literature shows that, in academic contexts, informal mentoring helps to integrate non-traditional students into mainstream academic environments (Burgstahler & Cronheim, 2001). Social supports can alleviate stress, and are especially important during the transition from high school to college where the support network they relied on over their high school years is often no longer available (Jacobi, 1991, p. 504). In my discussions with the study participants, it became clear that disabled students in senior years or those who had already graduated were in a strong position to provide mentorship, advice and motivation, and thus, became an important resource persons to other disabled women students:

> I got motivation from those who are ahead. When I came here as a first year student, there were others who were ahead of me. They used to sit us down and tell us the survival techniques in this place, and when we had problems they were always there to help. (Shani)

> There are some friends who have completed their programs and I go to them for advice whenever I face challenges. I get encouraged and I feel that, if my friends made it, I, too, can. So I feel like trying also. They are a great source of inspiration. (Afya)

Evident in these excerpts is the value of mentoring as a factor in disabled women's success in university. Shani and Afya found the availability of disabled role models and peers within the university an empowering and critical survival tactic. Research shows that while, previously, mentoring was more narrowly associated with academic preparation and success of graduate students, today, the practice is increasingly used as an approach for enhancing the retention, enrichment and completion rates of undergraduate students (Jacobi, 1991, p. 505). This practice is widespread across North America and is often particularly targeted at minority student populations (Gary & Booker, 1992; LaVant, Anderson & Tiggs, 1997). Such mentoring programs often focus on emotional and psychological support,

158

and on direct assistance with career and professional development (Jacobi, 1991, p. 510). Despite this background, the universities under investigation in this study have no formal mentoring programs, and study participants reveal that their support networks were made up of informal mentoring efforts initiated mainly by students[24].

Personal factors

Other respondents attributed their success to their own hard work, determination (Smith & Nelson, 1993; Ash et al, 1997), and to their self-belief. Field, Sarver and Shaw (2003) argue that self-determination is a central organizing concept in evaluating post-secondary programs for students with disabilities. Self-determination comprises a combination of skills, knowledge, and beliefs that enable a person to engage in goal-directed, self-regulated, autonomous behavior. It requires an understanding of one's strengths and one's limitations, as well as a belief in oneself as a capable and effective individual (Field, Martin, Miller, Ward & Wehmeyer, 1998, p. 2). Self-determination is vital to disabled students' successful academic transitions and outcomes (Wehmeyer & Palmer, 2003). The majority of studies focus on teaching disabled persons about making their own decisions (Zhang & Katsiyannis, 2002). Although little attention has been paid to examining self-determination as a success factor in disabled women's lives in the university, these study participants' narratives demonstrate that self-determination drives disabled women students' achievements. Shani points to her self-determination when she notes:

> I was determined to make it ... Because when you enter Ongozi University, the first semester is such that, if you are the kind of person who easily gives up, you will give up. Because first and foremost, you don't know anyone. Ongozi is so big. You don't know where the lecture halls are, there are no books in Braille. As much as you are supposed to go to class, you don't know where the class is, ... you don't have a friend to take you to class. So you have to be determined those first days.

Shani's narrative points out ways in which determination and resilience enabled her to deal with the challenges she faced as a visually impaired student. She speaks of the difficult conditions and environment specific to Ongozi University that disabled students face, and notes that these negative experiences can easily drive disabled students to "give up" their higher education pursuits.

Johari of the University of Khafee also links her success to belief in herself and to self-determination: "I have been successful because I believe in myself; disability or no disability I can make it." When I asked Johari to explain the genesis of her determination, she replied:

> I guess more of my religion and my principles have inspired me to have a sense of belief and faith in myself. For example, in my religion, Islam, we believe that if you want anything you can make it. With God you can make it, you can get anything that you want.

Johari identifies discipline and religiosity as key elements informing her determination to succeed.[25] Islamic teachings have provided her with important lessons that have inspired her to work hard and to succeed. Although there is limited research on the role of spirituality as a contributing factor to disabled students' success in higher education, particularly in an African context, studies pointing to spirituality and education in general in Africa show that spirituality gives people meaning and conditions their thoughts and behaviors (Dei, 2002; see also Wane & Neegan, 2007). Johari's narrative reveals that her religious beliefs shape how she thinks of herself and of her abilities. Her observations indicate that spirituality is a fundamental dimension of students' being and cannot be ignored in educational activities (Belousa, 2006, p. 216).

Financial supports

All the disabled women students commented about the significance of financing for higher education and its implications for their access, participation and success. In particular, respondents spoke of the government's extension of Higher Education Loans Board (HELB) funds to disabled students as a positive step that has contributed to their access to, and success in university (although, as we shall see later, the level of funding provided in this loaning system is inadequate to meet the education costs of these students).[26] Access to bank and cooperative loans, fundraising from friends and community members, and sponsorships from NGOs are other important sources of finance cited by the participants. When asked to explain the factors that have enhanced her success in the university, Dhahabu replied:

> The factors that have enabled my success include fees contributions, whereby we get HELB loans and also some financial support from another organization.

When the private student sponsorship program (as explained in chapter two) was introduced in Kenyan universities, students who joined university

160

as self-sponsored students were not eligible for government student loans. This policy has changed over the years, but still very few self-sponsored students qualify for HELB loans. Public universities, however, lobbied on behalf of disabled students for the extension of coverage under the HELB program, hence Dhahabu's observation that they are "able to get student loans" but only after proving that they have a disability.

Participants from both Ongozi and Khafee universities reported that their institutions offer a general bursary open to all students, but stated that this bursary was means-tested and did not provide specific support for disabled students. In this respect, Aziza from Ongozi University observed:

> The university has some forms of financial assistance in the form of bursaries, but it is not specifically for disabled students. Disabled students have to apply like other students and have to compete with them. Thus, getting it is another problem. Then they need evidence, such as an admission letter, to see if a student is able to pay fees. One has to provide a fees statement, and if one has a balance, they can't get the assistance. They consider how much one has. Also, they don't give much. They give approximately KShs. 3, 000. And then there is the ministry bursary, which it is also very hard to get. These give around KShs. 20, 000. (Aziza)

This policy illustrates that disabled students have limited options when it comes to accessing scholarships and bursary funds for their education. Consequently, the majority of disabled students rely on student loans and on support from their parents. Friends and sponsors (usually non-governmental organizations) also assist in financing these students' education. The research findings show that most direct entry students interviewed had applied for HELB loans, while the mature entrants who took study leaves got loans from their banks or from cooperative unions.

> I am in the regular program so I get the HELB loan. I also get support from my parents ... (Mkufu)

> I was getting the HELB loan. We tried and went through the university and then after proving that we had a problem with the vision, they accepted to assist me, although they were saying I was over age - is it 25 years they say? But they finally agreed to assist. They were giving me around KShs. 35,000 per year, and I could use my salary too. (Lulu)

Mkufu talks about relying on student loans and on support from parents to finance her education. On the other hand, because she is on study leave from her jobs, Lulu pays for her education, using HELB loans and personal savings. Lulu's situation also provides an example of some of the difficulties students can encounter in securing an HELB loan. Lulu had to prove her physical impairment as well as convince the organization to relax its age-limit policy. Currently, the HELB policy is that, if a student is not disabled and above 25 years, they cannot qualify for a loan to enable them to go to university. The government fails to recognize the fact that students follow different paths to get to university, and they do not acknowledge that setting an age cap when administering HELB loans is discriminatory to non-traditional students.

Both Shani and Nadra noted that external Non-Governmental agencies as well as individual sponsors supported disabled students in meeting their education expenses:

> There is an NGO (name of NGO) ... I applied one time and they boosted my fee for one semester and then my parents chipped in with the rest. So that is how I survive. (Shani)

> I had a sponsor but he passed away. He was my father's friend. He came from (name of country). Actually he had been sponsoring me since high school but he died in 2002. Since he had no children, he just wrote a will in my father's name, and that is the money I use to pay my school fees. (Nadra)

The other mechanism through which study participants finance their education is through *harambees* (fundraising events). Hawa gets support from friends and through these fundraising events:

> At the moment I can say I finance my education through fundraising and friends. ... And then there is the CDF which I applied for but they haven't responded. I am still following up. (Hawa)

Harambee is a Kiswahili word used to reference a practice in which local communities in Kenya voluntarily pool together their funds for private or public projects (Chieni, n.d; Mwiria, 1990). *Harambee* fundraising is also a common way of assisting individuals or families who face financial challenges to pay medical bills, or to pay for any other financial needs. The respondent also talks about constituency development fund (CDF) as a possible source of finances. The CDF is an annual budgetary allocation by the Central Government to each of the country's parliamentary jurisdictions, the "constituencies," which was established in the year 2003 (Kimenyi, 2005). According to the Kenya Institute for Public Policy and Research (n.d.), CDF aims at:

... controlling imbalances in regional development brought about by partisan politics. It targets all constituency-level development projects, particularly those aiming to combat poverty at the grassroots. The fund comprises an annual budgetary allocation equivalent to 2.5% of the government's ordinary revenue. ... 75% of the fund is allocated equally amongst all 210 constituencies in the country. The remaining 25% is allocated as per constituency poverty level. A maximum 10% of each constituency's annual allocation may be used for an education bursary scheme. (www.kippra.org/Constituency.asp)

Notwithstanding this statement about the possibility of utilizing CDF fund for educational bursaries, few of the students interviewed were aware of such provisions. Increased awareness about the existence of these funds would provide another valuable avenue by which students could fund their academic studies.

Institutional supports

Services such as medical care; support from university-based and student-run religious groups or from the disabled students' organization; provision of facilities such as wheelchairs, Braille machines and library support are all important components of participants' success in the university. Pointing to medical care, Faizah, an undergraduate student at Ongozi University, whose impairment is a result of an illness that requires constant monitoring and sometimes results into frequent hospitalizations, explained:

> One thing I can talk of is medical care. The college actually takes care of sick students. We have the health unit here which takes care of those minor conditions/ailments and when you get very sick they refer you to [name of hospital]. They actually do follow up since they will pay the bills if a student is admitted. This has assisted me because I have been hospitalized in [name of hospital] like four times. Every year I am actually admitted and they pay the bills. So, actually, they have really supported me in that respect. It would have been very expensive.

Faizah found the students' healthcare plan offered by the university beneficial. She observed that without such a plan it would have been very expensive to meet her medical expenses. In Kenya, medical care is not free. User fee (cost-sharing) was introduced in 1989 under the World Bank-initiated structural adjustment programs (SAPs). This has had consequences for access to and for quality of healthcare for the poor citizenry. Even though service provision in government dispensaries has remained free of charge, in reality it is not free, as patients have to pay for drugs from their pockets. This means that access to quality healthcare in Kenya is accessible mostly to the middle class and affluent individuals.

With regard to student-run organizations (faith-based groups and the disabled students' association), participants remarked that the religious groups, for instance, offered support by organizing readers, while the disabled students' organization advocated for disabled students' needs and hence contributed to the successes of the women in university:

> Because we don't have the brailed books, societies like the Catholics, S.D.A and Christian Union have also been organizing for us readers to help us read printed books and notes. The university also does so. They put notices up calling for people to volunteer as readers and then ask them to register at the resource center. (Nadra)

> There is good support from associations, such as Ongozi University Disabled Students' Association, which is helping us with advocacy with the university administration. (Aminia)

Other institutional factors that participants noted as contributing to their success in the university were provision of facilities such as wheelchairs and crutches for physically disabled students; provision of Braille machines and transcription services for visually impaired students, and provision of transport and accommodation services:

> Those who use wheelchairs are given chairs, and these are repaired by the university when they break. And for us who use Braille machines, they give us the machines which we have to return at the end of the program. They also repair them or give us replacements if they break down. (Aminia)

> Sometimes they write for us the materials and handouts in Braille when they are sending information to students so that we can also have a copy for ourselves. And during exams they write them in Braille. If we have written some work for lecturers in Braille they transcribe it into print so that the lecturers can read the information we have given to them. (Shani)

> Because the lecture halls are far apart they give us those tuk-tuks to move us around because the severely physically disabled and the totally blind cannot go alone to those far places. Personally, I

think I could not be going to class if they were not there. They come for us in the hostels and take us to class and then bring us back. (Dhahabu)

They give us accommodation. Disabled students are given single rooms. ...and then for me having somebody - an assistant I can stay with in the room - is good, although they told me that that was not their policy. I don't know how other students have been surviving, or maybe they have not had someone with severe physical disability like me. (Dada)

For Aminia, Shani, Dada and Dhahabu, services such as transport, accommodation, and readers offered by the university (mainly Ongozi), and the advocacy role played by the disabled students' organization in their universities is vital to their success in the university. It is important to note, though, that the majority of the participants from the University of Khafee were unhappy with the accommodation and transportation facilities in their university, as illustrated in their narratives in the barriers section below.

SUCCESS BARRIERS

In their description of success factors, the women indicated that family, friends, peers, finances and institutional supports contribute to their success in the university. This section looks at the barriers to disabled women students' success. The barriers are a blend of social, economic, cultural and political factors, and include: poverty/financial constraints; risks of sexual abuse and harassment; incidences of discrimination; inadequate learning materials/resources and accessibility challenges. These barriers may also be attributed to the overall under representation of disabled women students in Kenyan universities.

Poverty/financial constraints

Studies examining affluence and its implications on women's education in Africa show that the socioeconomic background of parents has an impact on the enrollment of females at every level of education (Logan & Beoku-Betts, 1996, p. 232). Literature on education in Africa also shows that poor families tend to send their sons rather than daughters to school (Kiluva-Ndunda, 2001; Logan & Beoku-Betts, 1996, p. 232). In Kenya, studies have shown that although both men and women students from higher socioeconomic backgrounds outperform students from lower socioeconomic backgrounds, the relationship between income and education is more fundamental for women students (see Eshiwani, 1983; 1984; Sifuna, 2006). Kiluva-Ndunda (2001) observed that traditional preferences to educate sons, following the assumption that girls will get married and therefore not offer much to their families in return, influences parents' choices to educate their female children. Additionally, Kiluva-Ndunda noted that the rising costs of education has exacerbated gender inequities in the provision of educational opportunities in Kenya and has become a major barrier to girls' education (p. 101). Consequently, most women students, especially in higher education, tend to come from families with higher socioeconomic status than their male counterparts (Hughes & Mwiria, 1989, as cited in Logan & Beoku-Betts, 1996, p. 232).

Furthermore, research shows that disabled women and children experience higher levels of poverty mainly because of structural inequalities in resource distribution (Barnes & Mercer, 2003, p. 143). Although education is seen as a means of addressing poverty, disabled girls and women have limited access to education, especially in low income countries, Kenya included (UNESCO, 1995 cited by Barnes & Mercer, 2003, p. 144). Participants in this study indicated that poverty impacts disabled women students' participation in higher education. Participants pointed out that the majority of disabled women that they knew with a university education either came from higher socioeconomic backgrounds or got some sponsor who paid for their education. The women articulated the different ways in which financial constraints impede their success in university. They noted that the majority of disabled women students in the university come from low socio-economic backgrounds and are self-sponsored students, meaning that they paid higher tuition fee, compared students admitted directly to university through the universities' joint admissions' board (JAB students). Although they got HELB loans, the money was not enough for their fee, accommodation, learning materials and general upkeep, as illustrated by Hawa and Lulu:

> Finance is the main problem because my parents are just small scale farmers and they don't have a good source of income. (Hawa)

> Most of us come from very poor families, yet we come here as self sponsored students, which mean we pay more. Right now, private stream students pay over 60,000 shillings. Imagine a person like me paying that much. I have a family and my three children also need school fees in high school and for other up keep. The HELB loan just gives us that *kalittle* amount that they give us, which is not enough. (Lulu)

Hawa and Lulu are talking about challenges that poor disabled students face in meeting high tuition costs in Kenyan universities. These high costs are an additional concern to mature disabled students who have families to support, as was the case of Lulu, who at one point had three children in high school. In Kenya, high school education is not free, students have to pay tuition and accommodation fees (for those in schools offering boarding facilities). Hawa and Lulu's concerns call for a review of the way higher education students in Kenya are supported. Maybe the ministry of education and universities should consider having disabled students enrolled as JAB students or they should extend more loans to them so that they are able to pay for their tuition. Without proper financial supports, many disabled students will not be able to attend university, even when they get admission, as Yakuti explained by:

> There are many disabled students who I know got admission to come to university, but because their parents cannot afford the fee, they decided to take them to colleges, which are cheaper and which run two-year courses. Others did not even go to those colleges because of lack of money. Some come, but may end up dropping out, if they don't get financial help.

Even for those that make an effort to enroll upon admission, it is still difficult to pay fees, and this affects their learning. Dhahabu explains some of the problems she faces when she has not completed paying fees:

> I haven't cleared the fee... before you get an exam card you are harassed in the exam room to the extent that sometimes you even end up missing the exam. ... you are disturbed in accommodation, your door is locked in the room where you stay, your beddings are taken away and you sleep on a bare bed.
>
> *Interviewer:* Who takes the beddings?
>
> *Dhahabu:* Housekeepers, they come and say they have been authorized by, I don't know - the manager. They come when you are in the room and so they pick when you are there ... You sleep on the bare bed until you pay; that is when they will return your beddings.

Dhahabu is speaking about the consequences of lack of finances on the part of disabled students once enrolled in university. She shows how students "play hide and seek" until they have their fees paid, lest their beddings be taken by accommodation staff.

However, even though economic constraints and poverty are a reality for many disabled students, Dada cautions against the notion of looking at

167

disabled people as poor people in need of charity, a practice that reinforces their marginalization in society. In her comments, she challenges the notion of presenting disabled people as subjects of charity who depend on handouts from well-wishers:

> They (disabled people) are poor, yes, but sometimes they also accept and think that they are poor. The mentality in society is all about disabled people being equal to poverty, and people with disabilities have been made to believe that. All that they want is handouts I don't know what we can do ... Some of these disabled people don't know that if you come to university somehow you can survive; they need to try to take risks and to persevere. It is possible to survive. I didn't know I could, but I have.

Dada critiques disabled people's understanding of self as stereotypically presented by the non-disabled society, without thinking what else they might be (Danaher, Schirato & Webb, 2000, p. 10). Goffman (1963) commented on how stigmatized persons have been socialized to accept the beliefs and values on which stigma is grounded when he noted:

> The standards they [the stigmatized] have incorporated from the wider society equip them to be intimately alive to what others see as their failing, inevitably causing them, if only for moments to agree that they do indeed fall short of what they really ought to be (p. 7).

Dada does not buy into these predispositions. She calls on disabled people to look at the stereotypical constructions of people with disabilities as an example of the limits that the non-disabled world imposes on disabled people and urges disabled people to look and to go beyond them. Dada advices her disabled colleagues to persist, in spite of the many challenges they may encounter in their efforts to access university education.

Fear/risks of sexual abuse and harassment

Risks of sexual abuse and harassment were also cited by study participants as some of their greatest challenges in the university. Literature shows that sexual abuse and harassment and premarital pregnancies contribute to the high drop out rates of schoolgirls in Kenyan high schools (Sifuna, 2006; Wane & Opini, 2006). Sexual violations of female students have also been documented in Kenyan higher education (Kamau, 1996; 2004; Omale, 2000; Sifuna, 2006). The disabled women students' stories in this study show that fears of sexual abuse and harassment caused them feelings of insecurity, making them cautious of their interactions

168

with male students. Study participants acknowledge that sexual abuse and harassment impact the number of girls transitioning from high school to post-secondary education. The consequences of abuse often include pre-marital pregnancies, which, in most cases, affect disabled girls' opportunities to access further their education. Thus the majority of the disabled women students identified "dealing with men" as one of their biggest challenges in the university:

> One of my greatest challenges is the men. Once the men realize that you have a certain problem, they will want to take advantage of your situation. So I have been very vigilant and I have been very aggressive, especially when I realize that that is the motive. So I put them off immediately. (Nadra)

In the above response, Nadra points to men's tendency to think of disabled women as "easy subjects to prey on" (see also Larkin, 1994; Wagner & Magnusson, 2005; Weiser, 2005), a practice they (men) see as part of being male exercising their masculinity (see Weiser, 2005). Nadra has, however, learnt to be firm and on guard, and notes that, if she does not defend herself, there are chances of being abused, which may disrupt her education (Leach & Machakanja, 2000).

Commenting on how risks of sexual abuse and harassment create fear and insecurity in disabled women, making it hard for them to walk on campus at night, and even making it hard to stay in their rooms without locking doors, Dhahabu stated:

> Sometimes you fear to walk around the university because, given that it is a university, there are so many things happening around you. You fear to walk alone because of fear of being raped. And now that I don't see, how would I walk alone? And there have been some rape cases on campus. Or sometimes I am in the room alone and I find myself fearing that maybe if I open the door someone will get in and will start beating me at night or raping me. You just fear. Or there are those people who may be wanting to read for you but when they arrive late you tell them you were supposed to come at this time. They may even tell you now you have to do for me this and that before I read for you - such incidences.

In the above narrative, Dhahabu points to disabled women students' feelings of insecurity on campus, especially during nights. Although she did not provide succinct evidence of how widespread cases of rape and/ or sexual abuse and harassment were on campus, she showed signs of being worried about her safety in our conversations. When asked about measures taken to ensure safety on campus, one of the officers interviewed from Khafee just gave a general statement emphasizing that campus was very safe and shrugged off disabled students' claims of possibilities of sexual abuse and harassment on campus. Such "politically correct" responses minimize the problem of abuse and leave students with no clear understanding of measures to take to ensure their safety, hence their fears and concerns. As Wane and Opini (2006) argued, loopholes in school structures, administration and leadership contribute to the increased cases of gendered violence in Kenyan schools (p. 55). There remain serious concerns regarding the ability of disabled women and women in general to pursue their education and complete it in a risk-free environment.

Discriminatory acts

Other disabled women students' narratives pointed to discriminatory experiences in club/association memberships; leadership; forming study groups and indifferent reactions from peers and family members. Some of these discriminatory experiences were linked to age differences and to having impairment. Speaking of age, Faizah narrated how younger students perceived mature students when they initially joined university:

When we came, these young ladies and men (referring to JAB students) felt like we are invading their assets, we are not supposed to be here, we are supposed to be somewhere else - we should leave this compound for them. But this is not the objective of the university. The university wants us to learn together. So long as you are able to pay, you have a chance to continue with your education. But then, because they are young, they tended to feel like that. So they used to talk about old people, calling them names. . However, you find that when these young people go to class they are not serious with studies, because they don't face the same level of problems, since they are being sponsored by their parents, and since they get HELB loans and are more comfortable. They even miss classes and go for outings, but when it comes back to class work and during exam time you find them panicking because they have not covered much and the old *wazees* (mature students) are sitted and relaxed. We don't have any luxuries, you have paid for your education so you are striving to achieve it. Unless you go out one weekend and see your family other times you are here with your books and doing your research so when they realized the *wazees* are doing better than them, that thing stopped, it is not there anymore. Now they are friendly, they come to visit, borrowing stuff, we work with them very well.

Faizah illustrates how younger students tended to look down upon older/mature students. She points to rifts that occurred between the two groups when they first joined university and how these rifts narrowed following good academic performance by mature students, and due to the latter's problem solving skills and life experience.

The disabled women students were not only discriminated against on basis of age but also on basis of impairment. Aminia talked about her experiences of discrimination in one of the academic clubs at the university:

> I wanted to join Red Cross but I was told I can't join it because of the practicals, whereby they said I had to see the blood when someone is cut. So I just decided to give up. I really wanted to join the club but I can't.

But is Red Cross only about practicals? Are there any other ways Aminia could have been involved in the club? It is clear here that impairment is superficially read and interpreted as inability. The club readers should have envisioned broader ways through which disabled students could contribute to and enrich this organization.

The problem of discrimination extended to student leadership and representations. Non-disabled students are reluctant to appoint disabled students as student representatives on claims that their impairment will deter them from performing their duties accordingly. As Fedha explained:

> When it comes to representing others in the university, there are those disabled students who have been vying but I have not seen any of them being elected. It is like they are kind of discriminated against because you can find some posters like maybe someone has been told like you, you don't walk, how will you run around and lead people when we are organizing for strikes? They even hold campaigns and talk like that.

Here Fedha shows how impairment is viewed as a deterrent to "effective leadership". Similarly, Dhahabu explains how impairment is also equated to "not [being] a good student" especially when lecturers require students to engage in cooperative learning activities:

> When you are in a class and people are forming groups, discussion groups or groups to write some kind of term papers or even doing research on a certain question, some people tend to choose themselves and leave the disabled students alone. You find that in most cases disabled students are in one group. Some students are not willing to make a group with you because they claim that they will be going to the library alone to look for the relevant books and

you won't be there so there is no much help you will provide. They won't accommodate you in their group.

All these narratives demonstrate the kind of non-disabled students' intolerance and tendency to look down upon disabled students just because of stereotypical assumptions that being disabled means being incapable. A fundamental task that remains is that of dismantling these ableist gazes that are deeply entrenched in the students' minds and in society as a whole.

Indifferent reactions from peers and family members

Although earlier on we saw that social supports, including peers, friends and family promoted disabled women students' success in university, some participants also identified these very factors as responsible for the barriers they faced in their education. Negative attitudes from peers, family members and society in general worked against some disabled women students' educational efforts. One respondent noted that non-disabled peers tried to discourage her from pursuing her education while another one suggested that she goes for surgical reconstructions to "normalize" her body:

> Sometimes I could meet people who are very negative and they discourage me from continuing with school. And when I was in Form One this lady wanted me to go do surgery so I could look more "normal" and yet I was not sick. ... But I didn't give up. Although when it comes to doing stuff, we could do it slower and take much more time, but it is okay. (Mkufu)

Why would non-disabled people discourage individuals with disabilities from pursuing an education? Why was this lady so much concerned about Mkufu's looks? Would that then mean that disabled people are unwelcome members of society who are either to be fixed and if "unfixable" be eliminated? The lady's observation about the need for Mkufu to go for surgery proves hooks' (1992) inference that there is "power in the looks". Non-disabled people are so caught up in a culture that emphasizes physical appearance as a form of cultural capital such that whoever doesn't match up to those looks is compelled to conform to, in Foucauldian terms, modern surveillance techniques (in this case surgery) so as to belong. Mkufu's response also confirms Goffman's (1963) assertion that the powerful in society set particular standards such that those who don't meet those standards (i.e. the normate – Garland-Thomson, 1997, p. 8) are considered "deviants" or "abnormal" and need to be "normalized". Here, the assumption is that there is something "wrong" with Mkufu's looks which may possibly translate into "limited chances of academic success". As Porter (1997) suggested, "... a disabled body is seen as lacking something essential, something to make it identifiable ... it is not quite a body in the full sense of the word, not real enough (p. xiii; see also Mitchell & Snyder, 1997). There is pressure to match a particular idealized image and having impairment is seen as a "falling short of this idealization". Pointing to the different ways in which disabled people may react to these "body image pressures" Wendell (1996) suggests that people with physical disabilities, may experience shame, self-hatred and a negative body image as a consequence of not "measuring up" to the cultural ideal that has been accepted and internalized (p. 91). They may wish for bodies that they cannot have, or they may reject the physical ideals as narrow and oppressive or they may fluctuate between these points. Mkufu chose not to conform to these physical ideals. Her narrative shows that she is contented with her body and with who she is and hence, challenged the stereotypical assumptions of "excellence" often reserved for the non-disabled bodies.

Participants also revealed that the "mis-reading and mis-interpretation" of the disabled body was not only a challenge in the wider society and in the education system but also within families. Aminia talked about how one disabled woman from her community was marginalized by her family:

> In our area there is another lady with a physical disability and the parents are not very well off. She did not even manage to go to school, not even to nursery, but the parents took other kids to school. She died in 2005. She was the fifth born in a family of six. Thcy didn't take her to school in the name of not having money but others were and they are now in fact working. Even the siblings who were working then did not support her; they didn't appreciate the way she was. Both of her legs were paralyzed she could not walk so she relied on people to move her around.

Aminia reveals the plight of a disabled woman who was discriminated against within her own family and who could not get the required support to help her lead an independent life. Evident here is how families make choices in terms of who to invest in because they have expectations of returns of some kind whether monetary or otherwise. Disabled persons, particularly women, are disadvantaged as it is presumed that they may not contribute much in return as disabled people are construed as lacking and excess. Rupturing societal structures that reinforce these biases is an essential part of the process of working towards full inclusion of disabled people in society both in practice and in policy.

Limited learning materials/facilities and resources

Study participants observed that lack of consistent readers, in the case of blind students, and the shortage of resources, such as books, Braille materials and sign interpreters for deaf students, affects their academic success. Speaking of readers, visually impaired students remarked that the absence of reliable readers affected their successful participation in the learning process.

> We could get readers at the beginning of the semester, volunteers, they could come - maybe five or six - but all of them are students and they also have their work to do. You could make a timetable with them but out of the five or six maybe only two may show up, keep the time and come and read for us; so reading was a problem. (Afya)

The above quotation illustrates the uncertainties visually impaired students have to deal with when it comes to accessing learning materials/ information that is in regular print. Since they rely on volunteer readers (who are often students) in the middle of the semester they also get busy and fail to honor their volunteer commitments. This leaves disabled students stranded at times. Others, especially the graduate students, are forced to hire private readers, which is expensive.

As for Braille materials and books and their high costs, Afya commented the following, particularly with regard to costs of materials:

> The college does not supply materials like Braille papers. One has to buy. I was taking religious studies and we wrote very many notes. So I was to spare may be KShs. 2,000 for Braille papers per semester. If I did not have those papers, I could not write the notes. And also the fact that there were no Braille books was a challenge when an individual wanted to read and there are no readers to help.

This insufficiency of resource books has effects disabled students' academic performances, as illustrated by Yakuti of Khafee University:

> Sometimes you go to the library to look for books and you don't get them immediately. It forces you to wait and all that time goes. Sometimes, by the time you get the book, it is close to the deadline and so it forces you to do the work in a hurry and sometimes you don't do it as you would like to because of time factor.

The women's voices above show how lack of sufficient resources works against these disabled students' learning needs. There are few reference books in the library. A lot of times the one or two copies available has to circulate among several students. By the time disabled students get it, they are unable to beat the set deadlines for their assignments, and have to do their assignments hurriedly, which compromises their quality of work and hence their performance. There is a need for the university to get more copies of reference books and to improve the loaning system, such that when a book is borrowed it does not circulate only among friends. There is also need to introduce a short loan services.

Physical access, accommodation and transport challenges

Participants from the two universities under investigation sometimes provided contrasting views about the accessibility, accommodation and transport services in their universities. Respondents from Khafee described their halls of residence as completely inaccessible and with no accessible washrooms. The same applied to the library, administrative buildings, and lecture halls:

> The hostels have nothing like ramps or elevators. As I told you, even the accountant is carried up the stairs. The library used to have lifts (elevators) but they are not functional anymore. ... The classes are sometimes held in the lower buildings and others in the tall buildings over there which have no lifts either. (Hereni)

At Ongozi University, halls of residence received favorable ratings in terms of access, but, even then, participants also pointed to some challenges that needed to be addressed. Dhahabu explained:

> I think there is also discrimination in the hostels, like these ones for the ladies. The rooms that are reserved for the visually impaired or the disabled in general are now being given to these (university students' organization) officials. So, us the visually impaired who are supposed to be in single rooms, we are meant to stay two or three, like here it should be one person but we are two; room six is a (university students' organization) official and they are not willing to come out; they should at least do something about it. *And have you reported this to the dean of students or to any other official?* Yeah, we have tried so much but they are not willing to come out, we don't know what is happening up there (meaning administration).

There is favoritism in offering accommodation services. Students are hierarchized and those in positions of power (student union officials) are given preference when it comes to allocation of single rooms, which are meant to be reserved for disabled students. This shows how power operates at the expense of disability.

With regard to transportation, study participants from Khafee noted that there were no such services organized by the university, whereas those at Ongozi remarked that the university was trying, even though these services had been deteriorating over the years:

> There is nothing like transportation for disabled students in Khafee. (Zumaridi-Khafee)

> The tuk-tuks are very few, only two and we are about 50, so they cannot help all of us. They are not always there. They have been breaking down with no replacements because they say there are no spare parts in the market. Subsequently, they are not reliable that much, especially when going to class. (Dhahabu - Ongozi)

> I don't know whether it is the bureaucracy in the University of Ongozi or if they are simply not willing to repair them; it is something that you fail to understand. (Shani -Ongozi)

In the above responses, participants are concerned about the continued deterioration of transport services for disabled students over the years. The women's comments show that the universities have failed to make the institutions accessible to disabled students. Dhahabu talks about failure to repair tuk-tuks because of the cost claims and lack of spare parts. Shani adds that she is not sure why access issues are not addressed by the university. At Khafee, when I talked to one of the officials during the interviews, she indicated that "no one really cared about disabled students" and that services such as transportation were not a priority for the university (Sauda). Evident in these findings is the fact that the universities fail to recognize that inaccessibility disables disabled students the more (Holloway, 2001). It also shows how, within the universities, "physical access means provision of "minimum" facilities rather than "optimal" facilities which are required to enable disabled students participate equally in the learning process" (DES, 1984, p. 1 cited in O'Connor & Robinson, 1999, p. 92).

Following these barriers, the women concluded that, for them, the notion of equality of opportunity is just a paradox, and is insufficient to counter the oppression that disabled women students face (see also Goode, 2007). Although the government and educational institutions emphasize the promotion of inclusion, there are many practices in place that reinforce inequities. In other words, securing equal educational opportunities (theoretically) for disabled women (a liberal feminist goal – see Acker 1994), has not necessarily addressed the problem of marginality that these women experience. In fact, the notion of equal treatment produces unequal outcomes because, and as shown in the narratives above, disabled women students continue to be subjected to "equal" yet exclusive admission criteria; high tuition costs; restrictions in terms of program and course choices; and participation in decision making processes, practices that leave them at the periphery in their universities. Consequently, the few disabled women students who make it to university experience tremendous challenges as they struggle to complete their degrees. This calls for a rethinking of ways to subvert the prolongation of ableism in educational institutions and in society as a whole. The section that follows examines how these women deal with the challenges narrated above.

RESISTANCE/COPING STRATEGIES

Study participants felt that the universities were, at times, responsive and at the same time irresponsive of disabled students' needs. Consequently, the women adopted different survival strategies to not only contest their subjugation but also to affirm who they were. The women's voices point to their struggles for a dignified identity in a disabling society that shows them oppression, rejection and humiliation (Apple, 1995, p. 104). But how do they do this? In what ways do they deflect the negativities they are bombarded with? What keeps them going in these struggles?

There are a number of strategies that the disabled women students employed to cope with the barriers they face. They utilize varied tactics to ward off the challenges they encounter, including: individual and collective assertions and advocacy; use of silence; spirituality and religion; self-affirmation; change of environment, and family and peer support, as survival mechanisms. These strategies are examined further as follows:

Individual and group advocacy

The disabled women students described how they took an "activist" role in challenging the status quo, in an effort to improve things for themselves and for other disabled students coming after them (Goode, 2007). They recognized the importance of developing self-advocacy skills and noted that speaking out was a powerful strategy for advocating for themselves and others and for making things change. Afya used the speaking out strategy to resist marginalization as follows:

> If I find a problem I speak it out and I am a person who is self motivated and I cannot get demoralized because of anything after all I encourage myself with the little I am able to do. Anything,

> like now you see I am able to do my own washing I don't have
> to go and look for people to come and to do it for me, I wash my
> room, I cook myself; if it is a matter of going to class, I pass
> like others. Maybe they could say _huyu alikuja_ university (this one
> came to university), she is just a fool wasting her money, but then
> I am excelling like anybody else and sometimes I am performing
> better than those who are saying, okay they are "normal".

Afya is describing how she used self assertion and advocacy to deal with the challenges she faced. She does so by doing stuff for herself and does not allow people to look down upon her because she is disabled.

Shani and Dada also explained that disabled students utilize speaking out and advocacy as a strategy to resist discrimination. Shani narrates how disabled students did speak out as a collective:

> When it came to campus, as I said earlier, we fought about it, we
> went to the heads of department and to administrators. It opened a
> way for others who were behind us, now they can do those courses,
> the languages.

Dada, on the other hand, describes how she spoke out through writing letters to the university administrators:

> You write letters to the V.C. asking them to do things like renovate
> this, fix that bathroom. I have a friend who helps me do that. I
> tell him what is missing and what I would wish to see done, then
> we sit and draft a letter requesting the V.C. to take action. He is
> someone from outside; he is a retired teacher and has a heart for
> the disabled.

Dada's narrative illustrates the role that allies could play in fighting oppression against disabled people in society. This friend worked to support Dada's goals and vision of challenging the marginalization experienced by disabled students.

Pointing to the essence of advocacy, Aminia observed that there is a need for disabled persons to come out and voice their needs and dissatisfaction: "people need to be told, we need to come out and say what we need because those people out there may not know what our needs are, so we need to tell them." She also reminded us of the importance of the notion of "nothing about us without us" (Charlton, 2000), when talking about representation and advocating for the needs of the disabled:

> I think that we need to be represented; people can't talk about

disability without knowing how it feels to be disabled; so the disabled need to talk about what it means about being disabled for it is the shoe wearer who knows where the shoe pinches.

Negotiating with the university administration through the disabled students' association was another strategy disabled students used. However, this has not been very fruitful as indicated by Dhahabu:

We have been looking to our association to help us, but now it is not working because as much as it tries to do so they have refused completely they say that there is nothing like talking; that we are supposed to give out money, to pay the fees; that they cannot hear us anymore. They see us as trouble makers [laughs]. And also we have been trying to approach the patron of our organization, like personally I tried to approach the patron who really helped me by giving me her mattress. But now there is no any other thing they can assist even themselves they will tell you to try and get money and pay your fees.

Dhahabu talks of ways in which disabled students engage in collective action to challenge the injustices they face. Barnes and Mercer (2003) observed that, for many disabled people, collective action may be seen as liberating and empowering. Dhahabu, however, notes that, in spite of this group action, the university remains adamant and unresponsive.

Use of silence and "let go" strategies

Other women used silence and letting go as a tool to resist oppression. Studies have shown that silence can be used as a resistance strategy. For example, Fordham (1990), writing from an American perspective, noted that academically successful African American girls used silence as an act of defiance or rejection of the low expectations of Black students held by many school officials (cited by Ward, 1996, p. 88). In this study, disabled women students used silence as a coping of resistance strategy in the following ways: (i) when the situation they were challenging involved a person in a position of power like a professor or university administrator and the women thought that the consequences may well be dire for them or for other disabled students were they to speak out; (ii) when they decided to acquiesce in relation to the situation they were faced with and rationalized it as part of life, and (iii) when they were being strategic and knew that their silence would pay off at that moment or in the near future. This was evident, for example, in Shani's case. When faced with the challenge relating to one of the professors who refused her to register for a course, Shani decided to keep quiet and let go of the discrimination:

> Actually I didn't report her. I didn't even think of reporting and looking at the kind of person she is, you know she is the kind of person, she is very arrogant and a don't care and you know for her being a professor; you know she sees herself being above everyone else ... because, in spite of her not being willing to teach me, it was surprising that my own classmates had problems with her too. Okay she almost told students, but to me, specifically, she had told me not to select that course. You know she is telling me now how do I teach you? I told her just try and verbalize.

The above quote shows how power is playing out. It is possible that Shani thought that speaking out about this professor could jeopardize her life and those of other disabled students, rendering them to become labeled as "possible troublemakers" to be watched out for as was shown in Dhahabu's comment above regarding the administration. This finding echoes Goode's (2007) observations about disabled students in the U.K. Goode found that some disabled students chose to be silent when faced with challenges because they did not want to be viewed in a negative way or to be "picked out" or recognized as someone "kicking up a fuss" (pp. 42-43). Shani might have felt that taking up the issue with other professors or with administrators would not have gone far, for the people who sit in the university senate and make decisions are this professor's colleagues and would be reluctant to comment critically on their colleague or point out flaws of "a system that feeds them." Thus disabled students' use of silence as a coping strategy is a result of their skepticism or distrust of the institution's willingness and commitment to challenging and changing the status quo. The students are not convinced that it is safe to face up to those in positions of power (James, 1994; 2001).

Yakuti also notes that, many times, disabled students do not respond to discrimination. She provided an example of election campaigns for student leaders, whereby, despite the negative comments from non-disabled peers, disabled candidates take it as "part of the campaign process." Yakuti provided an example of one physically disabled lady who was vying for the position of a secretary in the student union and how other non-disabled students made fun of her using clutches and wanting to be their leader. When asked what this disabled lady did, Yakuti replied:

> I have never seen any step being taken, and I did not see her take any step actually. Because - what will you do in that case? You

just say it is kind of political and you cannot say anything but keep quiet and accept things as they are.

Many disabled students do not take any steps because they have limited choices with regard to what to do. They just let things pass by and accept it as part of life.

On some occasions, the participants chose to use silence as a coping strategy because, if they spoke out, they might lose future support from their non-disabled colleagues. This was true of visually impaired students who rely on their peers for assistance with reading print material. When these peers failed to turn up, the disabled students did not raise their voices on them because they would need them in the future. Commenting on the challenge of readers, Aziza stated:

Well, there is nothing you can do to them; you have to be smart. If you try to call someone and he/she is not turning up, you just keep quiet. Because if you talk bad, the next day they will tell each other and you will not have a reader may be for the rest of the term.

For Aziza, being silent is being "politically correct", for there could be negative consequences if the disabled students speak out. Even so, silence can also be problematic. bell hooks (1988) sees silence as a tool of oppression, noting: "… silence is the condition of one who has been dominated, made an object; talk is the mark of freeing, of making one subject" (p. 129). One may then wonder, is the women's choice to remain silent a way of endorsing domination and, thus, perpetuating oppression? How would they challenge power and oppression when they choose to retract and remain silent? It is argued in this study that the women demonstrate that their decision to use silence in certain situations is not an innocent decision. For many of them, silence is more of a matter of survival than speaking out (Brigham, 2007).

Religion and spirituality

Study participants also turned to religion and spirituality to cope with the everyday struggles they were faced with. Religion and spirituality helped shape the women's identities, which, in turn, helped them to better navigate and to cope with the dominant ableist cultures and practices in the university (see Watt, 2003). The women talk about relying on prayers and on their beliefs and relationship with God, in dealing with negative attitudes and challenges associated with having a disability (see Shorter-Gooden, 2004). Religion and spirituality allowed the women to connect with a higher being for empowerment, sustenance, humility, resilience, encouragement and understanding of the self. For example, Dada explained how religion helps her deal with rejection:

> It [religion] gives me a more positive outlook and I can deal with rejection. I have had to deal with self rejection because when someone tells you, like when you request someone to come and push you and they say no, in the past it used to kill me, but now I just look at them and pity them.

In Dada's case, religion helps her to redefine herself in positive ways, especially when faced with rejection (Watt, 2003). Similarly, Mkufu explained that her religious beliefs help her to deal with harassment from males:

> Thank God I am born again. I show them[the men] that they should not take advantage of me ... most of the time I go like, there are very many ladies on campus and they are very beautiful, I think you can go for them.

Mkufu's observations indicate that religion helps her to challenge the notion of "men will be men" and to stand up for herself.

Pointing to the essence of spirituality in her life as a disabled woman, Pete noted that spirituality/religion gives her a form of identity and that it is also a source of self-esteem:

> Spirituality defines you, because once you are defined, because God is not a respecter of persons and God just loves you like any other person. So you know your place with God. Even if you are not accepted in the family, you know you are accepted by God, it will give you that identity that you need, that acceptance, that belonging...it gives me that extra identity...

Pete remarks that spirituality provides guidance and structure for her existence (see Schultz, 2005). It offers purpose and meaning in her life. Through spirituality, Dada is able to see her disability as connecting and expressing a purpose and meaning in life, "a vehicle to discover God's purpose" (Schultz, 2005, p. 1287). It helps balance her life (see Wane, 2002).

However, in as much as religion was a source of empowerment and a crucial survival mechanism, some participants were critical of religion and perceived it as a source of discrimination against people with disabilities. Hawa remarked:

> Sometimes they actually help [religion] but, to some extent, when

you go to church maybe when they are giving posters in church for youth events or something else they don't consider the disabled; and even (leadership) posts in church are often not given to disabled people. And you wonder why, because this could be a place to be included.

Afya disagreed with Hawa's observation about religion being discriminating and therefore unfriendly to people with disabilities:

Well, you know the buildings have been put up by the community, and the community has not been sensitized about disability, so most buildings are not accessible and that one can be a fact. But saying that you are not being considered in church or what, it all depends on one's attitude because, actually, where I go I don't find anything odd because my attitude is not to be sympathized with by those people. So long as I am able to reach the church, get into the hall and have a seat, I don't have any problem. In my situation I don't stand when others are standing because I am not looking at what people are doing but what I am able to do. If I can't stand I will not stand because we are praying to God. We are not praying because we can stand or kneel. If you go sit listen to the word, share with others you are okay. So for those who complain about discrimination in church I don't know what I can say, I don't find anything wrong with the church.

What the women's responses above show is that religion/spirituality provides internal buffers with which these students "counter marginalization" (see Shorter-Gooden, 2004, p.411). Spirituality is a source of their resilience. The women's observations confirm what findings from studies relating to critical or long-term illnesses suggest. That is, spiritual coping strategies involving relationship with self, others, God or nature helps individuals to cope with their ailments (Baldacchino & Draper, 2001). Baldacchino and Draper (2001) suggest that this may be because of finding meaning, purpose and hope, which may nurture individuals in their suffering and thus help them cope with their circumstances (see also Kaye & Raghavan, 2002). Perhaps more research on religion/spirituality and disabled women in higher education may help us to better understand how these aspects can help improve the lives and experiences of disabled women in university.

Self acceptance and perseverance

Dada talked about self-acceptance and taking pride in who she is as an important survival strategy. Dada emphasizes on self-acceptance as key to survival of any disabled person:

> There have been very many challenges on top of having a disability, but I don't see my disability as a challenge. It is now part of my life. But what has kept me going is God and also that sense of worth that motivates me. I feel I have a lot of potential but it comes out of knowing myself and that sense of being motivated to do even better. And then I also feel that my being in this situation is not in vain. I would want people to learn something out of it. Because if I am just there and I am challenged and I just got through my life and that is it, then what am I in this situation for? I want it to be for something. That is why, if I get a forum, I will share it. I want somebody to know that it is possible. And I also want someone to know that we are no different, we are the same, just like any other people, we achieve just as much. Disability is not inability; we can do just as much as any other person can do...

Having a positive sense of self-worth is key to boosting Dada's self-acceptance. Susan has come to terms with who she is and accepted it. She appreciates her disability and wants others to learn something from her situation. Studies on minority students show that an understanding of self and one's identity are critical factors that contribute to academic success (Codjoe, 2006; Dei, 1996a; Dei, James, Karumanchery, James-Wilson & Zine, 2000). According to Susan, and to use Codjoe's (2006) words, "self-affirmation challenges conventional wisdom" (p. 41) that disability is inability or disabled people are different.

What is more, for participants like Karuli from Khafee University, perseverance and patience is what has kept her going. She acknowledges that life can be full of challenges but with patience one can make it:

> Actually, there are two things that have kept me going, perseverance and patience. Those have really helped me because you know in this world there is no way you can live a smooth life all along, you have to come across ups and downs and you have to persevere so as to achieve what you want, yeah and also patience; patience pays. Because if you don't learn to be patient, okay you can find yourself doing some other things that are not good.

It is, thus, clear that religion and spirituality enabled the women to view their disability and challenges positively (Schultz, 2005, p. 1293). The participants see themselves as having a purpose in life and therefore are important members of society.

Change of environment/withdrawal

Some participants decided to move away from the environment (e.g. transfer schools) where they experienced barriers. Lykes (1983) called such a coping response "purposeful indirect coping". That is, the affected individual "responds deliberately but in a way that does not relate to solving the problem by, for example, changing one's goal and finding solace in a different pursuit" (cited in Shorter-Gooden, 2004, p. 411). This was true of Mkufu, a physically disabled student at the University of Ongozi, who explained how she refused to go back to her high school following the discrimination she experienced and had to change schools:

> I was very young and I responded in a radical way by not wanting to go back to that school again. So I refused *kabisa, kabisa* (completely) I told my parents I am not going back to that school I just want to transfer. That was after two terms in the school. I felt it was affecting me as I could not concentrate; most of the time I was just crying.

Mkufu asked her parents to transfer her to a different school because of the negative experiences she had. When asked if she was the only one who was disabled in the school, Mkufu noted that they were only two: "And as it happened the other one had a surgery and was not in school most of the time. So it was as if I was the only one." In this case she felt lonely and lacked someone she could identify with and/or relate to.

The "own and the wise": Disabled people and family

Goffman observed that a stigmatized person stands alone to face an unaccepting, prejudiced society noting:

> ... a discrepancy may exist between an individual's virtual and actual identity. This discrepancy when known about or apparent spoils his social identity; it has the effect of cutting him off from society and from himself so that he stands a discredited person facing an "unaccepting" world. (p. 19)

Goffman (1963) further noted that the stigmatized also find "sympathetic others who are ready to adopt their standpoint in the world and to share with them the feeling that they are human and essentially normal in spite of appearances and in spite of their own self-doubts" (pp. 19-20). Goffman described these "sympathetic others" as the "own and the wise" (p. 19). According to Goffman, the "own" are those who share the stigma. "Knowing from their own experience what it is like to have this particular stigma, the "own" provide the disabled individuals information, support, acceptance

185

and the comfort of feeling at home (p. 20; see also Ingram & Hutchinson, 1999, p. 99). In this study, we have seen that the disabled women student sought advice from other disabled women and men who had gone through university on how to deal with the challenges they were facing. They met as individuals or in groups to advice and empower one another.

The other category that Goffman (1963) talked about is the "wise". Goffman described the wise as individuals supporting the stigmatized; that is, non-disabled individuals whose personal situations made them privileged to the secret life of the stigmatized individual and sympathetic with it. Wise individuals treat the stigmatized individual as "normal" in spite of the stigma (Ingram & Hutchinson, 1999). In this study, the disabled women students point to family, who they felt were nonjudgmental and respectful, could be classified as the wise. The women talked of family members – parents, siblings, spouses and relatives – that offered support which kept them going in university and hence contributed to their success.

Dada's family also helped her establish a firm background and believe in herself, which also assisted her to look at life more positively:

> What also helped me were my parents and my siblings they just told me I have to do things. Like my father would tell me you have to start earlier. The only problem you have is your legs [laughs] and so you have to start earlier. And really I am actually very time conscious if I have to do something by this time, I will be doing it. Because I don't want people to disqualify me when I am not time conscious because they imagine it is because of my situation, I don't want people to do that, so I have to try twice as much.

Zumaridi kept on going because of support from her family:

> I have very supportive parents. They brought me here, pay my fee and provide me with the things that I require and have never doubted that I could not make it just because of the mere fact that I have a disability, never. My parents are very understanding, we talk and they ask me what I need and they support me to achieve what I need and are capable of achieving.

Thus, in moments of challenge, the women learnt to tap into their families for confidence, support and encouragement.

Friends

The women also realized that having good rapport with other students was crucial for their success. At some point they had no choice but to be "politically correct". It was like they were forced to keep friends and be good to them otherwise it would be a challenge. For example, mature disabled students had to find a way of understanding especially the younger students in order to survive when it comes to seeking readers to help them reading print materials. They made every effort to reach out to young JAB students, understand their thinking and behavior and accept them as they are so as to develop and nurture good relations with them. This is why Shani and Lulu had to do some "reaching out" and also try to create and keep good relations with friends and peers:

> You also have to at least gather some friends around you who will also be helping you in your reading especially before those other volunteer s are distributed to read for you. (Shani)

> One of things that has helped me, comparing my age [laughs] I am over 40 and here most of the people, students are very young, they are JAB students. Something that has helped me to at least learn to interact with this people is to be low, to know how to interact with them, learn their psychology and take them the way they would like to be taken. (Lulu)

> You just have to know how to relate to people and even though ... I am the kind of person who is quiet, but for you to survive, you have to reach out. Like if I don't have someone to get me to class, you just start your journey and you get someone on the way and you tell them to get you to class and then they go back to their businesses. Otherwise if you don't survive that way there is no way you are going to make it. So you have to be someone who is reaching out. (Shani)

In dealing with challenges mobility, some disabled women students sought help from friends and peers:

> We ask our fellow students to take us to those various lecture halls we are supposed to go to. I used to have a very nice neighbor in the hostels, so those first weeks, she used to wake up, take me to class and then come back to so she could go where she was going and then from class, I will find my, as in get someone to get me back to my room. That is how I survived. (Shani)

> May be you just request your friends to read for you. Although not all of them are cooperative to read for you so sometimes you remain without the full information on what was learnt on that day. (Dhahabu)

Shani and Dhahabu indicate that when the tuk-tuks that are supposed to ferry students from one point to another are not available because of break downs, delays or high demand, friends help them to get to class. Friends also are handy when it comes to academics and finances. As Hawa observed:

> Like now when I was coming to school I had to ask for may be a little fundraising from friends to meet my school fees because our source of income is very low it cannot make me actually, it cannot allow me to go and pursue further education. So I ask for funds from friends and the church. (Hawa)

Hawa, therefore, sought help from friends, community and family when dealing with financial challenges. All these strategies helped the women to carry on with their university education and to some extent informed the hopes and plans they had for the future.

CONCLUSION

This chapter has pointed to some indicators of attention being given to disabled students and at the same time indicators of neglect in their higher education pursuits (O'Connor & Robinson, 1999). The women appreciated the various forms of supports they received from within and outside of university, which enhanced their success. Without a doubt, family, friends, peers, supportive faculty helped these women to develop the resilience necessary to fight off the challenges they faced. They, for example, encouraged, mentored, advised and supported the participants both morally, emotionally, socially and financially. Disabled role models provided mentorship and advice, encouraging disabled women students to challenge the status quo and believe that "it is possible and doable." This support is fundamental to their retention rates. This finding suggests a need for universities to set up formal mentorship programs so as to provide information and supports to disabled students.

Conversely, the women also highlighted the factors that have limited their participation in university, including poverty, sexual abuse and harassment, discrimination, lack of sufficient learning resources and a constraining physical environment. With regards to poverty and discrimination, participants pointed to financial constraints and talked of feelings of divisiveness and distinctions on the part of disabled and non-disabled students because of the differences in fee charges. The women talked about financial barriers which distinguishes the "haves" and "have-nots" when it comes to access to higher education for disabled students and even the non-disabled. Such class differences have implications on transitions from high school to university, persistence and completion rates on the part of disabled women. There is the affirmative action rule that allows students from arid and semi-arid areas to join university with fewer points, and as regular students (JAB students), thereby paying lesser fee, but this is not allowed for disabled students. Participants feel that this is unfair as they also have "special" circumstances that contribute to their limited access to curriculum and to full participation in the learning process like their non-disabled counterparts. Their argument is that similar affirmative action should be extended to cover disabled students, or the government should diversify the curriculum and put in place accommodation to facilitate successful learning of the standard curriculum.

Being disabled and older exacerbated the marginalization that disabled women students experienced. Afya narrated how mature students experienced discrimination from younger non-disabled peers. The younger students found it a bit "odd" studying with these mature students some of whom had been their teachers in their elementary and high school years. However, the mature students, following their experience, were able to deal with this marginalization and to eventually develop great relationships with the young students.

There are divergences in findings from the two universities when it comes to physical access. For instance, the University of Khafee had hardly any accessible buildings while the University of Ongozi's halls of residence were viewed favorably. Some buildings at Ongozi – the new administration block, the library and some lecture halls – were described as being fairly accessible. With respect to transportation, Ongozi students hailed the presence of tuk-tuks in spite of their limitations such as constant breakdowns and non-committal drivers. Student with severe physical disabilities using a wheelchair, like Dada who may need some form of lifting, found tuk-tuks an unsuitable form of transportation. She recommended a revaluation of in-campus transportation so as to accommodate students with severe physical disabilities. These findings to some degree suggested that the universities have not taken access as a responsibility but have to be reminded all the time. Disabled students have to identify the limitations and to inform the administration before they take a step. Is it not the responsibility of the university to do regular inspection and to see what is missing and fix it? Improving physical access should be looked at as a university duty and responsibility. Holloway (2001) argued that "disabled students should be viewed as having a range of learning needs that have to be met through different teaching and learning styles and supports and not as a liability" (p. 608; see also Ridell, 1996). For participants at

Khafee, in particular, the slow response of the university to addressing physical access issues made these students feel that the university was either neglecting them, or putting the needs of disabled students as a low priority to the university, or the university did not just understand their needs (see O'Connor & Robinson, 1999).

Finally, the students in this study developed strategies to cope with the challenges they faced. They demonstrate resilience in pursuing their degrees. Their voices showed how they have persisted in spite of struggling to raise fees, deal with prejudice and discrimination, lacking sufficient learning resources, facing difficulties with physical access, accommodation and transportation, lacking representation, fears of abuse, etc. Their struggles and resistance can be viewed as a political fight for their own individuality as well as for a minority group. Higher education is a battleground where these disabled students struggle to find space for themselves and defend their rights (see Najarian, 2008). As we will see, there are some policy initiatives in place that address these rights but more needs to be done.

CHAPTER SEVEN

Policy Issues and Institutional Practices

This chapter analyses institutional policies and practices pertaining to disability and to disabled students, as revealed in the institutional documents reviewed (university strategic plans, student handbooks and university websites), together with the interviews conducted with the four university officers. The chapter focuses on what the reviewed documents say (or do not say) about disability and disabled students, and compares these findings with the narratives of the university officers interviewed. It is evident that gaps do exist between what is documented and what is actually practiced. The officers interviewed point to some fundamental issues that higher education institutions need to address in their efforts to improve access to higher education for disabled students. What follows is a synthesis of the issues that emerged from the review of the university websites, the student handbooks, and the strategic plans prepared by the two universities.

UNIVERSITY WEBSITES

The websites of both Khafee and Ongozi universities contained information about the history of the universities; the vision and mission statements of the universities; their structure and governance; their admission policies; the degree and diploma programs offered by the universities; the constituent colleges, schools, faculties, and departments at the universities; interfaculty transfers and program deferments, and information on student welfare and scholarships.

Worth noting is the fact that, unlike that of the University of Ongozi, the University of Khafee's website provided a breakdown on the numbers of students enrolled in different programs (undergraduate, postgraduate diplomas, masters, PhD) and their graduation rates for the different years. These numbers did not show how many of the students were disabled, nor did they show their ages, ethnicities, religion, or socio-economic status. There was a gender breakdown and it provided evidence that women continue to be underrepresented in higher education and in employment in Kenya. Indeed, Kamau (1996; 2004) and Sifuna (2006) observed that gender differences in higher education and in formal employment in Kenya persist, in spite of the country's impressive progress in expanding access to education since independence. For example, in the 2006/2007 academic

191

year, there was a total of 36, 991 students (14, 257 females and 22,734 males), and a total of 1, 411 faculty members (325 females and 1, 086 males) at the University of Khafee. Gender representations with regard to faculty remained dismal, such that only 23% of the faculty were female, compared to 77% males. Women were also underrepresented in management levels. Although the University of Ongozi did not provide comparable statistical breakdown, studies have shown that gender differences in Kenyan higher education institutions remain pervasive (Bunyi, 2004a; Kamau, 1996; 2004; Onsongo, 2006).

Another element featured on the websites of the two universities is student welfare. Both institutions have a Dean of Students who oversees the department of student welfare. The office of the Dean of Students offers services and programs that include chaplaincy; counselling; disabled students' services; student placement services; entertainment; students' orientation programs, and operations of students' organizations. The office also liaises with charitable organizations, university administration and the Higher Education Loans Board. The focus of this office is to enhance student welfare and to address students' needs.

Of interest in this study are the services offered to disabled students. Neither of the websites offered detailed accounts on the forms of supports and services available for disabled students. The University of Ongozi website did mention that students with physical challenges or otherwise would receive assistance and services such as translating brail material into print, provision and repair of wheel-chairs, and the co-ordination of tuk tuk[27] transport on the campus. On the other hand, the University of Khafee did not mention anything about disabled students on their website. They only stated that there is a special student advisor who assists students facing academic, financial or social problems by providing advisory, counselling and guidance services. But why is information on disability so limited in these websites? Who are the intended audience/ users of this scanty information? What does this tell us about disabled students and technology and the visibility and recognition of disability as an equity and inclusion issue in the universities?

In the precious two chapters above, the disabled women students narrated their struggles to access information from the World Wide Web. This is mainly because the technology in their universities is dated. The few computers available are largely customized for use by students without disabilities. Disabled students are forced to look for alternatives in non-governmental organizations particularly at the World Bank facilities, and this hampers service provision for disabled students in Kenyan universities. Indeed, Mason (1996) observed that the challenge of technology and brain drain makes it difficult to carry out core activities such as teaching and research in African universities. Although the universities identified the ability to compete globally with other universities as one of their strategic goals, it is not clear how this competition will be manifest in the face of inadequate information and in the face of the dissemination that is too wanting to empower and to support their students. Or are disabled students not part of the student population in universities that are planning to become competitive? Despite the fact that information technology has the potential to increase the perception and experience of "ability" by disabled people (Stienstra, 2002), the costs associated with its use inhibit disabled students' ability to access and to use it.

STUDENT HANDBOOKS

The student handbooks in both universities were prepared and distributed by the office of Dean of Students. The handbooks provided information on the history and background of the universities, on governance and on officers of the universities, information on the constituent colleges and faculties of the two universities, departments and programs of specialization; library services; university bookshop; university fees; student welfare services, and on the functions of the offices of the Dean of Students.

University of Khafee student handbook

The University of Khafee student handbook was updated in 2005. The handbook had a small blurb describing disability, indicating that university programs and services are open to all students with disabilities to receive optimal benefits from the university experience. Within and outside of the university, the Dean of Students strives to provide auxiliary services and equipment for students with disabilities, and also conducts awareness activities that help address these needs. Therefore, upon entry, students with disabilities are encouraged to report to the Dean of Students office to have their "needs assessed" and attended to.

As for accommodation, the student handbook explained that students with disability are to be accommodated on the ground floor of specified halls in single rooms unless otherwise requested. The handbooks further indicated that modifications have been made to rooms and to equipment in those halls of residence to meet the needs of the students. The office of the Dean of Students also provides transport to and from lecture halls. These observations, however, contradict what the women narrated in chapter seven and also what the officers said, as will be seen in the subsequent sections. The disabled women students interviewed noted that the halls of residence at the University of Khafee were inaccessible and disabled students kept on pushing staff in charge of accommodation to assign them ground floor rooms. There were also no transportation services provided for the disabled students from the halls of residence to class and vice versa. Although in the handbook, it is acknowledged that there is a shortage of residential spaces because of the high number of applications leading to situations where students have to share rooms and common facilities from time to time, those available have not been modified to accommodate disabled students, nor have efforts been made to help these women utilize lower level floor rooms in the halls of residence.

University of Ongozi student handbook

The student handbook for the University of Ongozi was last updated in 2004. The handbook identified the need for the office of the Dean of Students to keep up to date information about all students (addresses and telephone numbers of home and next of kin), but did not mention the need to identify whether these students had learning needs, disabilities, or their gender etc., and the kinds of supports offered to them. There was also information on student arrests by police, student travel, mail and the students' center (facility for student recreation, meeting places etc); student organizations; clubs and societies in the university and their roles, and information on the guidance and counselling services unit at the university. The unit provides counselling services relating to subject combinations; study habits; examination; stress reduction; physical and mental handicaps, including special needs; emotional strains and social adjustments difficulties. The unit also provides counselling on interpersonal and inter-group relationships, on health matters which are not directly related to a physical cause, and on family life education. But, as seen from the disabled women students' voices in chapters six and seven, not many students utilize these services.

It is, thus, clear that, although university statements in various documents appeared encouraging, a sign that the institutions were very pro-inclusion, it may not have been the case. In fact, several disabled students indicated that they were not aware of the existence of counselling services for disabled students on their campuses. The universities could have good intentions, but when they have a handful of disabled students, they have to prioritize their services and to work within their limited budgets. That way, addressing disability becomes an "add-on" issue.

As for hostels and accommodation, the handbook provided rules and regulations governing the conduct and discipline of students in the halls of residence and on campus. Although the handbook did not mention physical access of the hostels, my interview findings with disabled students revealed that the halls of residence at Ongozi were fairly accessible, compared to those at Khafee. In addition, the officers in charge of accommodation at Ongozi made efforts to assign disabled students single rooms and on ground floor levels. There were, however, cases where some disabled students (those with mild physical disabilities) that were on the ground floor level too, but in shared rooms.

STRATEGIC PLANS

The strategic plans for the universities reviewed covered the years 2005 to 2015. In these plans, both the universities identified mission and vision statements emphasizing provision of quality in education to their students and fostering academic excellence. As core foci of the universities, the strategic plans listed teaching and learning; innovation; research and development; consultancy; governance, leadership and management; human resources; infrastructure, including Information and Communication Technology (ICT) and library services; partnerships and linkages/marketing and publicity; finance; student affairs, including image/marketing and publicity, planning and implementation; monitoring and evaluation.

In the plans, both universities recognized teaching and learning as the fundamental businesses of the universities. The institutions pledged to offer quality education and innovative academic programs and curricula to promote scholarship. They also emphasized quality assurance in relation to teaching methods; assessment; and supervision; modes of delivery; curriculum; management and student admission, with a view to attaining world class status. Lacking in these impressive statements is an explanation of who is included and who is excluded, and how these goals will be attained. An examination of the contents in the implementation plan revealed that nothing was mentioned on tailoring the curriculum and assessment modes to meet the needs of disabled students, yet these are some of the key challenges that disabled women students alluded to in their narratives on barriers to their success in university (chapter seven). To paraphrase Boxall et al. (2004), there is a need for these universities and others to have teaching, learning and research in the universities and in the education system as a whole reflect the concerns and agendas of disabled students, rather than the disabling agendas of the academy that exclude them. Only by addressing these exclusionary practices would the "cracks in the walls of the academy be repaired and, hence, the equitable addressing of the learning needs of disabled students" (p. 103).

Noticeable in the plans is the importance of innovation, research and development for these universities. Both institutions are committed to creating an enabling environment and policy framework that promotes research and development so as to remain competitive in knowledge production and also to contributing towards national development (in spite of the prevailing financial challenges). But even with this commitment to research, some programs are favoured at the expense of others when allocating research funds. Amani of the University of Ongozi provided an example of how this favouritism operates when he noted:

> *Interviewer:* If you look at research in this university where do you find much of their research emphasis and how does research on disability rank?
>
> *Amani:* Disability issues come second or third or let me say last.
>
> *Interviewer:* And does that affect you in any way?
>
> *Amani:* Of course it does. It affects our effort to advance our department. For example, just a few weeks ago we got a letter from the administration saying that our research - okay we wanted to do a study that would sample districts in terms of poverty and food and link it to disability; .... And our proposal was okay, but during funding distribution, other proposals were selected for funding, ours was put aside. They said it was one of the wonderful proposals they had seen relating disability to poverty and food production, but it was not funded. So, in essence, what I am saying is that disability has not been taken as a serious topic. There is no positive stand with the financiers.

Evident in the above quotation is how, with limited funding, administrators make choices on what to fund. Research in the sciences is prioritized and such prioritizations demoralize faculty and staff in arts and humanities programs, inhibiting their creativity and ability to contribute to knowledge production, policy and practice. Science and technology are seen as the doorway to the much needed "development" in low income countries, and funds are dedicated to research in this field. This finding compels one to question what counts as "important knowledge" and what does not; which programs are best placed to lead to development and which ones do not, and what is development anyway; what is likely to generate income and allow universities to become competitive and what will not. Favouring sciences creates hierarchies and subjugates other knowledge (arts and humanities).

What is more, the universities acknowledged that the goals of teaching, learning, research and innovation cannot be successfully attained without sound leadership. Consequently, the universities proposed to review the existing governance structures and systems so as to serve the challenging, dynamic and competitive environment in which they are operating, and also to develop a governance system that will enable the universities to realize visionary, transparent and innovative leadership and management. But again, who are the leaders? To what extent are disabled people involved in the management of the universities? Findings from the interviews with disabled students and officers showed that there are hardly any disabled people in management positions in the two universities. Disabled people should be involved if inclusive "sound leadership" is to be attained. As O'Connor and Robinson (1999) argued: "Disability is too common in society for it to be left to non-disabled "experts". If policy is to be credible and effective, it has to be an in-built feature of these strategic plans. This is because making university education accessible to disabled students is not only about making the physical environment accessible or providing support services or modifying/differentiating instruction etc. It is also about "allowing disabled students (people) to speak for themselves and be involved in the provisions that are made for them" (Corlette & Cooper, 1992, p. 27 cited by O'Connor & Robinson, 1999, p. 92).

The strategic plans also showed that human resource development as well as human resource management and utilization are central to the successful functioning of the universities. Staff and faculty motivation and productivity are critical to the successful functioning of the universities, while low morale and poor work ethics adversely affect staff commitment and service delivery. It was recommended that systematic training and capacity building of staff be undertaken to empower them to discharge their roles effectively. Even so, the kind of training to be provided and the target staff remained unclear. Besides, the universities recognized that there was a serious shortage of high-calibre academic staff in the country. The universities would look into recruitment, promotion, motivation, retention, staff mindset, and staff rationalization, with the aim of producing a productive workforce that is creative, motivated, efficient and effective. The universities will also strengthen and sustain implementation of gender, marginalization, HIV/AIDS and disability policies.

The strategic plans also captured some of the challenges facing the universities in terms of resources and facilities. These include laboratories, libraries and information and ICT infrastructure. These facilities need to be developed or improved so as to attain world class standards. Infrastructure and physical facilities need to be expanded, rehabilitated and maintained (especially teaching space/lecture rooms, offices, laboratories and other utilities). However, considering the fact that most of the buildings remained largely inaccessible, there were no clear plans on how to improve them or how to implement the principles of universal design when, for example, putting up new buildings.

Another element specified in the strategic plans is improving technology to enhance teaching and learning, especially with regard to teaching materials, and availing of equipment, such as computers, LCD or overhead projectors, to enrich teaching and learning, as well as improving library services and space. In terms of ICT, there is inadequate provision of software and hardware, lack of trained personnel, limited connectivity and poor maintenance, which negatively impacts not only learning but also research activities. But improving ICT provision will also require that the technology be made accessible to disabled students. An analysis of these plans showed that the biggest gaps in the plan is not just the "how" of addressing the plans, but also who is responsible for addressing the plans and how the needs of disabled students would be met. For example, one of the areas identified by the officers was the need to improve computer technology so as to enhance research for disabled students:

> For instance, in the library, even though we have one of the talking computers next door here, they are using it mostly for teaching. We want to improve that so that there are some in the library. I know World Bank now has some in their library in town. When we went there, they informed us that we were free to use it and that our students could go to use it and access the internet when they want. But we are so far from town - those trips back and forth - we have challenges of transport too. So it will be nice to have access on campus. It would be nice to provide particular resources for those programs on campus with a view to improving the capacity of our students with disability to do research. As we talk about the future of the university, I hope that one time we will truly improve on this. As a research institution, this is an area we really need to improve on. I know we are teaching the students how to use those computers and, thus, creating awareness of their existence, but as of now, usage is limited because we have only one computer and the students cannot even practice properly.

Neema's observations above are in line with what Karuli and Shani reported with regard to technology in chapter six. Shani observed that the computers at Ongozi have no JAWS program, which makes it difficult for visually impaired students to use them. Karuli of the University of Khafee added that, even though their library has computers, they are not well connected and students find it hard to access online journals and other resources. This is one area that the strategic plans failed to address. Although they referred to improving Information and Communication Technology (ICT), it was more of a general observation with no specific measures on how to address the needs of disabled students.

The two universities value partnerships and linkages, and are conscious of their images in the global context. They want to expand networks and partnerships at local, regional and international levels in order to reposition themselves in the global arena as vibrant and competitive institutions of higher learning. The universities thus emphasize strengthening community outreach and community service through various programs and activities so as not to remain "ivory towers" in society. In order to compete with other institutions, they also have to market and publicize themselves with the aim of enhancing their corporate images and identities. But who is included and who is excluded in this "corporate" image? Whose agendas are prioritized in these endeavours? Which knowledge qualifies when it comes to competitiveness and which does not? These are issues that universities should consider, if they are to develop their faculties and/ or departments equitably, and if they are, subsequently, to involve their students and professors correspondingly.

One of the questions this study sought to answer was how disabled students financed their education. In the strategic plans, finance is identified as an important component for the two universities. The plans do not, however, mention extending financial supports to struggling students, particularly disabled students. Instead, they focus on how to generate income. The universities emphasize not running deficits but continuing to operate a balanced budget, while at the same time trying to pay off debts owed. The strategic plans identify ways in which universities would increase revenue and fiscal health (by increasing internally generated revenue and engaging in fundraising and soliciting support from donors, including the private sector, community members and other stakeholders).

Limited focus on sponsorships and bursaries supports the disabled women's assertion that even if they gain admission, they cannot afford to attend university because they do not have the means to pay. Those who are able to make it, and are unemployed, either get sponsorship from NGOs or from well-wishers, while others are supported by their parents/ family members. Contrary to observations by staff that disabled students get concessions and bursaries, the women's narratives in chapter six show that disabled students continue to experience financial challenges and administrators sometimes use discouraging language (e.g. no more babying them, pay like others, no favouritism) to "put the students off" whenever they request for those concessions. This is not to minimize the important role the universities have also played in negotiating HELB extension to disabled students. However, we also need to bear in mind that HELB support for disabled students remains insufficient. The disabled women students interviewed appealed for additional funds to cover remaining tuition fees and to meet accommodation and other living expenses.

Student welfare is the other strategic issue identified in the plans. Accommodation is referenced as one of the significant challenges that the universities have to deal with. Both universities are committed to improving student accommodation and catering, and to initiating a student-centred support system, including student work study programs. Suggestions of work study programs are great but are rarely enforced. None of the disabled women reported participating in this program, or in the research assistantship and tutorial fellowships that were once offered to graduate students. In fact, when Shani, the graduate student at Ongozi, inquired about them, she was told that they had been scrapped because of lack of funds.

The University of Ongozi pledged to enhance student leadership, moral and spiritual values as well as sports and games, and to strengthen guidance and counselling for students. The university wanted to improve provision of health services, particularly with respect to HIV/AIDS counselling and prevention campaign; drug abuse prevention and prevention of sexual harassment, and institution of violence prevention programs and mechanisms. It also catered for disabled students by providing services such as a special section in the library for the blind, special computers, sign language specialist, tuk tuk vehicles to ease movement within the campus, but these services need to be honed. The university also recognized the importance of equality of opportunity and indicated that there should be no discrimination on the basis of color, creed, tribe, race, gender and region of origin, physical disability, political affiliation or financial circumstances.

The findings from the documents were corroborated with interviews with university officers and also with the narratives of the disabled women interviewed. What follows is an analysis of the themes that emerged from the interviews with the officers. Some of their narratives confirmed the disabled women students' observations discussed in chapters six and seven, while others were at variance with what the women said or with what is written in the documents.

VIEWS OF UNIVERSITY OFFICERS ON DISABILITY AND DISABLED STUDENTS

Officers from Ongozi University indicated that their institution made commendable efforts in addressing the needs of disabled students, while those from Khafee acknowledged that there were significant limitations in supporting disabled students.

Facilitating access and supporting disabled students

In our discussions with disabled women about the services provided by their institutions, they mentioned hostel services, learning resources and transportation. A few talked about financial support in the form of bursary, although only a minority of them received this bursary. When I asked the officials about the forms of support that their universities provide to students, those from Ongozi named admissions of disabled students to university through the "parallel" programs and advocacy as some of the ways they enhance these students' participation in university education. Amani of Ongozi University remarked:

> What we have done as a department is to go beyond the "normal" admission and cut points set by the JAB for all universities. The JAB sets criteria for admission. Other than that, we have found that there are many disabled students who do not get in so we go into high schools and ask for minimum university qualification which is usually C+. Those who have C+ and were not admitted through JAB, we ask them to apply, and we get them in through that special admission by the university. The deans allow that special admission so we ask the schools to send us a list of students and we admit them. So we do it outside JAB.

Amani explained further how they reach the disabled students to get them to apply to university:

> *Interviewer:* How do you contact these students in high school, do you go to specific schools?
> *Amani:* We go through the Kenya Society for the Blind (KSB), the Kenya Society for the Deaf (KSD) and Society for the Physically Handicapped (SPH). We involve them in sending us the information. We also request them to send us lists of the schools and students.
> *Interviewer:* Don't you find this approach limiting? For example, what about students who live in rural areas, if they have attained a C+ but do not even know that these societies exist? How do you get to reach such students?

> *Amani*: That is why I am saying that we have also direct connection to schools, we tell the principals to send the lists. There are not many secondary schools for the disabled in Kenya.

A drawback to the recruitment approach described above is the assumption that disabled students are only found in special education schools. Such an approach may result in exclusion of disabled students in mainstream schools who may have attained an aggregate of a C+ but could not get admission to university and are not registered with any of the societies mentioned by Amani (KSB, KSD or SPH). Amani failed to recognize that the recruitment process was limiting. The University of Khafee did not have an equivalent recruitment program for disabled high school students but it allowed parallel admissions. Future studies should examine the recruitment, advertising and admission practices of postsecondary institutions in Kenya.

Advocacy was the other form of support that the officers provided on behalf of disabled students. Sauda of the University of Khafee provided an example of how this is done:

> We do students advocacy. Usually, when we ask for funding for students with disabilities, they don't want to give you funding, because they (referring to administration) don't understand the needs of disabled students. So you have to explain to them and to advocate for these students. We had to talk about things such as having ramps in the buildings. Sometimes you could see students being carried up the stairs by others because there are no ramps and this is not good.

Neema of Ongozi added that they advocate for disabled students inside and outside of the university regarding academic and non-academic issues:

> This office of student welfare, non-academic, it is non-academic although it spills over when there is concern. We liaise with academic officers as well as teachers ... we also teach. In addition, we handle non academic issues especially relational, roommate problems, parent relations, etc. When people are sick, we make a point of seeing them, following up to see how they are doing, and we get in touch with parents. We also organize for the student to be taken home, if need be, etc. We liaise with the HELB people, we are the ones who sign for them to get loans or who appeal on their behalf, should they require extra loans, because, again, the financial needs are becoming more and more critical. The poverty rates are hitting us the hardest I think. So we argue that the students need more than they have given them when we see that a student requires more, we talk on their behalf. ...We also

liaise with different bodies like groups that provide Braille paper. This is a challenge mainly for visually impaired students. We try and look for those papers and machines so that they can have the resources on time. The Kenya Society for the Blind is the group that usually help us with papers. ... There are also some activities like world cycling day that are held once a year. We liaise with them so that our students can participate. We have also held conferences with different groups that sensitize our students on HIV/AIDS and we liaise with those groups so that our students are also sensitized on the dangers of some of these social issues that we take for granted.

Neema further noted that officers at Ongozi also liaise with parents/ families of disabled students to support them:

We liaise with the family also. We believe that if there is a problem the best way to assist the student is to bring on board the parent because that would complete the circle of support system. When supporting the student, sometimes you find that the trouble began at home. So we try and bring the parents on board. The students can also come in and say hey, I can't deal with my parents, please can you talk to them on my behalf. So we call them and discuss the issues. The parents also come here and say hey, my son/daughter is having a problem and I am unable to resolve it. So we bring them together and try to see if we can assist bridging the gap.

Evident in the above responses is the recognition of the importance of advocacy, positive relations and support as predictors of academic success for disabled students (see Dennis et al, 2005). These officers are committed to building bridges between students, the university administration and their families, and to ensuring that their needs are addressed by the university.

The "university for disabled students"

When explaining the kinds of supports and services offered to disabled students, there was a tendency to point to the University of Ongozi as the "university for disabled students". Akil, an officer at the University of Khafee remarked:

Majorities of these students go to Ongozi because, for a long time, that university has been providing services for them. We have a few, but not as many as Ongozi, and most people think that, that is the university for disabled students.

Here, the assumption is that Ongozi University is better suited and better equipped to accommodate, teach or enhance access to higher education for disabled students. Amani, an officer at Ongozi also commented that disabled students "belong to Ongozi":

Amani: Here at Ongozi we are lucky because we are the most important institution of higher learning that accommodates disabled persons. Most of them are here. You will not find many disabled persons going to get education in other universities. ... If they are there, they are there by accident, because this is the university for the disabled.

Interviewer: Could you speak more to that?

Amani: Firstly, the university started offering (name of program and year it started). But even before that Ongozi is known to have admitted especially many blind students. Many of them come here. They opt to come here because of the special care they get. We have a resource center for them. There is a resource center for blind students and any other disabled student... The dean of students is the one who takes care of the welfare of all students, therefore, there is a section that deals with disabilities. Then there is the administration that has provided the tuk tuks for transportation from their hostels to classes and from class to class, dining hall, library and all that. So that helps out.

Amani remarked that Ongozi is "where disabled students belong" because they are taken care of. His observations are remarkable, yet problematic. One may be tempted to think that disabled students do not belong to other universities. It is like the other universities are for non-disabled students and therefore only Ongozi has "partitioned" its space to accommodate disabled students and they are "expected to belong to this partitioned space" (see Dear, Wilton, Gaber & Takahashi, 1997). Amani's remarks demonstrate the kind of boundary maintenance going on in higher education institutions which defines who belongs and who does not belong and where. His response projects how attitudes towards disability could restrict the ability of disabled people to move freely or to seek admission in other universities in the country. While Ongozi is to be hailed for making efforts to accommodate more disabled students, it should not be presented as the "university for disabled students". Such labelling may encourage other institutions in the country to maintain their reluctance to open their doors to disabled students and to keep referring them to Ongozi. All Kenyan universities have the responsibility of fostering equal access and inclusion for all students in their institutions.

Numbers of disabled students in the university

None of the officers from either university could provide an accurate picture of the numbers of disabled students enrolled in their universities. The officers provided general estimates of the population of disabled students in their institutions. For example, Neema of the University of Ongozi answered:

> We have about 50 students. I think 30 are visually impaired, I am not so sure. The others are different types of impairment some are hearing and some are physical.

Similar challenges in accounting for the enrolments of disabled students were evident at the University of Khafee. None of the officers knew the population of disabled students in their institution. Sauda of the University of Khafee noted:

> I joined the university in 1986, and at that time we had very many disabled students. There are those students with audio, visual and physical disabilities. The numbers of visually impaired students were many. You remember we had the Ordinary-level and Advanced-level system of education. So it happened that one didn't have to necessarily do sciences in secondary school. So when the student went for Advanced-level they could do the art subjects, and more people who were visually impaired could go for courses like arts and such like.

Akil of the department of student affairs at Khafee noted:

> As of now, I do not have any actual numbers, but all I know is that the numbers have reduced tremendously over the years because of the curriculum, but the exact numbers, I don't know. But they are there – physical, visual, hearing impairments – they are there and these are the most common.

Elaborating on how curriculum changes from the 7-3-2-3 system to the 8-4-4 system have impacted the enrolments of disabled students at university, Akil commented:

> When you look at the high school curriculum and also at the university's approach to teaching students with disabilities, they may not have enough facilities and resources to enable them admit these students. For example, a few years ago, I heard of students, for example in engineering, who are disabled and who stated that the whole set up was not to their advantage. It is a bit of a challenge. Some felt threatened by that whole set up. Although this person I could say had not a very severe physical disability, he felt that the sitting arrangement and the use of equipment was a bit of a challenge to him. So it is at high school

and also in the university where adjustments need to be made. But the 8-4-4 system apparently, because of its emphasis on the practical subjects, seems to be discouraging disabled students like the visually impaired when it comes to those subjects.

Amani added:
> The curriculum that changed has implications, because there could be more courses that these students have to handle and they disadvantaged the disabled students like those who are blind.

The officers had no accurate information on the number of disabled students enrolled in their universities. They, however, agreed that curriculum changes had a negative impact on the participation of disabled students in higher education. This observation was also made by the disabled women students in chapter six. Although it could be argued that some students (especially those with invisible disabilities) may be reluctant to reveal their impairments, leading the officers not to know about them, one wonders why the other students are not accounted for. Inadequate records on the number of disabled students enrolled in the university results in significant under-planning and under-provision of services that are meant to assist the students to succeed in their university education (see Morris, 1999).

Finances and program completion

The disabled women students interviewed identified finances as a key impediment to their successful participation in higher education. Indeed, the officers confirmed that finances are a challenge for most disabled students. Even so, there were contradictions when explaining the financial supports provided by the university. Amani of Ongozi insisted that the university provided concessions for disabled students:

> They are usually given concession by the university, some of them, not all of them. There are some who are given scholarship by private bodies and there are others who privately finance themselves.

Amani talked about disabled students getting special tuition payment plans. The women acknowledged that such a plan existed previously, but was phased out under the new management. Amani further maintained that the university was lenient to the students when it came to fee payments. When asked if he was aware of any disabled students who had dropped out of university due to finances, he claimed that the university was lenient:

> Well, I think the university is a little lenient to them. For example,

I have a student who has a bill of about KShs. 200,000 ($CND 3,500) and she is graduating in December. She is a wheelchair user and the university has allowed her to continue, despite this high balance. So they are not chased away.

There are divergences in what Amani is explaining and what the disabled women students reported in their narratives. In chapter five, Dhahabu, a visually impaired student explained how students' beddings are taken away and/or students are not allowed to sit for their exams when they have not cleared fees. Even Neema, an officer at Ongozi, confirmed that students do not sit for exams if they have fee balances:

We have cases, for example, last year, we had students with high fee balances, and now there is a requirement that students cannot sit for their exams before they complete paying the fees. Some of them were students with disabilities, two visually impaired students, I think, but I know one girl sorted out her problem. I don't know what happened to the other. So they are challenged in their own ways, just like other students, but they are mostly challenged in relation to the fees issue, which is common even for the non-disabled students.

Neema also stated that there is a bursary but acknowledged that it was not specifically for disabled students:

Neema: We also have an internal bursary that is helpful; it is university found and augments the "have-nots."
Interviewer: Is it for disabled students only?
Neema: Not necessarily, they apply, depending on their need, so they have to provide supporting documentation for their needs, one of which is disability, that goes into the record, and that needs to be supported. So it is on merit, I can say.

Even though disability was identified as one of the needs considered in administering the bursary, only a handful of the women I interviewed had received the bursary, despite their applying for it every year.

The discrepancies in the information provided by the two officers are evidence of either a lack of information sharing within the university or the reluctance to acknowledge that there is a problem with the way the university is treating disabled students. Communications and keeping up to date information on changes happening in the university that affect disabled students would improve if university staff, faculty and administrators work collaboratively in supporting disabled students.

Aside from financial limitations, challenges of program completion were also exacerbated by the implementation of structural adjustment programs (SAPs), which made educational costs unbearable for disabled students, the majority of whom came from low socio-economic backgrounds. As Amani reiterated:

> Most disabled persons come from very poor families. With the cost sharing, families with disabled children/students are struggling. It is a big disadvantage. That is why we ask for concessions, bursaries, and even ask that we educate these students for free instead of asking them to pay.
>
> *Interviewer:* And what has been the response?
>
> *Amani:* Not too bad. We have been told that they are considering it and we are hoping it is going to work some day.

Literature shows that SAPs have worsened the cycle of poverty in many African countries (Dei, 1998; Okeke, 2006; Okolie, 2003). Governments are spending less and less in basic services such as education and health and other development activities while downloading the costs of these services to families that were already struggling. The result has been increased perpetual inequalities and exploitation in society, as the poor continue to suffer while the rich grow richer (Stone, 1999). The effects of SAPs are an example of the many reasons why scholars have argued for the re-examination of the question of development and outsider interventions in addressing disability in low income countries (see Stone 1999; Momm & Kong, 1989, cited by Stone, 1999, p. 6).

Disability awareness and policy

Like the disabled women students, the officers interviewed agreed that the universities have no clear policy/statement on disability. The officers acknowledged that lack of such a policy has implications on how disability is articulated and dealt with, and on the nature of support offered to disabled students in their institutions. When I asked Amani whether the University of Ongozi has a disability policy, he replied:

> *Interviewer:* Does the university have a policy or statement or guideline on disability?
>
> *Amani:* Not really, that has to come from us and I don't think we have one.
>
> *Interviewer:* Why, when you have had the program running for all these years?
>
> *Amani:* Well, maybe that is what your book will help us to spell out; you will come help us develop something like that, a policy on

disability and on how they can be assisted. We have not reached there, no.

Neema, too, acknowledged that Ongozi has no clear disability statement or policy, other than what is mentioned in the students' handbook and on the university website:

Interviewer: Does this university have a policy on disability?

Neema: You know, look at the administration, the administrators are at the top there and no elevator. Can you imagine a person on wheelchair going up there? I have seen a girl being carried up by other students. Those are some of the things that need to be pointed out to the administration. Somebody needs to see you, be accessible. But they are putting up a new building, I don't know if they have considered making it accessible. The thing is, we are able now, but with the accidents on these roads today, you never know. What happens even to a person who is in that big position and they get into that situation, can they get into their offices? Disability is not something that is confined to certain individuals only. It can happen to anyone and when it comes we need to be aware and to deal with them accordingly. We must acknowledge the situations and the problems we have in our society.

Neema's response speaks to Linton's (2006) declaration that disability is a universal characteristic and no one in society is immune to it (see also Davis, 2002; Garland-Thomson, 2002). Neema appeals to administrators in her university to rethink disability and make their offices accessible to disabled students/people.

Considering the fact that not much was mentioned about disability in the documents reviewed, I asked the officers to explain how they sensitized their students and other university members about disability. Amani of Ongozi responded:

So far, we have not done that, but we are doing curriculum review and are suggesting a unit that can be offered to all students in education and to the whole faculty or school of education so that they are introduced to disabilities; when they go out they will at least have some awareness on disability. And in that curriculum we are suggesting that B. Ed students specializing in other subjects do one unit in special education.

Interviewer: Why not for all students in the university regardless of the kind of course/programs they are doing?

Amani: We shall get there but we thought of starting from our own faculty or school and then we can be an example to the rest of the university. You know change takes time and you need to push little by little for these things to happen.

Neema, however, strived to include disability issues in her teaching:
I had a class a year ago with physically impaired students, visually impaired and hearing impaired students. I used this example to explain what we are talking about in real life situations. I mentioned integration and showed how in that class we had disabled students and what we could do. So it was a good illustration. And when it came to school management, which is my subject, we talked about the head teachers' role and teachers' role in providing for the needs of students. For instance, if you have a low vision student in your class and they can't see the chalkboard, what do you do? What interventions do you put in place for a student on a wheelchair? ... So we sensitize the teacher candidates to look out for some of these issues.

In spite of these efforts to incorporate disability issues in the curriculum, Neema felt that the formulation of a university policy on disability was vital:
Interviewer: So are you then saying that the university needs such a policy and what should it look like or entail?
Neema: Definitely, they should. The policy needs to address questions like are we inclusive? What does inclusiveness mean? What does inclusiveness entail in as a far as access is concerned?

For Neema, disability awareness and self-reflection are necessary steps to legitimating inclusion and access, and to spelling out what educators could do to minimize or to eradicate marginalization of disabled students in our institutions and everyday practices.

Evaluating approaches to dealing with disability

In their evaluations of how the universities faired in providing services to disabled students, the officers reflected on issues such as admission, transportation, resources and the physical environment. Officers from Ongozi felt that their institution had tried but more needs to be done. Those from Khafee acknowledged that the university lacked in many areas and needed to give serious thought to better addressing the welfare of disabled students in the university.

For Amani, some of the achievements the University of Ongozi had made in addressing the needs of disabled students were in the areas of admission, fee plans, transportation and setting up a resource center for disabled students:

> The university has gone an extra mile to admit these students, give concessions for fees ... Although they do not give them the certificates; they allow them to finish their courses. There is also transportation to ease movement from class to class. The resource centers for the disabled students have also been helpful. There is also computer for the blind and one of our teachers teaches these students to use computers.

Neema also commented that Ongozi had tried to improve physical access:

> Other than the administration which is inaccessible, I think they have tried in some of the other locations. For example, in the lecture rooms, they have installed the ramps and they are wheelchair accessible; they are improving in that area.

On the other hand, the officers also pointed to the shortfalls of their universities and administrators' reluctance to address the needs of disabled students:

> Who cares about disabled students? There is nothing much being done to address their needs I would say. When I was in the office of student affairs I tried to negotiate with the administration so that these students get services such as transportation but now these things are never there. Nobody cares about disabled students. (Sauda, Khafee)
>
> ... Nobody is there to advocate for them, nobody cares that much. Like, if a student becomes blind, they say, take them to (name of university)... So you have to talk to the dean of the faculty where the students are to see what they can do. (Akil, Khafee)

When I asked what more could be done, Neema offered the following suggestions:

> We all teach or work with these students. I would appreciate a policy that sensitizes the entire staff. Whoever works in the university has to be sensitized because they deal with these students at one point or another. The entire student body also needs to be aware of issues of disability. I think every year we need to have orientation, and to put disability as part of the orientation program, so that

one is sensitized from the first year...They get to know these things from the word go. And then, in the library we should provide space for them to read. There is some, but this is for everybody. We need to reserve space for them. So, I think, providing information and sensitizing the whole university is something the administrators need to look into. It has to start from the top and trickle down ... The other thing is to also try and push the administration to come up with a disability policy.

Sauda, Akil and Neema recognize that the measures their institutions have taken to handle disability are insufficient. They propose a rupturing of the prevailing "don't care attitude" towards disability and putting in place sound leadership, awareness programs, resources and services improvements, and formulating systematic policies to deal with the constraints that disabled students face.

Equality of opportunity

The disabled women students felt that equality of opportunity was just an empty bubble. However, for officers such as Amani, the universities had helped tackle equality of opportunity:

> When we go an extra mile to have them admitted meaning when the cut off is at B we can go for B- and C+ although to us it is equalization of opportunities, affirmative action. That is how we get them (Amani).

Neema considered equality of opportunity from a physical access perspective:

> Equality of opportunity means creating an accessible environment. It could be a case of entry into a building; for example, if a person in a wheelchair ... is called for an interview and it is on 8th floor and he/she cannot access the building what will happen to them? We need to create an environment which even disabled people can access.
>
> *Interviewer:* So do you think the university extends equal opportunities to disabled students?
>
> *Neema:* You know, given the degree of awareness, I will say they are trying, because we can start by asking, are the administrators aware of the issues? If they are not aware, then you cannot really say the services are provided or not provided. Because if they are not aware, you cannot really hold them responsible because some things you just dismiss and later when you are made aware you

provide them. For example, when (name of administrator) was here he initiated transportation services for disabled students. So it took an administrator at the very top to see that need and to address it. And I think from there we have to improve more and more.

Neema's observation points to how power plays out in provision of services. It took someone in a position of power to implement transportation services for disabled students. Neema continued to claim that if those in power do not know, we cannot blame them. However, Vernon and Swain (2002) assert that "not knowing and making assumptions are themselves disabling" (p. 83).

Disability and society

The definition of disability is often contested. Although my study adopted a social model approach to defining disability, study participants had their own perceptions of what disability is or is not:

> You are disabled if you cannot do what your peers are doing and therefore you may need assistance. But if you can do what others are doing it does not matter if it is limbs that you do not have … (Amani)

> I think a lot of it is in our own vision, our own expectations; our own making; our own expectations. … We tend to measure people according to our expectations; we have our own assumptions about disabled people or children. So, in one way or another, we show it directly or indirectly that they are not achievers, from the way we talk to them; treat them; address them, and in all ways. And we keep them that way, instead of providing them with opportunity to excel. We need to identify areas where they can excel, and when we identify these, we can then work with our expectations. (Neema)

In that case Neema argued that it is we, the people - society - that create disability. Amani too argued that society creates disability:

> Society indeed creates disability in various ways. We have, for instance, mentioned accessibility. We cause people not to reach or to access the services by not providing means for reaching there, you see. And maybe treatment also. The way we treat disabled people, the attitude itself, the attitude we project, when providing services for disabled persons is very negative, yeah and, of course, has effects. There are mainly negative effects, stemming from the fact that we see the disability before seeing the person. For example, when you see Nick,, you just think, no, he is disabled. You start

sympathizing instead of empathizing with the person and you are wondering, "can he even do one two three?" while he does them so well. Like he can swim better than you and I.

Similarly, Sauda of the University of Ongozi commented on how societal barriers could be disabling:

There is need to remove the barriers that limit participation of disabled persons in society. Look at, for example, our public transport. It is very insensitive to disabled persons. How would someone using crutches or wheelchair get into those buses or *matatus* (public service vehicles)? It is a problem. So those things need to be looked into.

The above descriptions match the social model of disability. The officers argued that societal attitudes and beliefs inform our understandings and perceptions of disability. Disability is read against a particular set standard (the normate – Garland-Thomson, 1997). The disabled body is given logic of its own and is always in view and on view (Oyewumi, 2003). It invites a gaze, a gaze of difference, a gaze of differentiation and plays a role in the construction of social status (Oyewumi, 2003; Goffman, 1963). Disability is, therefore, a socially constructed and institutionalized phenomenon and not a product of individual failings (Barnes, Oliver & Barton, 2002). This may explain why disability-related discrimination has become so systematized and why it remains pervasive in institutions of higher learning, as exemplified by Amani:

Definitely, discrimination is common ... Examples have been given in classes where a teacher brings a diagram and says, look here, this is xyz, but fails to give extra explanation, disregarding that he has blind students in a class. That has happened.

Interviewer: How do you assist in such cases?

Amani: When students complain about that, we call the chair of that department and alert them so they alert their staff that we have blind students who need extra explanations when teachers are teaching, and the response has been very positive. Several times the chairs have informed their staff about the need to assist those students. Even then, not everyone will be willing to go that extra mile by doing various things to help these students. So, in that case, complaints are still heard here and there. But, overall, I would say that a number of lecturers have tried to help out.

Amani's narrative illustrated that disability discrimination may not necessarily be overt but also covert. It could also be exercised intentionally or unintentionally. This is why creating disability awareness in these institutions is imperative.

CHALLENGES FOR OFFICERS

The officers were conscious of the challenges they faced working with disabled students. They cited fear on the part of disabled students, scarcity of resources, together with societal prejudices and high unemployment of disabled graduates, as some of the limitations they were faced with. Neema of the University of Ongozi termed her challenges as "practical challenges", noting:

> This office has really made me more aware of many issues relating to the day to day practical challenges. For instance, my window there, we open it. And if we don't open it all the way flat on the wall, you will have a blind person hit into it straight in the face. So it is actually living day to day and putting myself and yourself in their shoes. Opening our door for instance, this is their corridor, they live across here, they walk over here in the corridor. I always look to see if the door is open in a certain way, and I have to secure the door firmly on the wall. So it has made me aware of some of the challenges, but these are just physical. I am also aware that there are also psychological challenges that these students experience, that you get to know when you talk to them one on one, and, of course, there are many that are not spoken. Some of them will not talk of them because they think that it makes them feel or confirm their disability; that is what I have picked on in some occasions; but I could be wrong also.
>
> *Interviewer:* In that case what do you do?
>
> *Neema:* During our general meetings I try to encourage socialization as much as possible, we talk general things and then get into the real issues. I also encourage the students to come and talk to me if they have problems; a problem said is a problem half solved. So I encourage interactions and at times even coming around and saying hello, although we really have very tight schedules, makes a difference.

Amani shared his frustrations about unemployment of disabled graduate students:

> The greatest challenge is when you graduate students and they come back a year or so and say they have not been employed that

is my concern, my greatest challenge; how can we have disabled persons graduating and going back to their families or parents and sitting there? You know, that is the hardest part for me to actually work with and I have gone beyond my duty to make sure that I look for jobs for these people personally in companies and private practice and advocating that equal opportunity for them to the employers.

When asked how employers respond, Amani replied:

You see employers are not keen on that and for them it is production and they see disability as some extra burden for them and will limit their productivity. So they rarely hire disabled people.

The other challenge had to do with lack of recognition and support of research on disability. As Amani observed: "the university's focus is mainly on the sciences, when it comes to research. We rarely get funds to run our projects, but again we cannot give up. We have to keep looking elsewhere for support and this is not easy."

Sauda, on the other hand, felt that the "don't care attitude" taken by the universities towards disabled students limits planning and service provision for disabled students:

You know, if the administration does not care, it is hard for those under them to plan anything for these students.

In raising this critique, Sauda challenged the university to rethink how they propagate discrimination in spite of commitments to promoting equal opportunities for all in accessing and in participating in higher education.

GENDER AND DISABILITY

Beyond the challenge of resources and attitudes, gender also exacerbated the challenges that disabled people experience in Kenya. DAWN Ontario (n.d.) observed that women with disabilities are discriminated against because they are women. Particularly for women with disabilities in developing countries, disability diminishes their chances to participate in society. Neema acknowledged that this is true even when one is non-disabled:

What I know is that, in the Kenyan population, there are very few women not just in university administration but in key decision making positions, and that is actually a problem. Ongozi is just a reflection of what is happening outside there. So we need to improve in that area, and make women more visible. I am happy that the president said during Kenyatta day that 30 percent of all public positions should be earmarked for women. That is a positive move, and if we can really do that, then we can see some changes maybe.

Amani added:

I want to see that difference made. For sure we do not have many disabled women and even the men in management. If we can have things changing and have more representations from disabled women it will be good.

Sauda of Khafee reiterated:

There are not even many disabled women in universities or with a postsecondary education, how do you get them into leadership? I think change has to start from the very lower levels, at the primary level. The university may not have a problem with adjusting the curriculum. The changes should start from primary through secondary school, then come to university.

The narratives above demonstrate how patriarchy is manifested in the Kenyan society. Gender is used to structure societal relations privileging men and rendering them powerful while women are less powerful. It is even harder for disabled women because it is taken for granted that they are to remain dependent on others in society (see Boylan, 1991).

Overall, the officers agree that attitude, finance, curriculum and resources are core barriers to the success of disabled students in higher education. The officers agree that a disability policy is necessary, both in the universities and nationally, in order to move any disability agenda forward. What follows are their suggestions on what could be done to improve the experiences of disabled students once enrolled at the university and also when transitioning to the world of work.

UNIVERSITY OFFICER'S CALL FOR CHANGE

In the views of the officers interviewed, for change to happen, moral, material/financial, and policy supports have to be formulated and implemented. These changes are to be instituted by the university, by disabled students and their parents/guardians, by employers, and by the government and other stakeholders.

Role of universities

Amani highlighted the need for other universities to open their doors to disabled students:

Instead of having all disabled students coming to Ongozi, I personally don't like that, I would want them to go to other universities, a university of their choice, instead of coming to Ongozi because that is where they have these facilities for the disabled. For me, it is very bad that we have concentration of disabled persons in Ongozi. I would want them out there but when they are here we make sure that they get the best to enable them succeed in their programs.

In addition to opening doors to disabled students, higher education institutions will also have to lead by example and make their physical spaces accessible to disabled students/people, as well as improve transport services within their institutions:

The physical environment can be improved. And also those tuk tuks are not enough but the idea is very good. We need more of them and more drivers for these tuk tuks. So there we can also talk of finances. There is not enough finance and we need to appeal to the university to give us more in that area. (Amani)

Universities should also sensitize their administrators, faculty, staff and students about disability:

We need to educate fellow professors on disability – create awareness so that the whole university gets to know how to deal with issues of disability. That awareness is very important. Tell other people throughout the university about disability … faculty should realize that a physically impaired person is as capable as anybody else to achieve. To be able to move around or to perform like the non-disabled, they only need extra help or other gadgets. The administrators also need to know that the cost of education is higher for disabled students because they need special extra gadgets to facilitate access to what non-disabled people take for granted. Thus, cost is something that the administrators should bear in mind, and they should put a little more effort to addressing the issue of expenses, for example, buy teaching aids and other special equipment needed. (Amani)

Administrators, staff and faculty should have a day with the disabled students, take a day off and walk through the campus and see what happens and just put themselves in the world of these students because some of these experiences you can't really talk of. You can't talk of everything, you must experience it. Let them walk with them to see some of the issues that they go through, because sometimes some people must touch and feel and even taste to actually internalize. So it is important to walk the path with them to see what their world is like to really understand the challenges they face. (Neema)

Above all, higher education institutions should create resource centers for disabled students or expand existing ones and hire qualified personnel to assist disabled students. They should as well include disabled students in making decisions affecting their lives:

We need a resource center, we need people who are trained to work with students with disabilities. And now, because of the education system, fewer and fewer disabled students are making it to university because of the practicals involved in the science subjects. That could be something to be looked into. (Sauda)

There is need to listen to these students' needs; to advocate for their needs, and also to sensitize the university community. (Sauda)

Disabled students need to be included in decision making in the university. We need to make sure that blind and physically impaired students are included in student welfare, student unions and all that, instead of isolating them. Because at the moment they are rarely involved in decision making processes although we have some in the union for the disabled students. (Akil)

Role of disabled students

The need for disabled students to advocate for themselves was also evident. This would augment the larger project of awareness raising and activism, which are central to working toward eradicating ableism in the universities:

Disabled students need to be assertive; continue showing that they are able ... If the teachers are teaching you and then you are able to take what they teach you like any other person, you are not disabled. So they should try and excel in other areas that other people have taken for granted. (Amani)

Amani wanted disabled students to keep challenging the barriers to their successful participation in university.

Parents

Capturing the role parents should play, Amani emphasized that parents have the potential to make or break it for their disabled children. They need to advocate for their disabled children:

> Parents should treat the disabled child as they treat the non-disabled child. They should not discriminate in any form. They need to include them in all aspects of life – play, going to the market, church, and any other social gatherings they think about, not hide them, just expose them and not to see the disability, but to see the person first ... Look for ways to assist them. (Amani)

Neema also noted:

> I think the parents also need to come out and talk about their own experiences with their disabled child. Because one thing, the society is very unkind, due to the fact that we have myths about disability. The parents need to understand that disability is not a curse and then come out and discuss their challenges as parents. What are the challenges of being a parent of a disabled child? So there are two levels there, maybe the academics need to come out and sensitize the parents, in a lot of *barazas*, about the disabled child or disabled persons in society and then from there, challenge them to come out and assist their children. The parents may be victims of the social stigma of parenting a child with a disability, so they need to come out and accept their situation. (Neema)

Government and employers

The officers suggested a need to increase pressure for employer accountability and transparency when it comes to employment equity. For instance, Amani reiterated:

> We have the disability act, it has recommended to the employers to leave a portion of say 5% to the disabled persons in their hiring. They should be followed up on this. And if it is taken seriously it will be nice.

Neema insisted on a practical government policy that takes into account disabled people:

> The government too nationally has to come up with a clear disability policy so that the entire country is aware. For example, when they are putting up buildings, they need to make them accessible for everybody. Look at our city planners, I was in town the other day, I think they want to put barriers in certain places and put fences. They dug holes and left them there, and the road is so busy, ... suppose your leg lands in one of these holes? Nobody even cares

or thinks that this is a serious health and safety issue. Like now they are chasing each other in town with hawkers and what have you, can you imagine what will happen if someone's leg enters there even those *askaris* (police) running after the hawkers? It is a danger for everybody, so we need to be sensitized on creating an environment that is safe and accessible. (Neema)

Amani is for practical inclusion:

I am for inclusion, I want to see practical inclusion, including all disabled persons in all aspects of life – schools, both in the rural and in cities – high school and primary- they need to be integrated. The universities too.

CONCLUSION

This chapter has shown that the institutions under investigation had inadequate concrete policies or statements on disability. Much of the interventions put in place resulted from advocacy by students and staff that work with them and largely depended on top administrators' responses to that advocacy.

It is no surprise that not much is said about disability in the strategic plans, given the corporatization and marketization trends being adopted by the universities. To use Bond's (1997) words, the universities under investigation are "under multiple assaults from continuing massification of higher education, staggering economy, political interferences and increasing emphasis on public accountability and excellence" (p. 3; see also Bond, 2001). Responses to these "assaults" have resulted in significant budget cuts and prioritization of services and programs in the universities. Amani provided an example of how these prioritizations have impacted research, whereby limited attention is paid to arts and humanities. Disability is not a "sexy" subject and is therefore low priority in the universities' research priorities (see Stone, 1999), a practice that leads to staff demoralization. When staff is demoralized it affects how they relate with students, especially those that need extra help. Yet, we have seen in chapter six that positive experiences with faculty and staff foster disabled students' academic success while negative experiences impede success. The strategic plans did not consider examining the causes of this demoralization and how to address it.

The chapter has also shown that for more disabled students to participate in university education there is a need for attitudinal, policy and structural changes at all levels of society. Such changes should not only reflect increased presence of disabled students in universities but also their increased participation in decision making processes and policy formulations (see also Puja, 2001). As the officers revealed disabled students are rarely involved in the everyday running of the university.

What is more, disabled students planning to attend higher education should be provided with information on what is available for them in those institutions, their rights and responsibilities as well as the responsibilities that higher education institutions have toward them. Being well informed will help these students to have opportunity to enjoy the benefits of the higher education experience without feeling excluded (see Office for Civil Rights, 2007). It is clear from the study findings that this information is scant, beginning from the websites of the institutions under study to the strategic plans and handbooks made available to students and to the general public.

CHAPTER EIGHT

Conclusion

This chapter summarizes the important findings outlined in the book. It interweaves the themes with existing literature to provide conclusions on the issues discussed. Some suggestions and directions for future research and for future policy and practice are also provided. Some of the issues revisited in this summary include what needs to be done to improve access to and participation in university education for disabled students. In this respect, focus is on the role of government, university managers, faculty and fellow students, and on the role of parents and society in general in enhancing the necessary improvements.

EMERGING ISSUES

Choice and agency

This research has shown that disabled women students have dreams of pursuing higher education. Although the women in this study experienced support in making choices to pursue university education, they also experienced significant struggles. These struggles included societal stigma; inadequate information, and lack of financial and educational resources.

Worth noting is the fact that the women's struggle to access university education is not "a mere rhetorical question. It is a question of affirmation and agency (the agency of self-empowerment)" (Nnaemeka, 1998, p. 384). They "refused to remain designated as passive recipients of charity and pity, and claimed the status of subjects with agency" (Hughes, 2005, p. 80). A look at the women's narrative experiences also reveals that those with power in society establish norms that order the lives of those without power (see Goffman, 1963). These findings corroborate Goffman's assertion that in society the dominant group's opinions (in this case the non-disabled) are often used to create hierarchies in society and stigmatize those who do not fit into those hierarchies. In this study disabled students were marked as inferior, different in ability, performance, and appearance and in so doing viewed as lesser than and consequently stigmatized (Goffman, 1963). This did not only happen in the university contexts but also in the wider society. That is, ableism is not only manifest in higher education but also in the wider society (Madriaga, 2007). On the other hand, the study findings also demonstrate that the disabled women students were not passive but proactive subjects. The women "came out" (Kallen, 1989)[28] and resisted the control and/or stigmatization they experienced in all aspects of their university life. Becker and Arnold (1986) argued that "stigmatized individuals find themselves in a continual struggle with negative attitudes and with the devalued status that accompanies them. As a result, they must constantly develop strategies of dealing with the stigma" (p. 49). The disabled women students interviewed utilized strategies such as spirituality and religion; family and peer support; advocacy; silence; self-affirmation, and changing the environment, in the process of exercising their agency.

The women noted that they had disabled peers, both within and outside school, who adviced and empowered them. This advice and empowerment made them feel supported and also helped them develop a strong identity as disabled women students and, consequently, a strong sense of self that helped them discover their abilities and talents. The women advocated for admission of more disabled women students so as to have a stronger community on campus. They clearly identified themselves as disabled and wanted to be surrounded by others who look like them. Their agency resided in their individual and collective endeavours, and was constantly shaped by the experiences they faced (see Stamp, 1986; 1989; Kiluva-Ndunda, 2001). The skill with which they managed their university experiences reflects their personal sense of agency.

Curriculum and interpersonal relations

The curriculum continued to carry out gatekeeping and normalizing functions (see Erevelles, 2005). The existing curriculum bears an ableist notion of "excellence" and recognition in education. This syndrome of excellence negates the question of "how" and by "whom", allowing a few select bodies (non-disabled) to claim excellence (see Murunga, 2005). Neither are disabled students compellingly represented in text nor in teachers' pedagogical approaches. Consequently, these students felt that the equity and fairness that education is supposed to foster is far from reality for many disabled women. In this context, university education in Kenya fails to live up to its goal of democratization (Dei & Shahjahan, 2008; Freire, 1994).

With regard to interpersonal relations, it is clear that the problem of disability lies, not only in the impairment of function and its effect on the disabled women students, but also in the area of relations with "normal" people (Hunt, 1998; Barton, 1998). Negative interactions informed by prejudiced attitudes and perceptions of disability as deviancy or lesser than left negative feelings of marginalization in disabled women students (see Jones et al., 1984). This marginalization went beyond provision of services, to how other students, faculty, staff, etc. perceived them and how they interacted with them.

Gender and disability

The research results show that traditional gender roles and stereotypes remain pervasive and persistent in the Kenyan society (see Moodley, 1999). Male dominance is an established reality in the country (see Murunga, 2005). Patriarchy informs the marginal representation of disabled women in higher education (Acker, 1994; Kamau, 1996). The peripheral existence of disabled women students in Kenyan university education is informed by happenings in societal apparatuses, including the family, leadership structures, religion, the economy, government etc., all of which work in favor of males. As Lulu demonstrated (chapter five), males are favored in educational pursuits, and this favoritism is informed by stereotypes of masculinity and femininity (role expectations of men and women) that define women as nurturers and men as the breadwinners (Gerschick 2000; Meekosha, 2004).

Administratively, the university management structures remained very androcentric in nature. While there were a few women in administration, they remained tokenized and the majority of the decisions were made by the very traditional patriarchs that have had a grip on power (Kamau, 1996; 2004). Thus, the increased presence of women in positions of power (administrative posts) did not necessarily bring about much change because the dominant and dominating patriarchal ideologies and practices to which women are subjected remained unchanged (Mara & Sagaria, 1993 as cited by Bensimon & Marshall, 1997, p. 14).

Consequently, disabled women (and women in general) continue to lag behind in educational attainment when compared to men. Although there were individual men who had defied existing patriarchal structures and supported disabled women to attain an education (e.g. in chapter five Shani's father; Hawa's father and siblings; Lulu's husband etc.), the wider societal structures remained intact and continued to suppress disabled women. Changing social structures and eliminating male domination and patriarchal structures are key to opening full access to knowledge and to the resources that disabled women need (Acker, 1994, p. 50).

Even so, and as Mikell (1997) rightly observed, African women sometimes find themselves in a paradoxical situation: that of "walking a political/gender tightrope" (p. 1). Mikell argued that African women are on the one hand concerned about "the sea of economic and political troubles facing their communities and their national "ships of state". On the other hand, they are also grappling with how to affirm their own identities while transforming societal notions of gender and familial roles" (p. 1). The disabled women in this study were not exempt from this paradox. At some point they seemed to be treading carefully when it came to addressing ableism. They had to balance between trying to address the question of gender and at the same time support the rights of disabled people without antagonizing their partnership in disability advocacy with disabled male students in the university. This finding, to some degree, speaks to Mikell's (1997) assertion that African feminism is "distinctly ... concerned with 'bread, butter, and power' issues than with issues such as female control over reproduction or variation and choice within human sexuality, or debates about essentialism, the female body, or the discourse of patriarchy (p. 4). Indeed, the disabled women students' words demonstrated that they were more concerned with how they (as a disabled people together with disabled men), could work towards gaining equal opportunities paralleling those of non-disabled students than emphasizing on the challenge of patriarchy.

Disability stigma/ableist schemas

The study findings show that physicality and "bodies matter" (see Butler, 1993). Pointing to physicality, Mitchell and Snyder (1997) observed that physical difference structures and pervades all aspects of our relational identities. In this study disabled students are imagined and read in a particular way (using an ableist lens). Non-disabled individuals formulate and disseminate ableist norms which define disabled individuals. These norms are translated into actions that produce messages on how disability is to be interpreted and acted upon. Disabled bodies are viewed as "abnormal" bodies. This is why when it comes to crucial aspects such as education, disabled people tend to be educated toward a particular goal. In this study, majority of the disabled women students were admitted into university to train as teachers and specifically special education teachers. Only a few went for other teaching specializations and/or other programs of study in general.

What these findings demonstrate, therefore, is that "markings on human bodies" are socially significant and that disability has to do with "embodied social signification" (see Loury, 2003, p. 334) whose outcomes encompass stigmatizing attitudes toward people with disabilities (see Goffman, 1963). Stigmatizing attitudes have negative impacts on disabled individuals in terms of education, social interactions, resource distribution and employment (see Tsang, Tam, Chan & Cheung, 2003). "Able-bodiedness"

226

is adored, while the disabled body is equated to "lack" (Shakespeare, 1994, p. 285). This adoration is evidenced in what is said and done to disabled students. As Ball (1990) remarked "discourses do not only embody meaning and social relationships but also constitute power relations" (p. 2). What is done and said to the disabled students in this study is an indication of the pervasiveness of ableism in society. For example, Shani (chapter seven), illustrated how ableist hegemony informs negative readings of disabled students (especially by some teachers/faculty) as a special group needing special attention – a group they do not know how to teach. Faculty, for instance, have the power to determine who is to enroll in a particular course and who is not to enroll etc. All these practices gesture how the disabled body is thought about and understood.

Overall, the lives and experiences of the disabled women students are guided by *ableist schemas* (conscious or non-conscious perceptions of disability and of the disabled body that inform people's actions and perceptions - borrowing from Valian's (1999) notion of *gendered schemas*, non-conscious hypotheses about sex differences that guide people's perceptions and behaviors (p. 2). Societal structures valorize "normalcy" through micro-structures, such as the curriculum, language, interpersonal relations, physical access, and other societal actions and practices etc., all of which are informed by the broader formalized macro-structures in society (see Hooks, 2005).

Colonization

Dei (2007) argues that "colonial" does not only imply foreign or alien but also imposing and dominating economic, social and political ideas and systems. Dei further argues that "colonizing practices create hierarchical relations while espousing a universality of superiority of certain knowledge systems and experiences" (p. 106) and for this study, privileging non-disabled bodies. Colonization has to do with the power of dominance which yields and maintains hierarchies (Dei, 2007). In the context of disabled women and higher education, "the intervention of colonialism created a situation where the earlier relatively powerful positions held by women were further eroded by the introduction of new power paradigms and opportunities, rooted in gender politics favoring men" (Obioma, 1998, p. 19).

Data in this study show how higher education in Kenya plays into the politics of "denying access" both consciously and unconsciously. Disability emerges as a site of difference and power (see Dei, 2007) and the university system in itself is a colonizing machinery. The history of disabled people in Kenya is rarely taken into account in teaching and learning processes.

If at all considered, it is done in a manner that demonizes African culture in favor of western values and perspectives. As observed from one of the interviews, professors tended to provide a one sided perspective of disability in Africa (negative) and the west (positive), leaving students to believe that the African culture is backward and inferior (Ntarangwi, 2003), and that disabled people were and are "outcasts" in all African cultures/societies (see also Amadiume, 2000; Dei, 2007; Fanon, 1967).

These findings show that Kenya's education system has not tailored "its content and pedagogy to the socioeconomic and cultural realities of its people capable of developing local solutions for local problems" (Ntarangwi, 2003, pp. 213 - 214). The country continues to uphold an education system that produces a people who consistently look to Europe and to North America for models of development and who, thus, fail to produce knowledge that matches their own social and physical environments (Ntarangwi, 2003). This situation calls for a change in the curriculum offered in African schools, to make it more relevant to African needs and conditions (see Dei, 2007; Wane; 2006; 2008).

Resilience

Listening to the narratives of the disabled women students, I wondered how they were able to succeed, despite the adversities they were faced with. A closer look at the discussion of success factors (chapter seven) indicates that a combination of personal characteristics and home and school factors contributes to the resilience of these disabled women students. Personal factors, including self-determination, hard work and self belief, were particularly core to the women's success (Litner et al, 2005 in chapter three). Because of self determination and (perhaps due to support from peers) the women were able to navigate the campus environment, make use of the resources available and advocate for more and, eventually, become part of the university culture. Additionally, in-school factors, especially supports from the universities, such as medical care, financial support, and provision of services and facilities for disabled students, also impacted the women's resilience. Family supports, together with other factors, such as spirituality, also helped the women to develop the essential resolve and persistence to succeed in university. These findings parallel Borman and Overman's (2004) results in their study of minority students in the U.S.A, which revealed that individual characteristics, such as self-esteem and school-related factors, including peer support, are important features associated with students' academic resilience (see also Jackson, Smith & Hill, 2003; Litner et al, 2005; Masten, 1994).

It is worth noting that results from Borman and Overman's (2004) study are not conclusive, as the research did not examine changes in the women's degree of resilience with program level or age etc. As Masten (1994) observed, resilience is a developmental process and, therefore, occurs over time (p. 6). It would be important to find out whether there are differences in academic resilience for disabled students, based on their gender, age, program level, type of disability etc.

RESEARCH AND POLICY CONTRIBUTIONS AND IMPLICATIONS

There are a number of issues that emerged from these studies which have implications for the current and future state of disability theory, research, policy and activism in Kenya. To start with, this study contributes to bridging gaps in disability research in low income countries. As noted in the introductory chapter, there is a dearth of literature on gender and disability in higher education in Africa. The study contributes toward making the voices of disabled women students in Kenya visible and from their own perspectives.

This study also contributes to literature, challenging views that disabled people are passive victims without agency (French, Swain & Reynolds, 2007; Hughes, 2005; Stone, 1999). The study shows that the disabled women students are hardworking individuals, committed to achieving "something"; they only need extra supports and appropriate accommodations.

The study contributes to research literature on the resilience of minority students in higher education contexts. It also opens up possibilities for further and more in-depth studies to enhance our understanding of resilience in disabled women students.

Research results contribute to the literature on intersectionalities. Findings demonstrate that disabled women students embody more than one social identity and that these identities intersect to inform their experiences in higher education. Referencing the experiences of Black women in America, Collins (2000) argued that Black women's oppression is not only interrelated, but is also bound together and influenced by experience of race, class, gender and ethnicity (p. 42). Data in this study pointed to the relational dynamics of gender, class, age, nature of disability (visible vs invisible), geographical location and ethnicity, and how these aspects shape the lives and experiences of the women.

From the literature on gender and education in Africa/Kenya, it became clear that research on gender and higher education seldom pays attention to disability issues. This study confirmed this omission and demonstrated how disabled women continue to experience further exclusion from the higher education corridors because of their gender and disability. These exclusions need redress through polices that advocate for inclusion of disability and disabled people in higher education research in Kenya.

Policywise, the study enabled an examination of occurrences relating to disability in Kenyan universities and, to some degree, an examination of government policies on disability. The study allowed an assessment of service provision for disabled students, existing gaps and what more could be done to bridge those gaps.

The study findings are also relevant to the Ministry of Health in Kenya. Most of the disabled women students' indicated that their disability was a result of illnesses that could have been prevented. For example, a number of participants talked about getting polio while others mentioned factors such as negligence or malpractice on the part of healthcare providers. These revelations are a crucial entrée into understanding how lack of or poor healthcare impacts on the lives and welfare of the citizenry and the need to improve and/or reform healthcare services in the country.

Furthermore, my research findings underline the need for universities to formulate, improve on and to implement a disability policy/statement that clearly outlines the nature and kinds of supports to be provided to disabled students. The findings demonstrate that ableism is a systemic problem in Kenya and that it is supported by various societal apparatuses. For this problem to be addressed effectively, everyone needs to act. However, the government has to take a lead role and also seek collaborations and partnerships with other societal institutions.

What is more, the narrative responses show that disabled women in rural areas of Kenya are being neglected. There is a need for both universities and government to reach out to these disabled students. The reaching out will require that the government rethink and reform its resource distribution modalities in the country. There are significant inequities in wealth distribution across the country and, as demonstrated earlier, disabled women from "have-not" provinces are the hardest hit. Non-governmental organizations involved in projects to support disabled students should also pay attention to these resource distribution discrepancies and assist these students in an equitable manner. The high costs of university education are one of the major barriers facing disabled women students in their access to and participation in university education. The introduction of the HELB program by the Ministry of Education and scholarships in an attempt to assist needy students is to be hailed. However, policies governing the awarding of these loans and scholarships need to be reviewed. As shown in chapter six, disabled students incur additional disability related expenses in their pursuit of higher education compared to non-disabled students. The ministry should take into account these additional costs and also consider providing additional funding to enable these students meet their educational expenses with lesser strain.

Theoretically, the study drew on a combination of frameworks to provide further evidence that patriarchy remains pervasive in the Kenyan society and that it negatively impacts the lives of disabled women students. This finding confirms what other existing studies on gender and education in Kenya have pointed to with respect to how male dominance in the country disadvantages women's participation in education, employment, leadership and overall societal activities (see Bunyi, 2004b; Kamau, 1996; 2004; Onsongo, 2006; Sifuna, 2006). On the other hand, the findings revealed that the disabled women do exercise their agency and also receive support from their male partners, parents, siblings and guardians, in spite of the prevailing patriarchy. This finding reinforces Obioma's (1998) and Oyewumi's (2003) emphasis that discussions on issues affecting women in Africa ought to be contextualized instead of being generalized using narrow Eurowestern interpretations of oppression of African women.

The study also proves how power operates in society. It shows how non-disabled people set the norms that disabled people (less powerful) have to conform to (Goffman, 1963). These norms are evident in the curriculum, physical access, policy etc. The women's voices also demonstrate how failure to fit into that "norm" leads to stigmatization and the implications on one's life chances.

Neglect of indigenous knowledge in theory, practice and policies and their possible contribution to the education and service provision for disabled people was evident in this study. Ogechi and Ruto (2002) showed that, in some indigenous Kenyan communities, disability is not an inability. Disabled people were integrated into society, as this was one of the expectations of an inclusive society (see also Kisanji, 1998). The literature reviewed demonstrated that in indigenous African societies women had their own ways of excelling that were disrupted by colonial structures and this is silenced in contemporary disability theorizing. Although I drew on the African feminist framework that captures some aspects of this history incorporating an indigenous knowledge framework may perhaps address this gap.

In terms of practice, among the many challenges facing the universities is the pressure to attend to the market and to expand, as articulated in their strategic plans. The universities are also committed to achieving technological standards comparable to those in institutions in western societies. For this reason, these universities find themselves quick to embrace initiatives that will generate money in the short-term. In the process, programs and service provisions, such as those for disabled students, are short-changed or, if at all addressed, are given short-term quick fix solutions. There is a need for a critical rethinking of the structures of oppression and marginalization that keep disabled students on the edges in the universities. Practical changes for long-term transformation are required. Universities cannot continue talking about inclusion without questioning the very structures that inhibit disabled students from being "full members" in these institutions.

The problem of ableism ought to be tackled in a holistic manner, starting right from the family level. Changes focusing on government and universities or other educational institutions alone would be insufficient. The government should reinforce the change. What is happening in higher education institutions is a reflection of the wider society and, indeed, the study participants' recommendations apply to all levels of society – university, government, family (parents) and disabled people.

The manifestation of power that marginalizes disabled students is buttressed by arguments of "not knowing." University administrators, for example, argued that they did not know the needs of disabled students and, therefore, often acted whenever those needs were brought to their attention. Vic Finkelstein (1998) described such occurrences as "ignorance of disability" (p. 37). This ignorance is characteristic in pedagogy, research, student relations, and financial support, and is tolerated because an "intellectual boundary" has been imposed around the world of disability, preventing critical interest in disability issues on the part of non-disabled education stakeholders – academics, researchers, students, administrators and government. This makes it difficult to protect voices of disabled people and to ensure that they are heard (Finkelstein, 1998). Kenyan universities should consider how their current policies and practices contribute to oppression of disabled students. This involves identifying, challenging and removing disabling barriers in their institutions (Barton, 1998).

In conclusion, this study has shown that there are commendable positive efforts being made to address the plight of disabled women students in their efforts to access higher education in Kenya. At the same time there are significant barriers to the success of these efforts that need to be addressed collaboratively.

LIMITATIONS AND FUTURE RESEARCH

This study was not without limitations. Methodologically, many disabled women students were glad to share their experiences. They hoped that, by putting their voices out there, they would educate the wider society and debunk the myths relating to inability. Challenges, however, arose when interpreting the findings. As noted in the introductory chapters, there are limited studies on disabled women in higher education in Kenya. This paucity of literature at times made it difficult when it came to supporting my analysis.

Moreover, this study drew on the experiences of disabled students in two public universities in Kenya. Even though one may argue that this is what is happening in other universities in the country, such conclusions may be inadequate. This is because, for example, private universities have different policies governing their operations. Drawing conclusions that this is what happens in their spaces too would not do them justice. Even with the public universities and, as seen with Khafee and Ongozi, there are differences in management and provision of services for students with disabilities.

Additionally, my research sample comprised of disabled women students who had been successful in attending university and who were able to stay in university and continue with their studies. This focus left important voices of women who were perhaps discouraged and, therefore, did not get to attend university or those who got into university and dropped out because of various reasons. Future studies should consider including these women's experiences.

The question of diversity in sampling was also limiting. First, and as noted earlier, I did not get to hear the experiences of women from the "have-not" provinces. Secondly, the sample was not representative enough of the diverse ethnic communities in the country. Since each ethnic community has different cultural practices informing their lives, the limited range of voices drawn on did not reflect these diversities precisely. Thirdly, there were a high percentage of participants with visual impairments in my study. This leaves out important voices (participants with other kinds of disabilities) that need to be heard. It is important that future studies address these shortcomings.

The other limitation relates to research ethics. Some women did comment that non-disabled persons exploit disabled people through research. It was difficult for me, and still is, to know how best to address these important concerns without reinforcing the women's repression. This challenge was also stated by Ryan (1998) in an examination of research with minority groups in the U.S.A. Ryan noted that "there have been arguments of academicians being "opportunistic intellectuals" who use the study of less privileged [groups] for economic and professional advancement [without] challenging the status quo (p. 97). Fester (1998) called these kinds of research engagements "academic colonialism" (p. 226). When I heard his comment, I wondered whether I was being an "academic colonizer?" How do I give back? In giving back will I be trading the "giving back" with their voices? How to give back remains a pertinent question for me. Nonetheless, this research was extremely educational, and I believe that universities, government and other institutions would draw on the findings to inform their practice, policy formulation and future research.

In spite of these limitations the study is strong in terms of drawing on a combination of frameworks, from diverse research participants' input, and from triangulating the results to understand the marginalization of a vulnerable group of students in higher education. The study's strengths also lies in bringing to light the marginalized voices of disabled women students, an aspect lacking in many of the research studies on higher education in Kenya.

As for future research, I will frame my suggestions in the form of questions to encourage further thoughts, research and practice. To start with, research results show that lack of finances contributed to limited access, participation and completion of university education for many disabled women. Many women suggested that there are disabled women in the community who would like to further their education but who cannot afford the costs. How is the government and postsecondary institutions in Kenya to address this challenge? The women and university officials explained that the government extends HELB loans to disabled students but these loans are insufficient to meet their tuition needs. This is because the majority of them join university as self-sponsored students. Should disabled students be allowed to join university as JAB students as part of the affirmative action policy? What would that mean for both disabled and non-disabled students (favoritism/compromising educational standards)? Findings from this study also demonstrated that the problem of access more often than not begins at the secondary school levels. What effect would the government considerations on subsidizing secondary education fees have on these students' access to postsecondary education? The government has put in place structures, such as HELB and CDF, to assist students from low income background to meet their education costs. How has the introduction of these programs impacted access to post secondary education for disabled students? Can such programs be extended to secondary schools?

Results also reveal variations in the degree and quality of support offered to disabled students in the two universities. Ongozi University seemed to have fairly well thought-out structures, compared to Khafee University. What lesson can other institutions learn from these findings? What would a model inclusive higher education institution in Kenya look like? How might inclusive policies be used to transform barriers to access for disabled women students? How best can disability be included, not only in higher education curriculum, but also in that of other levels of education?

How do universities plan to address questions relating to representation of disabled persons in their administration and service provision? At the University of Ongozi, findings demonstrated that more attention is paid to visually impaired students, compared to other disabled students. How would this concern be addressed?

This study focused on access and on participation of disabled students in public universities in Kenya. How do private universities compare with public ones in their approaches and policies to support disabled students?

Thinking of cultural/indigenous knowledge, what role can indigenous knowledge play in improving the lives of disabled persons and women in particular in Kenya? Given that in indigenous societies women had their own ways of excelling that were disrupted by colonial structures, can this be reclaimed in contemporary Kenya? How can its reclamation benefit disabled women? Studies addressing these questions may perhaps help generate an indigenous feminist disability framework that questions knowledge construction and dissemination in the field of disability studies. Although I drew on the African feminist framework that captures some aspects of history and indigenous knowledge, it was not conclusive and did not clearly address aspects such as ethnicity and religion.

Most of the students interviewed had visible disabilities, except for one who had epilepsy. Studies have shown that many disabled students with invisible disabilities are reluctant to self declare their disabilities because of fear that "coming out" (Kallen, 1989; Linton, 1998) might jeopardize their applications (Baron et al., 1996; Borland & James, 1999). This observation was also made by Akil of the University of Khafee who noted that students with mental illnesses seldom come for support to their office. How can universities address this fear?

Notable findings relating to informal mentorship emerged in discussions relating to interpersonal relations. Research, especially from North American contexts, has shown that formal mentoring programs promote retention and success of minority students (LaVant, Anderson & Tiggs, 1997). Although this finding can be generalized to draw conclusions that mentorship contributes to disabled women students' success in university education in Kenya, there is a need for further research to determine what structure of mentoring would work best for disabled students and by whom, before drawing comparative conclusions.

Since oppression of disabled students appears through the whole education system, further research – perhaps longitudinal in nature – should examine whether there are any changes in education access for disabled students, following the introduction of free primary education in 2003. Would there be more, do we have more disabled primary school graduates? Did the introduction of free primary education impact on the gendered and ableist attitude toward education provision in families? Are more disabled students, especially women, transitioning to secondary schools and to post-secondary institutions?

Lastly, while the women's narratives pointed to their interaction with non-governmental organizations and bodies such as the World Bank, this study did not examine the role of these actors in providing services to disabled people in the country or how they contribute to addressing the challenge of education access and its implications on disabled people. Future research should consider a critical analysis of the roles and approaches of these organizations in relation to disability discrimination.

RECOMMENDATIONS

Based on the results of this study, there are a number of observations and recommendations that one could make, which are in line with what the study participants alluded to as well. First, there is a need to acknowledge that disability is not inability. With proper supports, disabled students can equally perform/achieve academically.

Moreover, there is a need to acknowledge that access to higher education for disabled women is not only a question of justice but also democracy (Olsson & Ullenius, 2001, p. 87). Higher education will help empower disabled women, provide them with role models and also give them a visibility in the academic arena as well as society in general (Olsson & Ullenius, 2001, p. 87). Therefore, there is a need for universities to review their practices and to put in place policies that promote inclusion of disabled women students in universities as also suggested by Losinsky et al (2003). These policies should take into account curriculum; pedagogy; assessment practices; the equipment that students need to enhance learning; physical access, attitudinal barriers; finances; technology, etc. (see also Barton, 1998).

The practice of full and equal inclusion of disabled women students in higher education in Kenya is in itself significant in gender education reforms in the country. Kenyan universities have a special role to play in fully engaging disabled women in all aspects of higher education if "real" reforms and inclusion are to be attained (see Bond, 1997, p. 2). Curriculum is particularly key because, while it is great to have a standard curriculum for all public schools and in universities (standard curriculum for programs being offered), it is not feasible to expect the same end results for the diverse students enrolled in these schools (Ntarangwi, 2003, p. 219). There is need to take into account students' diverse learning needs and to address them accordingly. University leaders (administrators) have a role to play here. As Bond (2001) remarked, "leadership exercised by persons of significant influence is a force that guides and can shape the institution" (p. 81). If the administrators take a lead role in addressing disability issues, other members of the university community are likely to follow their footsteps. This is because "leadership responsibility resides both in the position and with the individual who holds the office at any point in time" (Bond 2001, p. 81).

Findings also show that great interpersonal relations made disabled students feel more comfortable and part of the university. Good relations also helped instill confidence in these students, thus contributing to improved self-esteem. There is urgent need for immediate development of policies and provision of disability awareness workshops within the university. This will help to improve student-student, student-faculty, student-staff relationships as a means to instill confidence and to support disabled students' academic progress (see MacFadgen, 2008). Considering that my research focused on educational institutions, I argue that teacher training and faculty and students need further sensitization and awareness about disability so that when they graduate and go out to the schools to teach, they promote inclusion and offer appropriate guidance and counseling to disabled students.

Kenyan universities should also make accessibility the cornerstone of any meaningful developments they embark on. Physical access issues were raised by the disabled women students as posing significant barriers to their success in university. These challenges need action from both the government and the universities. Therefore, in addition to the existing Persons with Disabilities Act (2003), there is need for a comprehensive policy that emphasizes the implementation of Universal Design rule both by the universities and government. This would advocate for making all buildings accessible, starting from government/public offices/institutions and educational institutions, be they private or public. These policies/ recommendations should be enforced through parliamentary legislation and should be taken seriously with a time frame, and with resources provided to carry out the for the required renovations to improve access to buildings in universities and government offices. These changes should be accompanied by government directives to housebuilders to build more accessible homes. They should also encourage landlords to convert the existing rental buildings into accessible spaces (see Barnes, 1990, p. 150).

Many disabled students graduate from university and seldom find employment. There is a need for transition programs to the job market. Such programs may entail setting up structured mentoring programs that hook up disabled and non-disabled senior students/graduates/those in the job market to help reduce discouragement and self-esteem issues; negative perceptions; stereotypes and prejudices. Such programs should be formalized in the universities to help disabled students.

Policies to foster inclusion of disabled people into mainstream society in Kenya are important, but they must target the participation of disabled people in their formulations and implementation. Although it is understandable that the government may not have sufficient resources to bring about radical changes in the lives of disabled people (see Barnes & Mercer, 2003, p. 145), there has to be a will to make changes. Disabled people's participation in society cannot be effective without institutional and government commitment to creating conducive and enabling environments to promote this participation. Most important is to utilize disabled people's experiences and expertise in these developments.

NOTES

(Endnotes)

1 Often times when the government of Kenya talks about disability and education, they have in mind the "special education approach". Special needs education targets vulnerable and disadvantaged children including those with disabilities, children with exceptionally difficult circumstances such as those living in streets, child labourers, abused children and those in correctional services; children of nomadic/pastoral communities and displaced/refugee children (Republic of Kenya, 2006; 2004).

2 Note that there are other models of disability – cultural, psychological, charity, administrative, political (Oliver, 1996) but in this discussion, I focus on the medical and social models which are the most widely discussed in disability writings.

3 An official language is a language given a special legal status in a particular country, state of other territory. Until 2010, English was designated by law as the official language and was, therefore, the most commonly used language in official settings in the country while Kiswahili was the national language. A nation's official language is the one used in the nation's courts, parliament and administration. A national language, on the other hand, is a language which has some connection – de facto or de jure – with a people. A national language may for instance represent the national identity of a nation or country (http://en.wikipedia.org). Under new Constitution, Kiswahili is now one of the two official languages in Kenya. Section 7 of the new Constitution declares Kiswahili and English as Lugha Rasmi (official languages) in Kenya (Thuku, 2010).

4 Kenya held its third multi-party elections on December 27, 2007 and three days later on December 30, 2007, Mwai Kibaki was declared the winner and sworn in as the president of Kenya. The leader of opposition party Orange Democratic Movement (ODM) Raila Odinga, accused Kibaki of massive rigging and doctoring the presidential results. International observers agreed that the voting was flawed and marked with massive rigging and even Kibaki's own election chief Mr. Samuel Kivuitu indicated in a press statement that he acted under pressure and was not sure who won the elections. Hours after Kibaki's declaration, violence erupted in most parts of Kenya, leaving over several people dead, thousands injured, hundred of thousands homeless and property worth millions of shillings in ruins allafrica.com/stories/200801110511.html). The violence continued

in spite of efforts and calls from the African Union (AU) and the international community to end the violence. Attempts by the AU chair John Kufuor to get the government and opposition to talk in early January failed and he handed over the task to former UN Secretary-General Kofi Annan. On January 22, 2008, Kofi Annan arrived in Kenya to mediate talks and in February 2008, an agreement was reached in which the post of a Prime Minister was created leading to the formation of a coalition government.

5 Some scholars have, however, argued that much of the commissions were set up whenever there was pressure to address educational issues in the country. For example, Amutabi (2003) observed that many of the education committees and commissions in Kenya appear to be appointed as response to certain pressures and crises to wade off public concern. This is because there was, and still is, a tendency to put aside the commission reports after the crises or pressure was over and, therefore, in most cases little or no action was taken with regard to the recommendations made (p. 141). There has been thus a sense of politicization of decision making in the education sector in Kenya since independence. Hence, the crises in the education sector in Kenya we see today (Amutabi, 2003).

6 It took the KANU government (the party in power then) about a decade to implement the first phase of its declared policy. It was not until December 1973, when the then President Jomo Kenyatta, through a decree, announced free education for the first four years of schooling in primary schools, that is standards (grades) one to four. The decree went further and provided a uniform structure of fees for those pupils in standards five to eight throughout the Republic. In 1978 the second president of Kenya Daniel Arap Moi also issued another directive for an additional free education for standard five to eight virtually declaring free primary education in Kenya (Amutabi, 2003, p. 131-133). This changed however in the early 90s with the introduction of cost-sharing and again changed in 2003 when the NARC government re-introduced free primary education.

7 Beginning the early 80s, parents in Kenya had to pay school fees to send their children to public primary schools in the country. This changed in 2003 when the government introduced free primary education for all. Because school fees were eliminated, more than 1 million children enrolled in public primary schools in Kenya and there have been problems of overcrowded classrooms. Plans are underway to introduce free secondary education for all.

8   The Sessional Paper No.1 of 2005 on " A Policy Framework For Education, Training and Research" aims at meeting the challenges of education, training and research in Kenya in the 21st century and commits the government to providing every Kenyan basic quality education and training (Republic of Kenya/Ministry of Education, 2006)

9   Wesonga et al. (2003) attribute the high enrolment of female students in private universities in Kenya to factors such as courses (most courses offered in these universities are in the humanities and social sciences, and women tend to be over-represented in these areas); the large numbers of female secondary school leavers with minimum university entry grades (C+) who fail to get admission into public universities and thus enroll in private universities; the high levels of discipline and good learning environments in private universities which reassures parents of their daughters' safety in college; and the cost of local private universities is still lower when compared to sending students to foreign universities abroad (p. 23 cited in Onsongo, 2007, p. 119).

10 Even so, some of the disabled women interviewed were in favor of segregated schools particularly during the early primary school years.

11 Maendeleo Ya Wanawake (in English - Progress for Women) is a nationally based organization formed initially in 1952 by a group of white settlers and administrators' wives who sought to advance the status of women according to Western values. They mobilized traditional women's work groups, trained them in childcare, hygiene, cooking, home sanitation, handicrafts, and other traditional activities (Oduol & Kabira, 2002, p. 385). The organization has since grown in membership and in focus. During the KANU regime, MYWO was closely monitored and co-opted by the ruling government so as to win members' support.

12 In Kenya, there are different levels teaching of teachers' training colleges as indicated in chapter two. There are colleges geared towards training primary school teachers only and these offer certificates in primary school; there are colleges that train teacher that can teach in both primary and secondary and are called diploma colleges and there are universities which offer a bachelor of education degree geared towards those interested in teaching primary, high school and college.

13 As discussed in chapter two, self-sponsored or parallel students

are students who join university through the private wing. They obtained a minimum of a C+ or have equivalent qualifications but could not get admission through the Joint Admissions Board so they pay higher tuition and do not qualify for government tuition subsidy.

14 Kenyan universities offer a concurrent degree in education which takes four years.

15 In Kenya, one can join an elementary teachers college for two years and be certified as a primary school teacher or a diploma teacher (after three years of training).

16 Lulu went through the 7-4-2-3 system of education before it was changed into the 8-4-4 in 1985.

17 In Kenya, standard three will be an equivalent of grade three in Canada. At primary (elementary) school level the term *standard* is used while at high school levels the word *form* is used and both imply grade levels.

18 Integrated schools include students with disabilities and those with other special needs with their non-disabled peers in the regular classroom.

19 The Kenya Broadcasting Corporation (KBC) is the state-run media (Radio and Television) organization of Kenya. It is state owned and was established by an Act of Parliament CAP 221 of the laws of Kenya to undertake public services. The main objective of the corporation is to inform, educate and entertain the public through radio and television services and thereby propagate all that consolidates national unity, peace, love and development (http://www.kbc.co.ke/info.asp?ID=1).

20 Subsistent farmers largely produce crops for home consumption and sometimes little surplus for periodical sales in the markets. They engage in seasonal trade and seasonal wage labour. Subsistence farmers largely rely on land as their chief means of production (see Nyakundi, 2005, p. 16).

21 The existing literature has shown that disability can add more strain to what is already a stressful situation (pointing to farming). In addition to the mental, emotional and physical stresses experienced by all farmers and farm families, when a disability occurs the economic viability of the farm may be affected due to the added costs of lifestyle, farm system and equipment modifications for the disabled person (http://www.parl.gc.ca/).

22 In January 2003, the Minister for Education, Science and Technology (MoEST) announced the introduction of Free Primary Education (FPE) in Kenya. All fees and any other tuition levies in public primary schools in Kenya were abolished. The government and development partners were to meet the cost of basic teaching and learning materials as well as wages for critical non-teaching staff and co-curricular activities. With the introduction of FPE, parents and communities were not required to build new schools, but rather refurbish and use existing facilities such as community and religious buildings. If they wished to charge additional levies, school heads and committees had to obtain approval from the MoEST. This request had to be sent to the District Education Board by the Area Education Officer, after a consensus among parents through the Provincial Director of Education, a fairly lengthy and tedious process (see Sifuna, 2005). However, while free primary education has increased participation, it has at the same time created considerable problems. It has exacerbated the problem of teaching and learning facilities. As a result of the high influx of new pupils, classrooms are congested. Many of the preliminary surveys seem to show that the existing facilities make a mockery of the free education program. Many school management committees feel that they are seriously constrained to improve the state of learning facilities due to the government's ban on school levies (see Sifuna, 2005)

23 Losinsky et al. (2003) defined accessibility not simply in terms of access to buildings, but also of the added time and distance by students using wheelchairs on the campus (p. 305).

24 Although there were academic clubs and students' organizations in which the study participants were involved and which sometimes offered support to them, these organizations were not established for mentorship purposes.

25 Some people see religion and spirituality as interconnected aspects while others distinguish them (see Dei, 2002). Some scholars argue that some people derive their spirituality from their religion (Palmer, 1999). Wane (2002), on the other hand, argues that spirituality is a natural process of life, a personal enterprise that is not to be achieved by reading books. Wane further suggests that, given the complexities entailed in defining spirituality, it is important that we view it in the context within which it is sustained and cultivated or used (p. 277). In this study, I use the two terms interchangeably to refer to a sense of wholeness and connection to

a higher source of power or being (see Miller, 1999; Palmer, 1999). This is because, from the interviews, the women indicated that their religious beliefs informed their spirituality.

26 HELB – The Higher Education Loans Board was established by an Act of Parliament (Act number 3 of 1995). At its introduction, only students at public universities were eligible for HELB loans. In July 2008, the government announced that all Kenyan students in university would be eligible for the loans (Otieno & Lauler, 2008). It would be interesting to find out how this loans provision has impacted disabled students' participation in university.

27 Tuk tuks are motorized rickshaws (three wheeler motor vehicles) commonly used as a mode of transportation (especially for taxi business) in India and Thailand. They are popular amongst tourists for their novelty value. Tuk tuks are occasionally faster than taxis in heavy traffic as weaving in and out is easier, but generally about the same or slower (http://www.into-asia.com/bangkok/tuktuk/).

Bibliography

Abagi, O. (1997). *Status of education in Kenya: Indicators for planning and policy formulation*. Nairobi: The Institute of Policy Analysis and Research.

Abagi, O., Owino, W., Sifuna, D. N., Waga, M., Ngome, C., Aduda, D., et al. (2000). *Implementing the report of the commission of inquiry into the education system of Kenya (The Koech Report): Realities, challenges and prospects*. Nairobi: Institute of Policy Analysis and Research. IPAR Special Report No. 3.

Abang, T. (1988). Disablement, disability and the Nigerian society. *Disability, Handicap & Society, 3*(1), 71-77.

Abberley, P. (1987). The concept of oppression and the development of a social theory of disability. *Disability, Handicap, and Society, 2*(1), 5-19.

Acker, S. (1992). New perspectives on an old problem: The position of women academics in British higher education. *Higher Education, 24*(1), 57-75.

Acker, S. (1994). *Gendered education: Sociological reflections on women, teaching and feminism*. Buckingham: Open University Press.

Acker, S. (1995). Carry on caring: The work of women teachers. *British Journal of Sociology of Education, 16*(1), 21-26.

Acker, S. (1999). Caring as work for women educators. In E. Smyth, S. Acker, P. Bourne & A. Prentice (Eds.), *Challenging professions: Historical and contemporary perspectives on women's professional work* (pp. 277-295). Toronto: University of Toronto Press.

Adeleye-Fayemi, B. (2004). Gender, sexuality, and popular culture in Nigeria. *Passages: A Chronicle of the Humanities, 8*, 1-2.

Adeyemi, M. B. & Adeyinka, A. A. (2002). Some key issues in African traditional education. *McGill Journal of Education, 37*(2), 223-240.

African Union of the Blind (AFUB), the Kenya Union of the Blind (KUB) & the Centre for Disability Rights, Education and Advocacy (CREAD) (2007). *State of disabled peoples' rights in Kenya (2007)*. Retrieved October 5, 2008 from http://www.yorku.ca/drpi/files/KenyaReport07.pdf.

Ainlay, S. C., Becker, G., & Coleman, L. M. (1986). *The dilemma of difference: A multidisciplinary view of stigma*. New York: Plenum Press.

Akatsa-Bukachi, M. (2005). *African feminism does it exist?* Paper presented at the Tanzania Gender Networking Program Gender Festival, September 5, 2005. Dar es Salaam, Tanzania.

Alder, N. (2002). Interpretations of the meaning of care: Creating caring relationships in urban middle school classrooms. *Urban Education, 37*(2), 241-266.

Al-haji, H. H. (n.d.). *Woman kind Kenya.* Memorandum presented to the Special Rapporteur on the Situation of Human Rights & Fundamental Freedoms of Indigenous Peoples in North Eastern Province, Kenya. Retrieved March 14, 2007 from http://www.wunrn.com/ news/2006/12_11_06/121806_kenya_special.html.

Allan, E. J. & Madden, M. (2006). Chilly classrooms for female undergraduate students: A question of method? *Journal of Higher Education, 77*(4), 684-711.

Amadiume, I. (1987). *Male daughters, female husbands: Gender and sex in an African society.* London: Zed Books.

Amadiume, I. (2000). *Daughters of the goddess, daughters of imperialism: African women, culture, power and democracy.* London: Zed Books.

Amosun, S. L., Volmink, L. & Rosin, R. (2005). Perceived images of disability: The reflection of two undergraduate medical students in a university in South Africa on life in a wheelchair. *Disability and Rehabilitation, 27*(14), 961-966.

Amutabi, M. N. (2003). Political interference in the running of education in post-independence Kenya: A critical retrospection. *International Journal of Educational Development, 23*(2), 127-144.

Anderson, D. W. (2004). *Human rights and persons with disabilities in developing nations of Africa.* Paper presented at the fourth annual Lilly Fellows Program National Research Conference on "Christianity and Human Rights", November 13, 2004. Samford University, Birmingham.

Anderson, G. (1989). Critical ethnography in education: Origins, current status and new directions. *Review of Educational Research, 59*(3), 249-270.

Anderson, J. (1970). *The struggle for the school.* London: Longman.

Apple, W. M. (1995). *Education and power.* (2nd ed.). New York: Routledge.

Apple, W. M. (2004). *Ideology and curriculum* (3rd ed.). New York: Routledge.

Ash, A., Bellew, J., Davies, M., Newman, T. & Richardson, L. (1997). Everybody in? The experience of disabled students in further education, *Disability & Society, 12*(4), 605-621.

Asch, A., & Fine, M. (1988). Introduction: Beyond pedestals. In M. Fine, & A. Asch (Eds.), *Women with disabilities: Essays in psychology, culture, and politics* (pp. 1-37). Philadelphia: Temple University Press.

Baldacchino, D. & Draper, P. (2001). Spiritual coping strategies: A review of the nursing research literature. *Journal of Advanced Nursing, 34*(6), 833-841.

Ball, S. (1990). *Foucault and education.* London: Routledge.

Baker, J. A. (1999). Teacher-student interaction in urban at-risk classrooms: Differential behaviour, relationship quality and student satisfaction with school. *The Elementary School Journal, 100*(1), 57-70.

Barile, M. (1996). Education and employment for the next millennium. *Women's Education des Femmes, 12* (2), 42-45.

Barnes, C. (1990). *Cabbage syndrome: The social construction of dependence.* Falmer: Lewes.

Barnes, C. (1996). Theories of disability and the origins of the oppression of disabled people in western society. In L. Barton (Ed.), *Disability and society: Emerging issues and insights,* (pp. 43-60). Harlow, Essex: Addison Wesley Longman Ltd.

Barnes, C. & Mercer, G. (2003). *Disability.* Cambridge: Polity.

Barnes, C., Mercer, G. & Shakespeare, T. (1999). *Exploring disability: A sociological introduction.* Cambridge: Polity Press.

Barnes, C., Oliver, M., Barton, L. (2002). Disability, the academy and the inclusive society. In C. Barnes, M. Oliver & L. Barton (Eds.), *Disability studies today* (pp. 250-260). Cambridge: Polity Press.

Baron, S., Phillips, R., & Stalker, K. (1996). Barriers to training for disabled social work students. *Disability & Society, 11*(3), 361-378.

Barton, L. (1998). Sociology, disability studies and education: Some observations. In T. Shakespeare (Ed.), *The disability reader* (pp. 53-64). London: Continuum.

Basse, M. (2010).*Census: Kenya has 38.6m people.* Retrieved November, 17, 2010 from http://www.nation.co.ke/News/-/1056/1000340/-/11114rlz/-/index.html

Becker, G. & Arnold, R. (1986). Stigma as a social and cultural construct. In: S. C. Ainlay; G. Becker & L. M. Coleman (Eds.), *The dilemma of difference: A multidisciplinary view of stigma* (pp. 39-57). New York: Plenum Press.

Belousa, I (2006). Defining spirituality in education: A post-soviet perspective, In M. de Souza, G. Durka, K. Engebretson, R. Jackson & A. McGrady. (Eds.), *International handbook of the religious, moral and spiritual dimensions in education* (pp. 215-230). New York: Springer.

Beoku-Betts, J. N. & Njambi, N. W. (2005). African feminist scholars in women's studies: Negotiating spaces of dislocation and transformation in the study of women. *Meridians: feminism, race, transnationalism, 6*(1), 113-132.

Bensimon, E. M. & Marshall, C. (1997). Policy analysis for postsecondary education: Feminist and critical perspectives. In C. Marshall (Ed.), *Feminist critical policy analysis: A perspective from post-secondary education* (pp. 1-21). London: Falmer Press.

Beresford, P. (1996). Poverty and disabled people: Challenging dominant debates and policy. *Disability & Society, 11*, 553–567.

Berndt, T. J. (1999). Friends' influence on students' adjustment to school. *Educational Psychologist, 34*, 15-28.

Bickenbach, J. (1993*). Physical disability and social policy.* Toronto: University of Toronto Press.

Boateng, F. (1983). African traditional education: A method of disseminating cultural values. *Journal of Black Studies, 13*(3), 321-336.

Bogdan, R. C., & Bilken, S. K. (1998). *Qualitative research for education: An introduction to theory and methods* (3rd ed.). Boston: Allyn and Bacon.

Bogonko, S. N. (1992). *A history of modern education in Kenya 1985-1991*. Nairobi: Evans Brothers.

Bond, S. (1997). *Service and self-respect: Women leaders in Latin American universities* (UNESCO Report ED-97/WS-41). Paris: UNESCO. Retrieved January 29, 2009 from http://unesdoc.unesco.org/images/0010/001091/109169Eo.pdf.

Bond, S. (2001). Culture and feminine leadership. In M. L. Kearney (Ed.), *Women, power and the academy: From rhetoric to reality* (pp. 79-85). Paris: Berghahn Books.

Borland, J., & James, S. (1999). The learning experience of students with disabilities in higher education. A case study of a U. K. University. *Disability & Society, 14*(1), 85-101.

Borman, G. D., & Overman, L. T. (2004). Academic resilience in mathematics among poor and minority students. *The Elementary School Journal, 104*(3), 177-195.

Boylan, E. (1991). *Women and disability*. London: Zed Books.

Boxall, K., Carson, I. & Docherty, D. (2004). Room at the academy? People with learning difficulties and higher education. *Disability and Society, 19*(4), 99-112.

Brigham, M. (2007). *An evening of serenity: Warming to the intersections of difference - circles of stories, knowledge, and laughter*. Paper presented at the departmental research series, Department of Sociology and Equity Studies in Education, Ontario Institute for Studies in Education, University of Toronto, February 16, 2007.

Brisenden, S. (1986). Independent living and the medical model of disability. *Disability and Society, 1*(2), 173-178.

Brueggemann, B. J., Garland-Thomson, R. & Snyder, S. L. (2002). Introduction. In S. L. Snyder, B. J. Brueggemann & R. Garland-Thomson

(Eds.), *Disability studies: Enabling the humanities* (pp. 1-12). New York: The Modern Language Association of America.

Buchmann, C. (1996). The debt crisis, structural adjustment and women's education: Implications for status and social development. *International Journal of Comparative Sociology, 37*(1/2), 5-30.

Bunyi, G.W. (2004a). Gender disparities in higher education in Kenya: Nature, extent and the way forward. *The African Symposium, 4*(1). Retrieved May 21, 2007 from http://www2.ncsu.edu/ncsu/aern/gendaedu.html.

Bunyi, G. W. (2004b). Interventions that increase enrolment of women in African tertiary institutions. *The African Symposium, 4*(3). Retrieved May, 19, 2007 from http://siteresources.worldbank.org/INTAFRREGTOPTEIA/Resources/grace_bunyi.pdf.

Burgstahler, S., & Cronheim, D. (2001). Supporting peer-peer and mentor-protégé relationships on the internet. *Journal of Research on Technology in Education, 34*(1), 59-74.

Burton, J. L. & McDonald, S. (2001). Curriculum or syllabus: Which are we reforming? *Medical Teacher, 23*(2), 187-191.

Butler, J. (1993). *Bodies that matter: On the discursive limits of sex.* New York: Routledge.

Cannella, G. S. (1999). The scientific discourse of education: Predetermining the lives of others - Foucault, education and children. *Contemporary Issues in Early Childhood, 1*(1), 36-44.

Carlson, L. (2005). Docile bodies, docile minds: Foucauldian reflections on mental retardation. In S. Tremain (Ed.), *Foucault, governmentality and critical disability theory* (pp. 133-152). Michigan: University of Michigan Press.

Carpenter, W. M. (1996). Female grotesques in academia: Ageism, antifeminism and feminists on the faculty. In V. Clark, S. Garner, M. Higonnet & K. Katrak (Eds.), *Anti-feminism in the academy* (pp. 141-165). New York: Routledge.

Cavet, J. (2000). It's a delicate thing: Coping with a hidden disability in mainstream schools. *British Journal of Special Education, 27*(3), 154-159.

Ceballo, R. (2004). From barrios to Yale: The role of parenting strategies in Latino families. *Hispanic Journal of Behavioral Sciences, 26*(2), 171-186.

Charlton, J. I. (1998). *Nothing about us without us: Disability oppression and empowerment.* Berkeley: University of California Press.

Chege, F. (2001). *Gender values, schooling and transition to adulthood: A study of female and male pupils in two urban primary schools in Kenya.* Unpublished doctoral book, University of Cambridge, U.K.

Chege, F. & Sifuna, D. N. (2006). *Girls' and women's education in Kenya: Gender perspectives and trends.* Nairobi: UNESCO.

Chieni, S. N. (n.d.). *The harambee movement in Kenya: The role played by Kenyans and the government in the provision of education and other social services*. Retrieved April 4, 2007 from http://boleswa97.tripod.com/chieni.htm.

Chimedza, R. (2000). *A situation analysis of children with disabilities in Zimbabwe*. Harare: UNICEF.

Chimedza, R. & Peters, S. (2001). *Disability and special needs education in an African context*. Harare: College Press.

Christenson, S. L. & Havsy, L. H. (2004). Family-school-peer relationships: Significance for social, emotional and academic learning. In Zins, J. E., Weissberg, R. P., Wang, M. C. & Walberg, H. J. (Eds.), *Building academic success on social and emotional learning: What does research say?* (pp. 59-75). New York: Teachers College Press.

Coates, R. D. (2008). Covert racism in U. S. A. today and globally. *Sociology Compass, 2*(1), 208-231.

Coleman, J. (1988). Social capital in the creation of human capital. *American Journal of Sociology, 94,* 94-120.

Coleridge, P. (1993). *Disability, liberation and development*. Oxford: Oxfam Publications.

Collins, P. H. (1998). *Black feminist thought: Knowledge, consciousness, and the politics of empowerment*. Boston: UnwinHyman.

Collins, P. H. (2000). Gender, black feminism, and black political economy. *Annals of the American Academy of Political and Social Science, 568*(1), 41-53.

Corrigan, P. (1998). The impact of stigma on severe mental illness. *Cognitive and Behavioral Practice, 5,* 201-222.

Creswell, J. W. (2005). *Educational research: Planning, conducting, and evaluating quantitative and qualitative research*. Upper Saddle River, NJ: Pearson Education.

Crosnoe, R. (2002). High school curriculum track and adolescent association with delinquent friends. *Journal of Adolescent Research, 17*(2), 144-168.

Crosnoe, R., Johnson, K. M. & Elder, G. H. (2004). Intergenerational bonding in school: The behavioral and contextual correlates of student-teacher relationships. *Sociology of Education, 77*(1), 60-81.

Danaher, G., Schirato, T., & Webb, J. (2000). *Understanding Foucault*. London: Sage Publications.

Darling-Hammond, L. (2000). *Solving the dilemmas of teacher supply, demand, and standards: How we can ensure a competent, caring, and qualified teacher for every child*. Kutztown, PA: National Commission on

Teaching and America's Future. (ERIC Document Reproduction Service No. ED463337).

Davis, L. J. (2002). *Bending over backwards: Disability, dismodernism and other difficult positions.* New York: New York University Press.

DAWN Ontario (n.d.). *Factsheets on women with disabilities.* Retrieved January 26, 2007 from http://dawn.thot.net/fact.html.

de Klerk, H. M. & Ampousah, L. (2003). Perceived images of disability: The reflections of two undergraduate medical students in a university in South Africa on life in a wheelchair. *Disability & Rehabilitation, 27*(16), 961-966.

Deal, M. (2007). Aversive disablism: Subtle prejudice toward disabled people, *Disability & Society, 22*(1), 93-107.

Dear, M., Wilton, R., Gaber, S., & Takahashi, L. (1997). Seeing people differently: The sociospatial construction of disability. *Environment and Planning Development: Society and Space, 15*(4), 455-480.

Deci, E. L., & Ryan, R. M. (1985). *Intrinsic motivation and self-determination in human behavior.* New York: Plenum.

Dei, G. J. S. (1996a). *African development: The relevance and implications of indigenousness.* Paper presented at the Learned Societies' meeting of the Canadian Association for the Study of International Development (CASID), Brock University, St. Catharines, Ontario, May 31 - June 2, 1996.

Dei, G. J. S. (1996b). *Anti-racism: Theory and practice.* Halifax: Fernwood.

Dei, G. J. S., James, I. M., Karumanchery, L. L., James-Wilson, S., & Zine, J. (2000). *Removing the margins: The challenges and possibilities of inclusive schooling.* Toronto: Canadian Scholars' Press.

Dei, G. J. S. (2002). Spirituality in African education: Issues, contentions and contestations from a Ghanaian case study. *International Journal of Children's Spirituality, 7*(1), 37-36.

Dei, G. J. S. (2004). *Schooling and education in Africa: The case of Ghana.* Trenton, NJ: Africa World Press.

Dei, G. J. S. (2007). Thinking and responding to difference: Pedagogical challenges for African education. In A. Mazama (Ed.), *Africa in the 21st century: Toward a new future* (pp. 99-130). New York: Routledge.

Dei, G. J. S., Asgharzadeh, A., Eblaghie-Bahador, S. & Shahjahan, R. (2006). *Schooling and difference in Africa: Democratic challenges in a contemporary context.* Toronto: University of Toronto Press.

Dei, G. J. S. & Shahjahan, R. (2008). Equity and democratic education in Ghana: Towards a pedagogy of difference. In J. Zaida, L. Davis & S. Majhanovich (Eds.), *Comparative and global pedagogies: Equity, access and democracy in education* (pp. 49-70). Netherlands: Kluwer Publishers.

Dennis, J. M., Phinney, J. S., & Chuateco, L. I. (2005). The role of motivation, parental support and peer support in the academic success of ethnic minority first-generation college students. *Journal of College Student Development, 46*(3), 223-236.

Deveaux, M. (1994). Feminism and empowerment: A critical reading of Foucault. *Feminist Studies, 20*(2), 223-247.

Driedger, D. (1996). Emerging from the shadows: Women with disabilities organize. In D. Driedger, I. Feika & E. G. Batres (Eds.), *Across borders: Women with disabilities working together* (pp. 10-26). Charlottetown: Gynergy books.

Duquette, C. (2000a). Experiences at university: Perceptions of students with disabilities. *The Canadian Journal of Higher Education, 30*(2), 123-142.

Durst, D. & Bluechardt, M. (2001). *Urban Aboriginal persons with disabilities: Triple jeopardy!* University of Regina Social Policy Research Unit. Retrieved August 23, 2007 from http://www.uregina.ca/spru/spruweb/spru_research.htm#NATIONS.

Eisenberg, M. G. (1982). Disability as stigma. In G. M. Eisenberg, C. Griggins & R. Duval (Eds.), *Disabled people as second-class citizens* (pp. 3-5). New York: Springer Publishing Company.

Eisemon, T. (1992). Private initiatives in higher education in Kenya. *Higher Education, 24*(2), 157-175.

Elimu Yetu Coalition (2007). *Statement on the status of education access in Kenya during the global week of action campaign for education 2007.* Retrieved March 18 2008 from http://www.education.nairobi-unesco.org/PDFs/Elimu%20Yetu%20Coalition%20statement%20GAW-2007.pdf.

Erevelles, N. (2005). Re-conceptualizing curriculum as "normalizing" text: Disability studies meets curriculum theory. *Journal of Curriculum Studies, 37*(4), 421-439.

Erwin, L. & Maurutto, P. (1998). Beyond access: Considering gender deficits in science education. *Gender and Education, 10*(1), 51-69.

Eshiwani, G. S. (1983). *Who goes to university in Kenya: A study of the background of Kenyan undergraduate students.* Nairobi: Bureau of Educational Research.

Eshiwani, G. S. (1984). *The education of women in Kenya, 1975-1984.* (ERIC Document Reproduction Service No. ED 284802).

Eshiwani, G. S. (1993). *A study of women's access to education in Kenya with special reference to mathematics and science.* (ERIC Document Reproduction Service No. ED 284802).

Esu, A. & Junaid, A. (2008). *Educational development: Traditional and contemporary.* Retrieved January 10, 2008 from http://www.onlinenigeria.com/finance/?blurb=536.

European Mollecular Biology Organization [EMBO] (2007). *Gender roles and not gender bias hold back women scientists.* Retrieved January 4, 2008 from http://www.uni-protokolle.de/nachrichten/id/147227/.

Fawcett, B. (2000). *Feminist perspectives on disability.*Harlow: Prentice Hall Pearson Education.

Ferri, B. A., & Gregg, N. (1998). Women with disabilities: Missing voices. *Women's Studies International Forum, 21*(4), 429-439.

Fester, G. (1998). Closing the gap – academic activism and academia in South Africa: Towards a women's movement. In O. Nnaemeka (Ed.), *Sisterhood, feminism and power: From Africa to the diaspora* (pp. 215-238). Trenton, NJ. African World Press.

Field, S., Martin, J., Miller, R., Ward, M, & Wehmeyer, M. (1998). *A practical guide for teaching self-determination.* Reston, VA: Council for Exceptional Children.

Field, S., Sarver, M., & Shaw, S. (2003). Self-determination: A key to success in postsecondary education for students with learning disabilities. *Remedial and Special Education, 24*(6), 339-349.

Finkelstein, V. (1998). Emancipating disability studies. In T. Shakespeare (Ed.), *The disability reader* (pp. 28-52). London: Continuum.

Finkelstein, V. (2004). Representing disability. In J. Swain, S. French, C. Barnes & C. Thomas (Eds.), *Disabling barriers – enabling environments* (pp. 13-20). London: Sage Publications.

Finn, J. D. & Achilles, C. M. (1999). Tennessee's class size study: Findings, implications, misconceptions. *Educational Evaluation and Policy Analysis, 21*(2), 97-109.

28 Foucault, M. (1974). *The archaeology of knowledge and the discourse on language,* translated from the French by A. M. Sheridan Smith. New York: Pantheon Books.

Foucault, M. (1975). *The birth of the clinic: An archeology of medical perception.* A. M. Sheridan Smith, trans. New York: Vintage Books.

Foucault, M. (1977/1995). *Discipline and punish: The birth of the prison.* New York: Vintage Books.

Foucault, M. (1980). *Power/knowledge and other writings 1972-1977.* New York: Pantheon Books.

Foucault, M. (1982). The subject and power. In H. Dryfus & P. Rabinow (Eds.), Michel *Foucault: Beyond structuralism and hermeneutics* (pp. 208-226). London: Harvester Wheatsheaf.

Freire, P. (1994). *Pedagogy of hope: Reliving pedagogy of the oppressed.* New York: Continuum.

French, S. (1993). Can you see the rainbow? The roots of denial. In J. Swain, V. Finkelstein, S. French & M. Oliver (Eds.), *Disabling barriers*

- *Enabling environments* (pp. 69-77). Thousand Oaks, CA: Sage Publications.

French, S., Swain, J, & Reynolds, F. (2007). *Understanding disability: A guide to health professionals.* Churchill Livingstone: Elsevier.

Frieden, L. (2003). *People with disabilities and postsecondary education.* Retrieved June 15, 2004, from http://www.ncd.gov/newsroom/publications/education.html.

Froschl, M., Rubin, E. & Sprung, B. (1999). *Connecting gender and disability.* Retrieved May 18, 2007 from, www2.edc.org/WomensEquity/pdffiles/disabdig.pdf.

Fulton, S., & Sabornie, E. (1994). Evidence of employment inequality among females with disabilities. *Journal of Special Education,* 28(2), 149-165.

Gall, J. P., Gall, M. D., & Borg, W. R. (2005). *Applying educational research: A practical guide* (5th ed.). New York: Longman.

Garland-Thomson, R. (1997). *Extraordinary bodies: Figuring physical disability in American culture and literature.* New York: Columbia University Press.

Garland-Thomson, R. (2002). The politics of staring: Visual rhetorics of disability in popular photography. In S. L. Snyder, B. J. Bruggeman & R. Garland-Thomson (Eds.), *Disability studies: Enabling the humanities* (pp. 56-75). New York: The Modern Languages Association Press.

Gary, L. E. & Booker, C. B. (1992). Empowering African Americans to achieve academic success. *NASSP Bulletin, 76*(546), 50-55.

Gathenya, W. T. (2003). *Alternative education: Provisions for "street children" in Kenya.* Unpublished doctoral book, University of Toronto.

Geda, A., de Jong, N., Mwabu, G. & Kimenyi, M. S. (2005). *Determinants of poverty in Kenya: A household level analysis.* Department of Economics Working Papers, University of Connecticut. Retrieved July 4, 2008 from http://digitalcommons.uconn.edu/cgi/viewcontent.cgi?article=1050&context=econ_wpapers.

Gerschick, T. J. (2000). Towards a theory of disability and gender. *Signs* 25(4), 1263-1269

Ghai, A. (2003). *(Dis)Embodied form: Issues of disabled women.* New Delhi: Har-Anand Publications.

Gilson, S. F., & DePoy, E. (2002). Theoretical approaches to disability content in social work education. *Journal of Social Work Education, 38*(1), 153-165.

Glesne, C. (1999). *Becoming qualitative researchers: An introduction.* New York: Addison Wesley Longman.

Glesne, C. & Peshkin, A. (1992). *Becoming qualitative researchers: An introduction.* White Plains, NY: Longman.

Goffman, E. (1963). *Stigma: Notes on the management of spoiled identity.* Englewood Cliffs, NJ: Prentice Hall.

Goode, J. (2007). Managing disability: Early experiences of university students with disabilities. *Disability and Society, 22*(1), 35-48.

Goodley, D. (2001). Learning difficulties, the social model of disability and impairment: Challenging epistemologies. *Disability & Society, 16*(2), 207-231.

Goodenow, C., & Grady, K. E. (1993). The relationship of school belonging and friends' values to academic motivation among urban adolescent students. *Journal of Exceptional Education, 62,* 60-71.

Groce, N. E. (1999). General issues in research on local concepts and beliefs about disability. In B. Holzer, A. Vreede & G. Weigt (Eds.), *Disability in different cultures* (pp. 285-296). New Brunswick: Transaction Publishers.

Hall, R. M., & Sandler, B. (1982). *The classroom climate: A chilly one for women?* Project on the Status and Education of Women. Washington, D.C.: Association of American Colleges.

Hasselbring, T. S. & Glaser, C. W. (2000). Use of computer technology to help students with special needs. *The Future of Children, 10*(2), 1-21.

Hattam, R. (2000). *Becoming somebody without school.* Paper presented at the Australian Association for Research in Education (AARE) Conference, Sydney. Retrieved May 2, 2007 from http://www.aare.edu.au/00pap/hat00013.htm.

Hay, C. M. (2005). Women standing between life and death: Fate, agency and the healers of Lombok. In L. Parker (Ed.), *The agency of women in Asia* (pp. 26-61). Times Center, Singapore: Marshall Candevish Academic.

Hibbs, T. & Pothier, D. (2006). Post-secondary education and disabled students: Mining a level playing field or playing in a minefield? In D. Pothier & D. Richard (Eds.), *Critical disability theory: Essays in philosophy, politics, policy, and law* (pp. 195-222). Vancouver: UBC Press.

Holloway, S. (2001). The experience of higher education from the perspective of disabled students. *Disability & Society, 18*(4), 597-615.

hooks, b. (1988). *Talking back: Thinking feminist, thinking Black.* Toronto: Between the Lines.

hooks, b. (1992). *Black looks: Race and representation.* Boston, MA : South End Press.

Hook, D. (2005). Affecting whiteness: Racism as technology of affect. *International Journal of Critical Psychology, 16,* 74-99.

Hops, M. (1996). *Attitudes towards disabled children in Botswana: An action research into the attitudes of students and Batswana in general.* Unpublished Research Project for a Masters Degree in Special

Educational Needs. Utrecht: Hogeschool van Utrecht/ Seminarium voor Orthopedagogiek.

Hovart, E. M. & Lewis, K. S. (2003). Re-assessing the burden of "acting White": The importance of groups in managing academic success. *Sociology of Education 76*(4), 265-280.

Hughes, B. (2005). What can a Foucauldian analysis contribute to disability theory? In S. Tremain (Ed.), *Foucault, governmentality and critical disability theory* (pp. 78–92). Michigan: University of Michigan Press.

Hunt, P. (1998). A critical condition. In T. Shakespeare (Ed.), *The disability reader* (pp. 7 – 19). London: Continuum.

Hurst, A. (1993). *Steps towards graduation: Access to higher education and people with disabilities.* Aldershot: Avebury Press.

Hurtado, S. (1994). The institutional climate for talented Latino students. *Research in Higher Education, 35,* 21-41.

Hurtado, S., Carter, D. F., & Spuler, A. (1996). Latino student transition to college: Assessing difficulties and factors in successful college adjustment. *Research in Higher Education, 37*(2), 135-157.

Imrie, R. (2000). Disability and discourses of mobility and movement. *Environment and Planning, 32*(9), 1641-1656.

Imrie, R. (2005). *Accessible housing: Quality, disability and design.* London: Taylor and Francis.

Imrie, R. & Hall, P. (2001). *Inclusive design: Designing and developing accessible environments.* London: Taylor and Francis.

Imrie, R. & Kumar, M. (1998). Focusing on disability and access in the built environment. *Disability & Society, 13*(3), 357-374.

Ingram, D. & Hutchinson, S. A. (1999). HIV-positive mothers and stigma. *Health Care for Women International, 20,* 93-103.

Ingstad, B. (2007). Seeing disability and human rights in the local context: Botswana revisited. In B. Ingstad & S. R. Whyte (Eds.), *Disability in local and global worlds* (pp. 237-258). Berkeley: University of California Press.

International Knowledge Network of Women in Politics (iKNOW Politics) (2007). *Gender in Kenyan politics.* Retrieved June 18, 2008 from http://www.iknowpolitics.org/node/4047.

International Labour Organization (ILO) (2004). *Kenya country profile – Employment of people with disabilities: The impact of legislation (East Africa).* Retrieved May 16, 2005 from http://www.ilo.org/public/english/employment/skills/disability/download/cpkenya.pdf.

Jackson, A. P., Smith, S.A. & Hill, C. L. (2003). Academic persistence among Native American college students. *Journal of College Student Development, 44*(4), 548-565.

Jacobi, M. (1991). Mentoring and undergraduate academic success: A literature review. *Review of Educational Research, 61*(4), 505-532.

James, C. E. (2001). Dialogue and resistance in the classroom. *CORE Newsletter 11*(1). Retrieved January 28, 2008 from, https://pi.library. yorku.ca/ojs/index.php/core/article/view/2491/1696.

Jarbrink, K., & Knapp, M. (2001). The economic impact of autism in Britain. *Autism : The International Journal of Research and Practice, 5*(1), 7-22.

Jones, E., Farina, A., Hastorf, A., Markus, H., Miller, D., Scott, R., & French, R. (1984). *Social stigma: The psychology of marked relationships.* New York: W. H. Freeman.

Kabira, W. & Nzioki, E. (1993). *Celebrating women's resistance: A case study of women's groups movement in Kenya.* University of Sussex: Institute of Development Studies Information Resource Unit.

Kallen, E. (1989). *Label me human: Stigmatized minorities and human rights in Canada.* Toronto: University of Toronto Press.

Kamau, M. N. (1996). *The experiences of female academics in Kenya.* Unpublished doctoral book, University of Toronto.

Kamau, M. N. (2004). Outsiders within: Experience of Kenyan women in higher education. *Jenda: A Journal of Culture and African Women Studies,* 6. Retrieved November 27, 2007 from http://www.jendajournal. com/issue6/kamau.html.

Kanogo, T. (2005). *African womanhood in colonial Kenya 1900–1950.* Oxford: James Currey.

Kariuki, K. (2006). She is a woman after all: Patriarchy and female educational leadership in Kenya. *Postamble, 2*(2), 65-74.

Kaye, J. & Raghavan, S. K. (2002). Spirituality in disability and illness. *Journal of Religion and Health, 41*(3), 231-242.

Kelly, V. A. (2004). *The curriculum: Theory and practice.* London: Paul Chapman.

Kenya Institute for Public Policy and Research (n.d.). *The democratic governance support program (DGSP) - Constituency development fund (CDF).* Retrieved May 4, 2008 from http://www.kippra.org/Constituency.asp.

Kenya Law Reports (n.d). *The Persons with Disabilities Act 2003.* Retrieved November 18, 2005 from http://www.kenyalaw.org/kenyalaw/ klr_app/frames.php.

Kenya Society of the Physically Handicapped (2001). *Disability, gender and education: Violence against women with disabilities in Eastern and Western provinces and factors affecting girls with disabilities to access education in Rift Valley province.* Nairobi: Kenya Society of the Physically Handicapped.

Kenyatta, J. (1965). *Facing mount Kenya.* New York: Vintage Books.

Kenosi (2000). *The education of pupils with special educational needs in Africa, looked at within the African Context.* Paper presented at the International Special Education Congress on "Including the excluded". University of Manchester, U.K. Retrieved, February 26, 2008 from http://www.isec2000.org.uk/abstracts/papers_g/grol_1.htm.

Kern, J. (1999). Meeting women's needs: Women and girls with disabilities in the practice of rehabilitation projects. In B. Holzer, A. Vreede & G. Weigt (Eds.), *Disability in different cultures* (pp. 251-267). New Brunswick: Transaction Publishers.

Kiluva-Ndunda, M. M. (2000). *Women's agency and educational policy: The experiences of the women of Kilome, Kenya.* Albany: State University of New York Press.

Kimenyi, M. S. (2005). *Efficiency and efficacy of Kenya's constituency development. fund: Theory and evidence.* Economics Working Papers, University of Connecticut. Retrieved June 28, 2007 from www.digitalcommons.uconn.edu/cgi/viewcontent.cgi?article=1052&context=econ_wpapers.

King, A. (2004). The prisoner of gender: Foucault and the disciplining of the female body. *Journal of International Women's Studies, 5*(2), 29-39.

Kinoti, K. (2008). *Kenya's elections: How did women fare?* Retrieved May 26, 2008 from http://www.awid.org/eng/Issues-and-Analysis/Library/Kenya-s-elections-How-did-women-fare.

Kisanji, J. (1993). Special education in Africa. In: P. Mittler, R. Brouillette, & D. Harris (Eds.), *World yearbook of education 1993: Special needs education* (pp. 158-172). London: Kogan Page.

Kisanji, J. (1998). *Culture and disability: An analysis of inclusive education based on African folklore.* Paper presented at the international expert meeting and symposium on Local Concepts and Beliefs of Disability in Different Cultures, Bonn, Germany. Retrieved April 5, 2006 from http://www.eenet.org.uk/key_issues/cultural/culture_disability.rtf.

Kithyo, I. M. & Petrina, S. (2002). Gender in school to school transitions: How students choose career programs in technical colleges in Kenya. *Journal of Industrial Teacher Education, 39*(2), 2-23.

Kiyaga, N., B., & Moores, D., F. (2003). Deafness in Sub-Saharan Africa. *American Annals of the Deaf, 148*(1), 18-24.

Koech, D. K. (1999). *Report on the commission of inquiry into the education system of Kenya: Totally integrated quality education and training (TIQET).* Nairobi: Government Press.

Koivula, N. (1999). Sport participation: Differences in motivation and actual participation due to gender typing. *Journal of Sport Behavior, 22*(3), 360-380.

Kotlik, J.W. & Harrison, B.C. (1989). Career decision patterns of high school seniors in Louisiana. *Journal of Vocational Education, 14*, 47-65.

Kozma, C. (2005). Dwarfs in ancient Egypt. *American Journal of Medical Genetics, 140*(4), 303-311.

Kwesiga, J. (2002). *Women's access to higher education in Africa: Uganda's experience.* Kampala, Uganda: Fountain Publishers.

Lamborn, S. D., Brown, B. B., Mounts, N. S., & Steinberg, L. (1992). Putting school in perspective: The influence of family, peers, extracurricular participation, and part-time work on academic engagement. In F. M. Newmann (Ed.), *Student engagement and achievement in American secondary schools* (pp. 153-191). New York: Teachers College Press.

Larkin, J. (1994). Walking through walls: The sexual harassment of high school girls. *Gender and Education, 6*(3), 263-280.

LaVant, B. D., Anderson, J. L. & Tiggs, J. W. (1997). Retaining African American men through mentoring initiatives. *New Directions for Student Services, 80*, 43-53.

Leach, F. and Machakanja, P. (2000). *A preliminary investigation into the abuse of girls in Zimbabwean junior secondary schools* (DFID Education Research No. 39). London: DFID.

Lenskyj, H. J. (2003). *Out on the field: Gender, sport and sexualities.* Toronto: Women's Press.

Lichtman, M. (2006). *Qualitative research in education. A user's guide.* New York: Sage Publications .

Linton, S. (1998). *Claiming disability: Knowledge and identity.* New York: New York University Press.

Linton, S. (2006). *My body politic: A memoir.* Ann Arbor: University of Michigan Press.

Logan, B. I. & Beoku-Betts, J. A. (1996). Women and education in Africa: An analysis of economic and socio-cultural factors influencing observed trends. *Journal of Asian & African Studies, 31*(3/4), 191-205.

Longmore, P. (2003). *Why I burned my book and other essays on disability.* Philadelphia: Temple University Press.

Lonsdale, S. (1990). *Women and disability: The experience of physical disability among women.* Basingstoke: MacMillan Press.

Losinsky, L.O., Levi, T., Saffey, K. & Jelsma, J. (2003). An investigation into the physical accessibility to wheelchair bound students of an institution of higher education in South Africa. *Disability and Rehabilitation, 25*(7), 305-308.

Loury, G. C. (2003). Racial stigma: Toward a new paradigm for discrimination theory. *The American Economic Review, 93*(2), 334-337.

Lunsford, K. S. & Bargerhuff, E. M. (2006). A project to make the laboratory more accessible to students with disabilities. *Journal of Chemical Education, 83*(3), 407- 410.

MacFadgen, L. (2008). *Mature students in the persistence puzzle: An exploration of the factors that contribute to mature students' health, learning, and retention in post-secondary education.* Accessed April 30, 2008 from: www.ccl-cca.ca/NR/rdonlyres/D17D6EC1-6894-4E65-A08F 1921E039DD32/0/MacFadgenFinalExecSummEAL2006.pdf.

Madibbo, A. I. (2006). *Minority within a minority: Black Francophone immigrants and the dynamics of power and resistance.* New York & London: Routledge.

Madriaga, M. (2007). Enduring disablism: Students with dyslexia and their pathways into U.K. higher education and beyond. *Disability and Society, 22*(4), 399-412.

Maerten, M. (2004). *African feminism, RoSA Fact Sheet*, No. 34. Retrieved November 26, 2007 from http://www.rosadoc.be/site/rosa/english/pdf/factsheetsenglish/34.pdf.

Malakpa, S. W. G. (2006). *The African association for special education and rehabilitation services (AASERS): A proposal.* Retrieved July 26, 2008 from http://www.inclusionflagship.net/Malakpa_Sep06.pdf.

Mama, A. (1995). *Beyond the masks: Race, gender and subjectivity.* London: Routledge.

Marah, J. K. (2006). The virtues and challenges in traditional African education. *The Journal of Pan African Studies, 1*(4), 15-24.

Margalit, M. (1990). *Effective technology integration for disabled children: The family perspective.* New York: Springer-Verlag.

Marks, D. (1999). Models of disability. *Disability and Rehabilitation, 19*(3), 85-91.

Marsh, J. C. (1997). *Planning, management and ideology: Key concepts for understanding curriculum.* New York: Routledge.

Marshall, C. & Rossman, G. (1999). *Designing qualitative research* (3rd ed.). Thousand Oaks, CA: Sage Publications.

Maskos, R., & Siebert, B. (2006). Self-determination: The other side of the coin. Reflections on a central but ambiguous term of the German disability rights movement. *Disability Studies Quarterly, 26*(2), 18. Retrieved May 2, 2008 from http://www.dsq-sds-archives.org/_articles_ html/2006/spring/maskos_siebert.asp.

Mason, D. (1996). *Strategic planning in African universities: Good practice guidelines for Vice Chancellors* (UNESCO Report ED-96/WS-30). Paris: UNESCO.

Mason, J. (2002). *Qualitative researching.* London: Sage

Mason, M. G. (2004). *Working against odds: Stories of disabled women's work lives.* Boston: Northeastern University Press.

Masakhwe, W. P. (2008). *Post-election violence and disabled people in Kenya: Issues for reflection and action.* Retrieved January 28, 2008 from http://www.independentliving.org/docs7/masakhwe20080124.html .

Martin, P. Y. & Turner, B. A. (1986). Grounded theory and organizational research. *The Journal of Applied Behavioral Science, 22*(2), 141-157.

Masten, A.S. (1994). Resilience in individual development: Successful adaptation despite risk and adversity. In M.C. Wang & E.W. Gordon (Eds.), *Educational resilience in inner-city America: Challenges and prospects* (pp. 3-25). Hillsdale, NJ: Erlbaum.

Mbire-Barungi, B. (1999). Ugandan feminism: Political rhetoric or reality? *Women's Studies International Forum, 22*(4), 435-439.

Mbiti, J. S. (1990/1991). *African religions and philosophy.* New York: Anchor Books.

McConkey, R. & O'Toole (1995). Towards the new millennium. In B. O'Toole & R. McConkey (Eds.), *Innovations in developing countries for people with disabilities* (pp. 3–14). Chorley, U.K.: Lisieux Hall Publications.

McHoul, A. & Grace, W. (1993). *A Foucault primer: Discourse, power and the subject.* Melbourne: Melbourne University Press.

McLaren, P. (1995). Collisions with otherness: Travelling theory, postcolonialism and the politics of ethnographic practice – the mission of the wounded ethnographer. In P. McLaren & M. Giarelli (eds). *Critical ethnography and educational research* (pp. 271-300). Albany:State University of New York Press.

McMillan, J. & Wergin, J. (2006). *Understanding and evaluating educational research* (3rd ed.). Sydney: Pearson.

McNay, L. (1992). *Foucault and feminism.* Cambridge: Polity.

Meekosha, H. (2004). *Gender and disability.* Retrieved October 27, 2008 from http://www.leeds.ac.uk/disability-studies/archiveuk/meekosha/meekosha.pdf.

Mero, P. T. (n.d.). *Self-reliance in education.* Retrieved September 22, 2007 from http://www.american-heritage.org/pdf/Self-Reliance.pdf.

Merriam, S. (1998). *Qualitative research andc ase study applications in education.* San Francisco, CA: Jossey-Ba ss.

Merrill, B. (1999). *Gender, change and identity: Mature women students in universities.* Aldershot: Ashgate.

Mianda, G. (2002). Colonialism, education and gender relations in the Belgian Congo. The *Evolue* case. In J. Allman, S. Geiger & N. Musisi (Eds.), *Women in African colonial histories* (pp. 144-163). Bloomington: Indiana University Press.

Michalko, R. (2002). *The difference that disability makes*. Philadelphia: Temple University Press.

Mikell, G. (1997). *African feminism: The politics of survival in sub-Saharan Africa*. Philadelphia: University of Pennsylvania Press.

Ministry of Education (2006). *Development of education in Kenya*. Retrieved June 19, 2008 from www.ibe.unesco.org/International/ICE47/English/Natreps/reports/kenya.pdf.

Mitchell, D. T. & Snyder, S. L. (1997). Introduction: Disability studies and the double bind of representation. In D. T. Mitchell & S. L. Snyder (Eds.), *The body and physical difference: discourses of disability* (pp. 1-34). Ann Arbour: University of Michigan Press.

Mondoh, H. O. & Mujidi, J. (2006). The education of girls in Kenya: Looking back and still looking forward. *CODESRIA Bulletin, 1 & 2,* 58-60. Retrieved December 19, 2008 from www.codesria.org/Links/Publications/bulletin1_06/page58-60-mondoh.pdf.

Moodley, R. (1999). Masculine/managerial masks and the "other" subject. In S. Whitehead & R. Moodley (Eds.), *Transforming managers: Gendering change in the public sector* (pp. 1-17). London: Taylor & Francis.

Moore, M., Beazley, S., & Maelzer, J. (1998). *Researching disability issues*. Buckingham: Open University Press.

Morris, J. (1991). *Pride against prejudice*. London, Women's Press.

Morris, J. (1996). *Encounters with strangers: Feminism and disability*. London: Women's Press.

Morris, J. (1999). *Hurtling into a void: Transition to adulthood for young people with complex health and support needs*. York, U.K.: Joseph Rowntree Foundation.

Mucai-Kattambo, V. W., Kabeberi-Macharia, J. & Kameri-Mbote, P. (1995). *Law and the status of women in Kenya*. International Law Research Center, Geneva, Switzerland. Retrieved June 6, 2006 from http://www.ielrc.org/content/a9501.pdf.

Mungai, A. M. (2002). *The quest for education in post colonial Kenya: My personal experiences*. Paper presented at the 46th Annual Meeting of Comparative and International Education Society, Florida, March 6-9. Retrieved July 8, 2008 from http://www.eric.ed.gov/ERICDocs/data/ericdocs2sql/content_storage_01/0000019b/80/1b/44/ec.pdf.

Murunga, R.G. (2005). African women in the academy and beyond: Review essay. In O. Oyeronke (Ed.), *African gender studies: A reader* (pp. 397- 416). New York: Palgrave Macmillan.

Musisi, N. B. (1992). Colonial and missionary education: Women and domesticity in Uganda, 1900-1945. In K. T. Hansen (Ed.), *African encounters with domesticity* (pp.172-194). New Brunswick, NJ: Rutgers University Press.

Mwiria, K. (1990). Kenya's harambee secondary school movement: The contradictions of public policy. *Comparative Education Review, 34*(3), 350-368.

Najarian, C. G. (2006). *Between worlds: Deaf women, work, and intersections of gender and ability.* New York: Routledge.

Najarian, C. G. (2008). Deaf women: Educational experiences and self identity. *Disability & Society, 23* (2), 117-128.

Nathani, C. N. (1996). *Development: Indigenous forms of food processing technologies. A Kenyan case study.* Unpublished doctoral book, University of Toronto.

Ndurumo, M. (2001). *Rights of persons with disabilities.* A paper presented to the Constitution of Kenya Review Commission at the Beach hotel. Retrieved February 18, 2006, from http://www. kenyaconstitution. org/docs/09ed002.htm.

Ndurumo, M. M. (1993). *Exceptional children: Development consequence and interventions.* Nairobi: Longman.

Ngigi, A & Macharia, D., (2006). *Kenya health sector policy overview.* Nairobi: IT Power East Africa.

Ngome, C. (2003). *Kenya.* In D. Teferra & P. G. Altbach (Eds.), *African higher education: An international reference handbook* (pp. 359-371). Bloomington: Indiana University Press.

Nicolaisen, I. (1995). Persons and non-persons: Disability and personhood among the Punan Bah of Central Borneo. In B. Ingstad & S. R. Whyte (Eds.), *Disability and culture* (pp. 38-55). Berkeley: University of California Press.

Njeuma, D. L. (1995). An overview of women's education in Africa. In J. Conway, J. & S. Bourque, S. (Eds.), *The politics of women's education: Perspectives from Asia, Africa, and Latin America* (pp. 123-135). Ann Arbor, MI: University of Michigan Press.

Nkinyangi, J. A. & Mbindyo, J. J. (1982). *The condition of disabled persons in Kenya.* Nairobi: Institute of Development Studies.

Nnaemeka, O. (1998). *Sisterhood, feminisms and power: From Africa to the diaspora.* Trenton, NJ: Africa World Press.

Noddings, N. (1992). *The challenge to care in schools.* New York: Teachers College Press.

Nora, A. & Cabrera, A. F. (1996). The role of perceptions of prejudice and discrimination on the adjustment of minority students to college. *The Journal of Higher Education, 67*(2), 119-148.

Nosek, M. A. (1996). Wellness among women with physical disabilities. *Sexuality and Disability, 14*(3), 165-182.

Nova Scotia Advisory Council on the Status of Women (2006).

Employability of women with disabilities: Breaching the disability wall. A brief to the standing committee on human resources, social development and the status of persons with disabilities consultations on employability in Canada. Retrieved July 8, 2007 from http://women.gov.ns.ca/pubs2006_07/EmployabilityBriefSept2006.htm.

Nyaigotti-Chacha (2004). *Reforming higher education in Kenya: Challenges, lessons and opportunities*. The inter-university council for East Africa at the State University of New York. Workshop with the parliamentary committee on education, science and technology Naivasha, Kenya, August 2004. www.iucea.org/publications/Reforming_HE.doc.

Nyakundi, P. (2005). *Rural Kenya's peasantry and the poverty reduction strategy paper (PRSP): Some implications*. Unpublished Master's book, Swedish University of Agricultural Sciences. Retrieved June 1, 2008 from http://www.sol.slu.se/publications/masters_29.pdf.

Nyerere, J. K. (1967). *Freedom and unity*. Dar es Salaam: Oxford University Press.

Oanda, I. O. (2005). New frontiers of exclusion: Private higher education and women's opportunities in Kenya. *JHEA/RESA, 3*(3), 87-105. Retrieved January 20, 2008 from http://www.codesria.org/Links/Publications/jhea3_05/oanda.pdf.

O'Connor, U., & Robinson, A. (1999). Accession or exclusion? University and the disabled student: A case study of policy and practice. *Higher Education Quarterly, 53*(1), 88-103.

Ochoggia, R.E. (2003). Persons with Disabilities Bill 2002: Implications concerning visual disabilities for academic library and information services in Kenya. *New Library World, 104*(7/8), 307-312.

Odden, A. (1990). Class size and student achievement: Research-based policy alternatives. *Educational Evaluation and Policy Analysis, 12*(2), 213-227.

Ogechi, N. O. & Ruto, S. J. (2002). Portrayal of disability through personal names and proverbs in Kenya: Evidence from Ekegusii and Nandi. *Stichproben: Wiener Zeitschrift für kritische Afrikastudien, 3*, 63-82.

Ogundipe-Leslie, M. (1994). *Recreating ourselves, African women and critical transformations*. Trenton, NJ: Africa World Press.

Okeke, P. E. (2006). Higher education for Africa's women: Prospects and challenges. In A. A. Abdi, K. P. Puplampu & G. S. J. Dei (Eds.), *African education and globalization: Critical perspectives* (pp. 79-92). Oxford: Lexington Books.

Oketch, M. O. (2004). The emergence of private university education in Kenya: Trends, prospects, and challenges. *International Development of Educational Development 24*, 119-136.

Okolie, C. A. (2003). Producing knowledge for sustainable development in Africa: Implications for higher education. *Higher Education, 46*, 235-260.

Oliver, M. (1990). *The politics of disablement: A sociological approach.* New York: St. Martin's Press.

Oliver, M. (1996). *Understanding disability: From theory to practice.* New York: St. Martin's Press.

Oliver, M. & Barnes, C. (1998). *Disabled people and social policy: From exclusion to inclusion.* London: Longman.

Olsson, B. & Ullenius, C. (2001). Making universities gender-aware: The Swedish experience. In M. L. Kearney (Ed.), *Women, power and the academy: From rhetoric to reality* (pp. 86-91). Paris: Berghahn Books.

Omale, J. (2000). Tested to their limit: Sexual harassment in schools and educational institutions in Kenya. In J. Mirsky & M. Radlett (Eds.), *No paradise yet: The worlds' women face the new century* (pp.19-38). London: Zed Press.

Omolewa, M. (2007).Traditional African modes of education: Their relevance in the modern world. *International Review of Education/ Internationale Zeitschrift für Erziehungswissenschaft/ Revue internationale l'éducation, 53*(5/6), 593-612.

Onken, S. J., & Slaten, E. (2000). Disability identity formation and affirmation: The experiences of persons with severe mental illness. *Sociological Practice: A Journal of Clinical and Applied Sociology, 2*(2), 99-111.

Onsongo, J. K. (2006). Gender inequalities in universities in Kenya. In C. Creighton, F. Yieke, J. Okely, L. Mareri & C. Wafula (Eds.), *Gender inequalities in Kenya* (pp. 31-48). Nairobi: UNESCO. Retrieved June 18, 2006 from http://unesdoc.unesco.org/images/0014/001458/145887e.pdf.

Onsongo, J. K. (2002). *Factors affecting women's participation in university management in Kenya.* A Study sponsored by the Organisation of Social Science Research in Eastern and Southern Africa (OSSREA).

Opini, B. (2008). Strengths and limitations of Ontario post-secondary education accessibility plans: A review of one university accessibility plan. *International Journal of Inclusive Education, 12*(2), 127-149.

Oriedo, T. (n.d.). *The state of persons with disabilities in Kenya.* Retrieved July 18, 2005 from   http://www.cec.sped.org/intl/state.

Osoro, B. K., Amundson, A. E., & Borgen, W. A. (2000). Career decision-making of high school students in Kenya. *International Journal for the Advancement of Counselling, 22*(4), 289-300.

O'Toole, B. (2000). The view from below: Developing a knowledge base about an unknown population. *Journal of Sexuality and Disability, 18*(3),

207-224.

Oyewumi, O. (1997). *The invention of women: Making an African sense of western gender discourse.* Minneapolis: University of Minnesota Press.

Oyewumi, O. (2002). Conceptualizing gender: The Eurocentric foundations of feminist concepts and the challenge of African epistemologies. *Jenda: A Journal of Culture ad African Women Studies, 2* (1). Retrieved December 19, 2007 from http://www.jendajournal.com/vol2.1/oyewumi.html.

Oyewumi, O. (2003). Introduction: Feminism, sisterhood and other foreign relations. In O. Oyewumi (Ed.), *African women and feminism: Reflecting on the politics of sisterhood* (pp. 1-24). Trenton, NJ: Africa World Press.

Owino, W. & Abagi, O. (2000). *Implementing the report of the commission of inquiry into the education system of Kenya (The Koech Report): Realities, challenges and prospects.* Nairobi: Institute of Policy Analysis and Research (IPAR), Kenya.

Papadimitriou, M. (2004). *What girls say about their science education: Is anybody really listening?* Oxford, U.K.: Trafford publishing.

Parker, V. (1999). Personal assistance for students with disabilities in HE: The experience of the University of East London. *Disability and Society, 14*, 483-504.

Parker, L. (2005). Resisting resistance and finding agency: Women and medicalized birth in Bali. In L. Parker (Ed.), *The agency of women in Asia* (pp. 62-97). Times Center, Singapore: Marshall Candevish Academic.

Paul, S. (1999). Students with disabilities in post-secondary education: The perspectives of wheelchair users. *Occupational Therapy International, 6*(2), 90-109.

Peat, M. (1997). *Community-based rehabilitation.* London: Saunders.

Pirinen, R. (2002). Catching up with men? Finnish newspaper coverage of women's entry into traditionally male sports. In S. Scraton & A. Flintoff (Eds.), *Gender and sport: A reader* (pp. 94-105). London: Routledge.

Porter, J. I. (1997). Foreword. In D. T. Mitchell & S. L. Snyder (Eds.), *The body and physical difference: discourses of disability* (pp. xiii-xiv). Ann Arbour: University of Michigan Press.

Preece, J. (1999). *Using Foucault and feminist theory to explain why some adults are excluded from British university education.* Ceredigion: Edwin Mellen Press.

Priestly, M. (2003). *Disability: A life course approach.* Oxford: Blackwell Publishing.

Psacharopoulos, G. (1994). Returns to investment in education: A global update. *World Development, 22* (9), 1325-1343.

Psacharopoulos, G. & Patrinos, P. (2004). Returns to investment in education: A further update. *Education Economics, 12* (2), 111-135.

Puja, G. (2001). *Moving against the grain: The expectations and experiences of Tanzanian female undergraduates.* Unpublished doctoral book, University of Toronto.

Ray, J. & Warden, M. K. (1995). *Technology, computers and the special needs learner.* Albany, NY: Delmar.

Republic of Kenya (1964). *Kenya education commission report part I (Ominde Report).* Nairobi: Government Printer.

Republic of Kenya (1988). *Report on the presidential working party on education and manpower training for the next decade and beyond (Kamunge Report).* Nairobi: Government Printer.

Republic of Kenya (1993). *A report of the taskforce on special needs education: Appraisal exercise.* Nairobi: Ministry of Education, Science and Technology.

Republic of Kenya (1998). *Master plan on education and training 1997 - 2010.* Nairobi: Government Printers.

Republic of Kenya (2003). *Ministry of Education Science and Technology report on the National Conference on Education and Training held at Kenyatta International Conference Center November 27th to 29th 2003.* Accessed January 8, 2008 from http://planipolis.iiep.unesco.org/upload/Kenya/Kenya_Report_Nat_conf_ed_training.pdf.

Republic of Kenya/ Ministry of Education (2006). *Draft policy on special needs education for children with disabilities. Nairobi draft – Methodist.* Nairobi: Ministry of Education.

Rhamie, J. & Hallam, S. (2002). An investigation into African-Caribbean academic success in the U.K. *Race Ethnicity and Education, 5*(2), 15-170.

Richardson, J .T. E. & King, E. (1998). Adult students in higher education: Burden or boon? *The Journal of Higher Education, 69*(1), 65-88.

Riddell, S., Wilson, A. & Tinklin, T. (2002). Disability and the wider access agenda: Supporting disabled students in different institutional contexts. *Widening Participation and Lifelong Learning, 4,* 12-26.

Rioux, M. (1991). *Rights, justice, power: An agenda for change, a culture of diversity, rights-based technology.* Retrieved March 2008, from http://www.enablelink.org/include/article.php?pid=&cid=&subid=&aid=841.

Rodriguez, N., Mira, C. B., Myers, H. F., Morris, J. K., & Cardoza, D. (2003). Family or friends: Who plays a greater supportive role for Latino college students? *Cultural Diversity and Ethnic Minority Psychology, 9,* 236-250.

Rotich, D. C. (2004). The affordability of school textbooks in Kenya: Consumer experiences in the transformation to a liberalizing economy.

Nordic Journal of African Studies, 13(2), 175–187.

Ryan, P. (1998). Singing in prison: Women writers and the discourse of resistance. In O. Nnaemeka (Ed.), *Sisterhood, feminism and power: From Africa to the diaspora* (pp. 197 -214). Trenton, NJ: African World Press.

Saito, S. & Ishiyama, R. (2005). The invisible minority: Under-representation of people with disabilities in prime-time TV dramas in Japan. *Disability & Society, 20*(4), 437-451.

Schick, F. (1997). *Making choices: A recasting of decision theory*. London: Cambridge University Press.

Schultz, E. K. (2005). The meaning of spirituality for individuals with disabilities. *Disability and Rehabilitation, 27*(21), 1283-1295.

Schur, E. M. (1983). *Labeling women deviant: Gender, stigma, and social control*. Philadelphia: Temple University Press.

Shah, S. L. (2005) *Career success of disabled high-flyers*. London: Jessica Kingsley.

Shakespeare, T. (1994). Cultural representation of disabled people: Dustbins for disavowal? *Disability & Society, 9*(3), 283-299.

Shakespeare, T. (2006). *Disability rights and wrongs*. London: Routledge.

Shakespeare, T., & Watson, N. (1997). Defending the social model. *Disability and Society, 12*(2), 293-300.

Shikwati, J. (2007). *Comment: Tapping into youthful energy*. Retrieved July 8, 2008 from www.bdafrica.com/index.php?Itemid=5821&id=1236& option=com_content&task=view.

Shorter-Gooden, K. (2004). Multiple resistance strategies: How African American women cope with racism and sexism. *Journal of Black Psychology, 30*, 406–425.

Sifuna, D. N. (2005). The illusion of free primary education in Kenya. *Wajibu – A Journal of Social and Religious Concern, 20*. Retrieved July 28, 2008 http://africa.peacelink.org/wajibu/articles/art_6901.html.

Sifuna, D. N. (2006). A review of major obstacles to women's participation in higher education in Kenya. *Research in Post-Compulsory Education, 11*(1), 85-105.

Slee, R. (2001). Social justice and the changing directions in educational research: The case of inclusive education. *International Journal of Inclusive Education, 5*(2/3), 167-178.

Sofola, Z. (1998). Feminism and African womanhood. In O. Nnaemeka (Ed.), *Sisterhood: feminism and power* (pp. 51-64). Trenton, NJ: Africa World Press.

Stage, F. & Milne, N. (1996). Invisible scholars. *Journal of Higher Education, 67*(4), 426-445.

Stamp, P. (1986). Kikuyu women's self-help groups. In C. Robertson & I. Berger (Eds.), *Women and class in Africa* (pp. 27-46). New York: Africana

Publishing.

Stamp, P. (1989). *Technology, gender and power in Africa.* Ottawa: International Development Research Centre.

Stienstra, D. (2003). *The intersection of disability and race/ethnicity/ official language/religion.* Retrieved November 18, 2007 from http://www. disabilitystudies.ca/Documents/Resaerch/Completed%20research/ Intersection%20of%20disability/Intersection%20of%20disability.pdf.

Stodden, R. A., Whelley, T., Chang, C., & Harding, T. (2001). Current status of educational support provision to students with disabilities in postsecondary education. *Journal of Vocational Rehabilitation, 16*(3/4), 1-10.

Stone, S. D. (1995). The myth of bodily perfection. *Disability & Society, 10*(4), 413-424.

Stone, E. (1999). Disability and development in the majority world. In E. Stone (Ed.), Disability and development: *Learning from action and research on disability in the majority world* (pp. 1-18). Leeds: The Disability Press.

Stone, D. L. & Colella, A. (1996). A model of factors affecting the treatment of disabled individuals in organizations. *Academy of Management Review, 21*(2), 352-401.

Strauss, A., & Corbin, J. (1998). *Basics of qualitative research: Grounded theory procedures and techniques.* Thousand Oaks, CA: Sage Publications.

Stubbs, S. (1994). *A critical review of literature relating to the education of disabled children in developing countries.* Cambridge: Cambridge University Press.

Suarez-Balcazar, Y., Orellana-Damacela, L., Portillo, N., Rowan, J. M. & Andrews-Guillen, C. (2003). Experiences of differential treatment among college students of color. *The Journal of Higher Education, 74*(4), 428-444.

Sudarkasa, N. (1996). *The Strength of our mothers, African and African American women and families: Essays and speeches.* Trenton, NJ: Africa World Press.

Taleporos, G. & McCabe, M. (2002). Body image and physical disability - personal perspectives, *Social Science and Medicine, 54*(6), 971-980.

Talle, A. (1995). A child is a child: Disability and equality among the Kenya Maasai. In B. Ingstad & S. Whyte (Eds.), *Disability and culture* (pp. 56-72). Berkeley: University of California Press.

Tamale, S. (1999). *When the hens begin to crow: Gender and parliamentary politics in Uganda.* Boulder, CO: Westview Press.

Tamale, S. (2004). Gender trauma in Africa: Enhancing women's links to resources. *Journal of African Law, 48*(1), 50-61.

Tamale, S. (2006). African feminism: How should we change? *Development, 49*(1), 38-41.

Taxis, J. C. (2006). Fostering academic success of Mexican Americans in a BSN Program: An educational imperative. *International Journal of Nursing Education Scholarship, 3*(1), 1-14.

Tembe, F., M. (2001). *People with disabilities and employment in Mozambique.* Retrieved November 8, 2008, from http://www.disabilityworld.org/11-12_01/employment/mozambi.

Teng'o, D. (2003). *Joining university: How it works.* Retrieved May 15, 2008 from http://www.nationaudio.com/News/DailyNation/14102003/supplement/SS1310-A-Gen@8@8.pdf.

Thomas, C. (1999). *Female forms. Experiencing and understanding disability.* Buckingham: Open University Press.

Thomas, C. (2004). Disability and impairment. In: J. Swain, S. French, C. Barnes & C. Thomas (Eds.), *Disabling barriers – Enabling environments* (pp. 21-27). London: Sage Publications.

Thomas, J. (1993). *Doing critical ethnography.* California: Sage Publications.

Thompson, A., & Dickey, D. K. (1994). Self-perceived job search skills of college students with disabilities. *Rehabilitation Counseling Bulletin, 37,* 358-370.

Tinklin, T & Hall, J (1999). Getting round obstacles: Disabled students' experiences in higher education in Scotland. *Studies in Higher Education, 24*(2), 183-194.

Titchkosky, T. (2003). *Disability, self and society.* Toronto: University of Toronto Press.

Titchkosky, T. (2007). *Reading and writing disability differently.* Toronto: University of Toronto Press.

Titchkosky, T. (2008). To pee or not to pee? Ordinary talk about extraordinary exclusions in a university environment. *Canadian Journal of Sociology, 33*(1), 37-60.

Tomlinson, S. & Abdi, O. A. (2003). Disability in Somaliland. *Disability & Society, 18*(7), 911-920.

Tompkins, C. H. (1996). *A critical ethnography of disability in women's lives.* Unpublished doctoral book, University of California, San Francisco.

Toroitich, I. K. & African Women and Child Information Network (2004). *Women rights as human rights in Kenya: A contradiction between policy and practice.* Retrieved June 5, 2007 from http://www.changemaker.no/filemanager/download/564/occ%20paper%20-%20womens%20rights.pdf.

Traustadóttir, R. (1990). *Obstacles to equality: The double discrimination of women with disabilities. Overview article.* Centre on Human Policy. Accessed May 8, 2008 from http://www.independentliving.org/docs3/chp1997.html.

Tsang, H. W. H., Tamn, P. K. C., Chan, F. & Cheung, W.M. (2003).

Stigmatizing attitudes towards individuals with mental illness in Hong Kong: Implications for their recovery. *Journal of Community Psychology, 31*(4), 383-396.

Turmusani, M (2003). *Disabled people and economic needs in the developing world: Political perspective from Jordan.* Aldershot: Ashgate.

Valian, V. (1999). *Why so slow? The advancement of women.* Cambridge, MA: The MIT Press.

Vernon, A. (1996). A stranger in many camps: The experience of disabled black and ethnic minority women. In J. Morris (Ed.), *Encounters with strangers: Feminism and disability* (pp.48-67). London: Women's Press.

Verstraete, P. (2007). Towards a disabled past: Some preliminary thoughts about the history of disability, governmentality and experience. *Educational Philosophy and Theory, 39*(1), 56-63.

Wagner, A. & Magnusson, J. L. (2005). Neglected realities: Exploring the impact of women's experiences of violence on learning in sites of higher education. *Gender and Education, 17*(4), 449-461.

Walters, D. (2004). The relationship between postsecondary education and skill: Comparing credentialism with human capital theory. *Canadian Journal of Higher Education, 34*(2), 97-124.

Wane, N. N. (2002). African women and spirituality: Harmonizing the balance of life. In N. N. Wane, K. Deliovsky & E. Lawson (Eds.), *Back to the drawing board: African Canadian feminisms* (pp. 275-291). Toronto: Sumach Press.

Wane, N. N. (2005). Claiming, writing, storing, sharing African indigenous knowledge. *Journal of Thought, 40*(2), 27-46.

Wane, N. N. (2006). Is decolonization possible? In Dei, G. S. J. & Kempf, A. (Eds.), *Anti-colonialism and education: The politics of resistance* (pp. 87-106). Rotterdam: Sense Publishers.

Wane, N. N. (2008). Mapping the field of indigenous knowledges in anti-colonial discourse: A transformative journey in education, *Race, Ethnicity and Education, 11*(2), 183-197.

Wane, N. N. & Neegan, E. (2007). African women's indigenous spirituality: Bringing it all home. In N. Massaquoi & N. N. Wane (Eds.), *Theorizing empowerment: Canadian perspectives on Black feminist thought* (pp. 27-46). Toronto: Inna Publications.

Wane, N. N. & Opini, B. O. (2006). An exploration of gendered violence in Kenyan schools. *Eastern African Journal of Humanities and Sciences, 6*(2), 44-66.

Watt, S. (2003). Come to the river: Using spirituality to cope, resist, and develop identity. *New Directions for Student Services, 104*, 29-40.

Wehmeyer, M. L., & Palmer, S. B. (2003). Adult outcomes for students with cognitive disabilities three years after high school: The impact of self-determination. *Education and Training in Developmental Disabilities, 38*(2), 131-144.

Weiser, J. (2005). *The discursive marginality of gender-based harassment in high schools.* Unpublished doctoral book, University of Toronto.

Wendell, S. (1996). *The rejected body: Feminist philosophical reflections on disability.* New York: Routledge.

Wesonga, D., Ngome, C., Ouma, D., & Wawire, V. (2003). *Private higher education in Kenya: Analysis of trends and issues in four selected universities.* Draft research report submitted to The FORD Foundation Office for Eastern Africa.

Whitehead, M. 2004. *Persons with disability: Study commissioned by the Corporate Planning Unit of the City of Joburg as a component of the human development agenda.* Johannesburg: City of Johannesburg. Retrieved May 2, 2008 from http://www.joburg.org.za/corporate_planning/disabled.pdf.

Willett, J. & Deegan, M. J. (2001). Liminality and disability: Rites of passage and community in a hypermodern society. *Disability Studies Quarterly, 21*(3), 137-152.

World Health Organization (WHO) (2008). *World report on disability and rehabilitation.* Retrieved December 10, 2008 from http://www.who.int/disabilities/Concept%20NOTE%20General%202008.pdf.

Wotherspoon, T. (2004). *The sociology of education in Canada: Critical perspectives* (2nd ed.). Toronto: Oxford University Press.

Yates, S. (2005). Truth, power, and ethics in care services for people with learning difficulties. In S. Tremain (Ed.), *Foucault, governmentality, and critical disability theory* (pp. 65-77). Michigan: University of Michigan Press.

Zhang, D. & Katsiyannis, A. (2002). Minority representation in special education: A persistent challenge. *Remedial and Special Education, 23*(3), 180-187.

Zeleza, P. T. (1997). *Manufacturing African studies and crises.* Dakar: Codesria Book Series.

Ziesler, M. (2002). Double discrimination against disabled women in rich and poor countries. *Disability World, 14.* Retrieved August 10, 2007 from http://www.disabilityworld.org/06-08_02/women/double.shtml.

Zine J. (2008). *Canadian Islamic Schools: Unravelling the politics of faith, gender, knowledge and identity.* Toronto: University of Toronto Press.

Zine, J. (2005). *Staying on the straight path: A critical ethnography of Islamic schooling in Ontario.* Unpublished doctoral book, University of Toronto